Religion:
Foundation of the Free Society

by Edmund A. Opitz

The Foundation for Economic Education, Inc.
Irvington-on-Hudson, New York

Religion: Foundation of the Free Society

The Foundation for Economic Education, Inc.
30 South Broadway
Irvington-on-Hudson, NY 10533
(914) 591-7230

Publisher's Cataloging in Publication
(Prepared by Quality Books, Inc.)

Opitz, Edmund A., 1914–
  Religion : foundation of the free society / by Edmund A. Opitz

    p. cm.
    Includes index
    Originally published 1994.
    ISBN 0-910614-92-X

    1. Religion—Economic aspects. I. Title

BR115.E3075 1996   261.8'5
                       QBI95-20867

Library of Congress Catalog Card Number: 95-083491

Second printing, 1996
Cover design by Beth R. Bowlby
Manufactured in the United States of America

Table of Contents

Introduction

by the Right Reverend Robert C. Harvey

I am honored to introduce *Religion: Foundation of the Free Society*, and hope it will help to bridge gaps and shore up foundations for those who want their lives to count. Its author, Edmund Opitz, brings wit as well as understanding to the study of economics. The good teacher's passionate concern is evident in his writing as well as discourse.

A silent question, "Why me?" has been pressing from the moment of his request and my acceptance. A line from the 119th Psalm keeps coming to mind, "I am small and of no reputation." Why would Edmund Opitz, who has made valuable contributions to the study of economics and religion, and who is acquainted with leading figures in both fields, ask this introduction by one who is an amateur at best—as well as a late arrival on both scenes.

One answer could be that in an age of specialization the amateur may not get so tangled in the underbrush as to lose sight of the forest *and* the trees. He may understand the connectedness of things in a way denied those whose vision—like that under a magnifying glass—discloses much of very little.

Since there would be personal reasons as well, I may mention one or two. Mr. Opitz and I are old friends. We are enthusiasts for the free-market economy; I believe we would both opt for liberty wherever there is assurance of its wise and responsible use. Each of us has been ordained to the ministry of the Church—he in the reformed tradition and I in the Anglican. Would either of us go so far as to call the market economy a divine institution? No.

Yet the laws by which a free market functions are of more than human origin. Edmund Opitz is as convinced as I that economic law perceived, understood and given free rein—permits a providential care for man's needs that far exceeds anything that the world in its wisdom has yet devised. While man's understanding is still so limited and sin so all-pervasive—making "In God we trust" a needful and deeply felt refrain—a few things involving freedom are sufficiently proven for us

1

to breathe grateful prayers of thanks. One is the capacity of free markets to satisfy human needs when so many mechanisms of human invention have brought inequity and failure. The stunning success, over a few short years, of market economics in Japan, Taiwan, South Korea, Hong Kong, and Singapore demonstrate how life-giving a belief in freedom can be, and how widely it has taken hold.

Not long after Edmund Opitz and I become acquainted—it was thirty years ago—I remarked that while reading Adam Smith's *Wealth of Nations* an awareness of priestly calling began to surface in my mind. The connection could have been accidental, but I think not. Adam Smith's thought is deeply religious. He deals with the needs of individuals *and* societies in terms of divine purpose and provision. So I accepted his work as giving substance to my *sense* of vocation, if not to the vocation itself. Since this happened fifteen years before Mr. Opitz' book, *Religion and Capitalism: Allies, Not Enemies* was written, it was Adam Smith who convinced me of the connection.

For a decade after the second world war, I had covered the central states for a Wall Street firm engaged in the management of mutual funds. I enjoyed the work, for it seemed an ideal way for ordinary people to become shareholders in our economy and nation. Since my previous work (aside from five years as an officer in Pacific Fleet destroyers) had been in sales rather than finance, I now devoted my hours in trains and planes to studying the mechanics of the market. This is how I came to read Adam Smith.

Till then I had been unaware that, during the Middle Ages, wages and prices were set by the Church rather than by State or marketplace. In retrospect that arrangement was regrettable, for it helped to make the Ark of Salvation a power-component in need of reform. This was true for much of Europe; it reflected the Western Church's eagerness to be "involved." Its attention to the divine immanence was in marked contrast to what prevailed in the Eastern Church—namely, a centering on God's transcendent glory.

The medieval arrangement gave a hint of what would take place in the command economies of our day. That primitive economy was hampered by the notion that there was only so much money—and so many jobs—to go around. The result was a skewing of justice itself; the "just price" and the "just wage" seemed more important than allowing the economy to develop organically—with participants at every level prospering along the way.

When, in our century, the socialists and Marxists appropriated the functions of the marketplace, the result was devastating. Uncontrollable costs and loss of incentive cut the availability of goods and services from a flow to a trickle. Worse still, it took three generations for one fatal flaw to become clear to all. At no stage in its production and distribution was the command economy able, of its own resources, to know the value of items on its shelves. Not until Marxism's demise did men realize how dependent the system had been upon the free world for help. Espionage aside, much information was available for the asking—in government publications, in *The Wall Street Journal*, in auto and appliance manuals and even in regularly updated Sears, Roebuck catalogues! But it was critically needed. Without the data issued routinely by free markets, the command economy would have been unable to function.

As the Dark Ages drew on to Renaissance the concept of economy had been reborn. But growth came in halting steps. Trade and commerce needed to assume some importance before underlying patterns became apparent. The idea of *oikonomia* (*stewardship*, lit. *house-rule*) had been limited to small communities. Its development was delayed by the fact that the concept of credit, which was well understood in ancient times, had not yet been resurrected. Nor had natural law ever been known to apply to the marketplace. Jobs and money supply, as already pointed out, were assumed to be invariables. The charging of interest on loaned-out money was treated as mortal sin.

Adam Smith gave the *coup de grace* to that mentality. He not only showed the way in which private initiatives could add up to public good, he demonstrated the workings of natural law in a field where men had never been aware of its presence.

When I appreciated that such law could exist in the social as well as physical sciences—and in a universal and self-enforcing way—I was filled with delight. I could see that, unlike the Moral Law (which had been divinely mandated in one time and place), economic law had waited to be discovered. It remained for Adam Smith and other economists to conclude that what they were observing was natural law applied to the field of economics. If so, it might possess the same authority and require the same obedience as laws governing the universe of chemistry and physics.

What relief such a discovery must bring the human race! No longer need we be burdened by bureaucracy and red tape. No longer need we require official imprimaturs on private agreements. Men could appreciate that from the beginning their Creator had provided means whereby private purposes could add up to public good. Accepting the divine hand in our economic activity, we need no longer proclaim "the good of the community" while putting fingers in our neighbors' pockets.

It took little reflection to realize that this was wishful thinking. The concept of private enterprise linked with free markets is only one of many economic models on the scene. Regardless of whether others are utopian, demonic or both, it would be extravagant to expect the world to genuflect to the free enterprise model simply because its laws have been laid down by God rather than man. Even *The Wealth of Nations* was regarded by many as "old hat" thirty years ago. The book was published in 1776. By comparison, the *Communist Manifesto* came in 1848, with *Das Kapital* following in three installments between 1867 and 1895.

By now, however, Karl Marx has had his day. His thought and the religion it mandated have received the same treatment Leon Trotsky meted out to the Mensheviks in 1918, "You are bankrupts, your role is played out. Go where you belong—into the dustbin of history." Such treatment, as we can believe, will be given finally to every command economy. Unfortunately it takes decades of war and social dislocation before such systems are revealed to be idols. By contrast Adam Smith's thought, though influential and widely praised, has never been tried on a national scale.

There are three ways in which assessments of Adam Smith's model seem to fall into place. The first will see freedom in the marketplace as being in harmony with the designs of the Most High. It will regard economic law as "Law" in the sense of being linked with God's providential purposes for mankind. It will hold that economic law, like the Moral Law, has been given for our benefit. It will accept that some of its benefits were reaped over a span of hundreds and thousands of years before man realized what it is and came to value its contribution to prosperity, order and world peace.

Another assessment would regard economic law as useful to know about and hopefully turn to profit. But that would be the limit of its importance. People of that mind would not dream of observing such law with the care they reserve for laws whose violation would put them behind bars or in a morgue. If such law were truly Law (they would hold) an infraction would bring, (a) an immediate consequent (b) measurably linking cause and effect, (c) denigrating a wrongdoer's honor, and (d) painful enough to discourage repetition.

Those holding such views might be scofflaws in regard to the Moral Code as well. The threat of punishment for violating the Moral Law is no more immediate or certain than for infraction of laws that constitute no crime. There are always those who want to take a chance. If punishment does come, entire generations may be passed by in the process—which is why people are sometimes made to suffer for the sins of those they never knew.

A third assessment would separate the Moral Law from those laws that are found in nature but were never mandated in the sense that God said, "This law is to be obeyed." Where natural law is not revealed, but simply waits for our discovery, a case may be made that it is no more moral than the laws of math or physics.

The eclectic view—such as the third seems to be—might satisfy those whose religion is essentially gnostic. Their search for the secrets of the universe could be carried on with the hope of giving man the upper hand both with nature and with God. It would treat the Lord increasingly as an outdated concept instead of what He is—the Source and Sustainer of all life.

Yet few, even among atheists, would deny that there are such realities as right and wrong, justice and injustice, and the need for restraint and moral force. If we appreciate that the Moral Law and the natural law, of their very nature, leave us as free to disobey as to obey, we can see a purposive linkage on the Creator's part between the kingdom of heaven and its counterparts on earth.

Not all religion can be true religion; at least some of it has got to be make-believe. By the same token, not all economic activity in free markets will be unwholesome; some of it will be productive for all parties involved. Where religion is true religion—bestowed, that is, by the One and Only God—and where economies are put to use by people whose motives and actions are just and good, there can be little question as to the linkage.

This, of course, has been Edmund Opitz' thesis—reflected in his work. Since he cannot play devil's advocate for what he himself advances, let us attempt it here and now. His thought needs to be proven in the way the Dahlgren Proving Ground *tests* or *proves* a naval gun.

In such an advocacy we must insist on the vast difference between a true religion and any economic system. The one must be concerned with people's souls, which is to say, with the transformation of their character and with their heavenly destination. The other is concerned with their well-being here on earth—and no more than that. On the surface they have nothing in common and appear to be antithetical.

Yet such is only a surface observation. In the Christian tradition—as in the Jewish—there cannot be one without the other. The Moral Law of the Old Testament insists that the salvation both of individuals and societies lies in obedience to God's commands. The purpose of men's life on earth—so far as the faithful are concerned—is chiefly to provide an arena for the training and proving of their souls. For those who give themselves willingly to God's covenant relationship, earth and heaven are linked in one great overarching purpose.

Curiously and happily, there can be fulfillment even for atheists (who allow no possibility of relationship with God) and sociopaths (who may accept His existence but are determined not to do His will). The atheist profits by the fact that a God-seeking society is well ordered; he must willy-nilly be a partaker of its good things. The sociopath profits by the fact that the godly society prospers and therefore offers tempting prey.

There can be—as today is largely evident—the possibility of beneficial consensus for devotees of all religions. It consists in the following—*as a universal ethic,* of what Jews, Christians and Muslims have accepted as being a mandate from God.

The precepts of the Ten Commandments strike a harmonious chord with the ethic of nearly every culture. Everywhere we find acceptance of its definition of human values and behavior. We find acceptance as well of men's need to give respect, obedience and worship to a Creator God. The chief difference between those who acknowledge the Ten Commandments as Law and those "outside the Law" has been that for the latter folk its rules apply only to their own people—while as commanded by God they apply to all mankind.

The point bears repeating. What God did on Sinai's height was to take a code that was already universal among tribes unknown to one another, and by direct revelation give it back to man as His command. It already was as nearly natural as a human law could be; now it was supernatural as well. It had been perceived as applying here and there; now it applied everywhere, having the approval not only of the vast majority of mankind but the authority of the One True God.

Yet even if men in all times and places accept the Ten Commandments' moral substance—which they do while continuing with the ritual aspects of their cults—there remains the fact that neither moral nor economic laws have seemed to be rigorously enforced. There are those who ignore or disobey the Moral Law yet seem to prosper without punishment. In the economic field there are whole nations who play fast and loose with the rules laid down for decent and just behavior.

In the field of private morality it is held that unjust behavior is sinful and therefore a barrier to eternal life. In the field of public morality (which includes economic behavior) no such declaration has been made. Nations and other man-made bodies are under no threat of hellfire. Their put-down can only be in the here and now. It may come from their own angry members or from rivals outside their borders. It may come from suicidal policies, degeneracy, boredom, sloth. Who is to say it is not from God?

Up to this point we have not closed our case for an alliance between religion and the free market economy. Let us attempt it now. It may be found in the readiness of men in the so-called free world to give support to moral *and* economic Law as an act of faith and an expression of good intent.

The fulfillment of our life on earth, according to Judeo-Christian precepts, requires not only obedience but the trust that God will bring order out of chaos. Similarly, our willingness to allow private enterprise in a market economy, free trade among nations and the placing of constitutional limitations on government—those commitments are also ventures of faith.

How can we be "one nation under God"? If faith can be a public as well as a private virtue, an economic good such as market freedom can be seen as an element in the Providence of God. As citizens of the "land of the free," we should be as committed to freedom in markets and contracts as we are to obedience of the Moral Law. For a just people there need be no conflict between the two. While our devotion to the market economy may not involve the saving grace that has to do with the soul's heavenward journey, I cannot think of dedication to sound principles of freedom as being selfish or idolatrous.

Actually, sound institutions serve the same function that a toy doll does for a little girl. The toy provides the child with the unconscious opportunity to exercise the care and affection that will stand her in good stead when she herself is a mother. The child's acted-out devotion to the doll is a providential means whereby a goal of earth-shaking importance may be obtained.

The marketplace is like that doll. It is no plaything, to be sure, nor can it be "just pretend." Yet those who use the market in good faith are doing more than provide a future for themselves. They are engaging in a process by which their society may be more just and more productive, and their country more secure.

We may hope that conformity with the Moral Law may bring its own chief end—the eternal life which is not the concern of this introduction. Regardless of the one, we do have hope of the corollary other—that a wise and faithful observance of economic law can lead to fulfillment of our ideals as "one nation under God . . . with liberty and justice for all."

Such a view is expressed by the Apostle Paul in a line that has secular as well as spiritual implication. In speaking of the first of the ethical mandates of the Ten Commandments, he calls it "the first commandment with promise." It is a striking example of private morality's working unconsciously for the highest public good, "Honor thy father and thy mother *that thy days may be long upon the land which the Lord thy God giveth thee*." Paul shows the New Israel to be solidly at one with what the Old Israel declares in its Proverb, "Righteousness exalteth a nation, but sin is a reproach to any people."

I cannot close without giving attention to what many believe to be the Western world's greatest need—the continuing vitality of the consensus from which its values have been derived and around which its energies have been focused. That consensus is so nearly congruent with the Judeo-Christian ethic as to be, in effect, one and the same thing.

To the degree our world is post-Christian it is also post-Jewish and post-Muslim, for the Moral Law is one. Yet even with the partial eclipse of Western religion, we may see that its three-thousand-year-old consensus on the truth and propriety of the Moral Law provides a God-given means by which a whole world's virtue and integrity may be restored.

I. RELIGIOUS ROOTS

Biblical Roots of American Liberty

The First Amendment to the Constitution forbids Congress to set up an official church; there was to be no "Church of the United States" as a branch of this country's government. Such an alliance between Church and State is what "establishment" means. An established church is a politico-ecclesiastical structure that receives support from tax monies, advances its program by political means, and penalizes dissent. Our Constitution renounces such arrangements *in toto;* the Founders wrote the First Amendment into the Constitution to prevent them.

The famed American jurist Joseph Story, who served on the Supreme Court from 1811 till 1845, and is noted for his great *Commentaries on the Constitution of the United States,* had this to say about the First Amendment: "The real object of the Amendment was, not to countenance, much less advance Mahommedanism, or Judaism, or infidelity, by prostrating Christianity; but to exclude all rivalry among Christian sects, and to prevent any *national* ecclesiastical establishment, which should give to an hierarchy the exclusive patronage of the national government."

The various theologies, doctrines, and creeds found in this country can thus be advanced by religious means only—by reason, persuasion, and example. Separation of Church and State means that government maintains a neutral stance toward our three biblically based religions—Catholicism, Judaism, and Protestantism, as well as toward the various denominations and splinter groups. These several religious bodies, then, have no alternative but to compete for converts in the marketplace of ideas. This is a good arrangement, good for both Church and State; it avoids the twin evils of a politicized religion and a divinized politics.

A Christian Nation

It has often been observed that America is a Christian nation—around which observation several misunderstandings cluster. We are a

From the July 1991 issue of *The Freeman.*

Christian nation in the sense that our understanding of human nature and destiny, the purpose of individual life, our convictions about right and wrong, our norms, emerged out of the religion of Christendom— not out of Buddhism, Confucianism, or primitive animism. And it is a fact of history that our forebears whose religious convictions brought them to these shores in the seventeenth and eighteenth centuries sought to create in this new world a biblically based Christian commonwealth. But it was not to be a theocracy—of which the world had seen too many! It was to be a religious society, but one which incorporated a *secular* political order!

The reasoning ran something like this. The human person is forever; each man and woman lives in the here and now, and also in the hereafter. Here, we are pilgrims for three score years and ten, more or less. Life here is vitally important for it's a test run for life hereafter. Earth is the training ground for life eternal. Such training is the essence of religion, and it's much too important to be entrusted to any secular agency. But there is a role for government; government should maintain the peace of society and protect equal rights to life, liberty, and property. This maximizes liberty, and in a free social order men and women have maximum opportunity to order their souls aright.

Separating the sacred and the secular in this fashion is a new idea in world history. Secularize government and you deprive it of the perennial temptation of governments to offer salvation by political contrivances. By the same token, things sacred are privatized as free churches, where the spiritual concerns of men and women are advanced by spiritual means only.

So, when it is said that America is a Christian nation, the implication intended is poles apart from what is meant when it is observed, for example, that Iran is a Shiite nation. The Shiite sect of Islam is a branch of the government of Iran. Other religions are not tolerated. Deviations from doctrinal orthodoxy are forbidden. The government punishes infidels because Shiism is Iran's official, authorized church. From time to time government uses the sword to gain converts. The government of Iran is not neutral with respect to religion.

In the United States, it is mandated that the government maintain a level playing field, so to speak, "a free field and no favor," where freely choosing individuals find their different pathways to God while government merely keeps the peace. This is what is really meant by the phrase, "Separation of Church and State." This oft-quoted phrase is frequently misunderstood as suggesting that religion and politics are incompatible, and that we should keep religion out of politics.

If we think of "politics" as several candidates wheeling, dealing, and slugging it out in an election campaign, it's clear that religion doesn't have a significant role in such a situation. And if we think of "religion" in terms of a contemplative meditating and praying in his cell, it's obvious that politics is absent. But there is no coherent political philosophy apart from a foundation of religious axioms and premises.

Religion and the Social Order

Religion, at its fundamental level, offers a set of postulates about the universe and man's place therein, including a theory of human nature, its origin, its potentials, and its destination. Religion deals with the meaning and purpose of life, with man's chief good, and the meaning of right and wrong. Thus, religious axioms and premises provide the basic materials political philosophy works with. The political theorist must assume that men and women are thus and so, before he can figure out what sort of social and legal arrangements provide the fittest habitat for such creatures as we humans are. So, some religion lies at the base of every social order.

It is the religion of dialectical materialism that is the take-off point for the Marxian theory and practice of the total state. Hinduism is basic to the structures of Indian society. Western society, Christendom, was shaped and molded by Christianity. Incorporated into Western civilization were elements from the Bible, as well as ingredients from Greece and Rome. This composite was lived, worked over, and thought out for nearly 1,800 years by the peoples of Europe. And then something new emerged and began to take root in the New World; it was the recovery of that part of the Christian story needed to ransom society from despotism and erect the structures of a free society wherein men and women might enjoy their birthright of economic and political liberty.

A vision emerged of a society where men and women would be free to pursue their personal goals, unimpeded by the fetters of rank, privilege, caste, or estate that had hitherto consigned people to roles determined by custom and command, not by their own choice.

The people who settled these shores during the seventeenth and eighteenth centuries were children of the Reformation driven by their need to worship God as it pleased them, according to their own wisdom and conscience. Believing that God had entered into a covenant with His people, they freely covenanted together to form churches. This was later called "the gathered church idea," seemingly endorsed by Jesus Himself in Matthew 18:20: "Where two or three are gathered together in my name, there am I in the midst of them."

The local New England church in the Puritan period had full ecclesiastical authority to ordain its minister and appoint deacons and elders. Its minister could celebrate communion, perform christenings, baptisms, and marriages, and conduct funerals—all on the authority of the local church. Each church was in voluntary fellowship with other churches, but in authority over none. The covenant pattern of the early New England churches was the paradigm for the federalist political structure erected two centuries ago. The West was moving from status to contract, as Sir Henry Maine would observe in 1861.

This concern for individual liberty in society was not limited to theologians. Tom Paine generally took a critical stance when dealing with religion and the church, but in 1775 in an essay entitled "Thoughts on Defensive War" he wrote as follows: "In the barbarous ages of the world, men in general had no liberty. The strong governed the weak at will; 'till the coming of Christ there was no such thing as political freedom in any part of the world. . . . The Romans held the world in slavery and were themselves slaves of their emperors. . . . Wherefore political as well as spiritual freedom is the gift of God through Christ." And Edward Gibbon, so critical of the Church in his history of Rome, nevertheless pays tribute to " . . . those benevolent principles of Christianity, which inculcate the natural freedom of mankind."

Our forebears of a couple of centuries ago regarded human freedom as a religious imperative. They loved to quote such biblical texts as: "Where the Spirit of the Lord is, there is liberty" (II Cor. 3:17), and "Proclaim liberty throughout all the land to all the inhabitants thereof." (Lev. 25:10) They struggled for freedom of worship; they fought for the right to speak their minds, and for a free press to put their convictions into written form. They also had firm convictions about private property. The popular slogan of the time was "Life, Liberty, and Property!" Property meant the right of private ownership. Adam Smith and his *Wealth of Nations* came along at just the right time—with what Smith called his "liberal plan of liberty, equality and justice"—to become the economic counterpart of the political ideas of the Declaration of Independence.

The Importance of the Individual

The central doctrine of the American political system is our belief in the inviolability of the individual man or woman. This is one of the self-evident truths enunciated in the Declaration of Independence: "We hold these Truths to be self-evident, that all Men are created equal, that they are endowed by their Creator with certain unalienable Rights, that among these are Life, Liberty, and the Pursuit of Happiness." The "equality" which is the key idea of the Declaration means "equal justice," the Rule of Law, the same rules for everybody because we are one in our essential humanity.

The reflections of H. L. Mencken on this point are intriguing as coming from a man usually critical of religion. In 1926 Mencken wrote an essay entitled "Equality Before the Law." "Of all the ideas associated with the general concept of democratic government," he wrote, "the oldest and perhaps the soundest is that of equality before the law. Its relation to the scheme of Christian ethics is too obvious to need statement. It goes back, through the political and theological theorizing of the middle ages, to the early Christian notion of equality before God. . . . The debt of democracy to Christianity has always been under estimated. . . . Long before Rousseau was ever heard of, or Locke or Hobbes, the fundamental principles of democracy were plainly stated in the New Testament, and elaborately expounded by the early fathers, including St. Augustine.

"Today, in all Christian countries, equality before the law is almost as axiomatic as equality before God. A statute providing one punishment for A and another for B, both being guilty of the same act, would be held unconstitutional every where, and not only unconstitutional, but also in plain contempt of common decency and the inalienable rights of man. The chief aim of most of our elaborate legal machinery is to give effect to that idea. It seeks to diminish and conceal the inequities that divide men in the general struggle for existence, and to bring them before the bar of justice as exact equals."

The freedom quest of Western man, as it has exhibited itself periodically over the past 20 centuries, is not a characteristic of man as such. It is a cultural trait, philosophically and religiously inspired. The basic religious vision of the West regards the planet earth as the creation of a good God who gives a man a soul and makes him responsible for its proper ordering; puts him on earth as a sort of junior partner with dominion over the earth; admonishes him to be fruitful and multiply; commands him to work; makes him a steward of the earth's scarce resources; holds him accountable for their economic use; and makes theft wrong because property is right. When this outlook comes to prevail, the groundwork is laid for a free and prosperous commonwealth such as we aspired to on this continent.

A Created Being in a Created World

We gaze out upon the world around us and are struck by the preponderance of order, harmony, beauty, balance, intelligence, and economy in the way it works. The thought strikes us that the explanation of the world is not contained within the world itself, but is to be sought in a Source outside the world. The Bible simply declares that God created the world, and when He had finished He looked out upon the world He had created and called it good. The biblical world is not *Maya*—as Hinduism calls its world; it is not a mirage or an illusion. Nor is the world of nature holy; only God is holy. The created world, including the realm of nature, is "the school of hard knocks." The earth challenges us to understand its workings so that we might learn to use it responsibly to serve our purposes. Economics and the free enterprise system teach us how to use the planet's scarce resources providently, efficiently, and non-wastefully—in order to produce more of the things we need.

Man comes onto the world scene as a created being. As a created being, man is a work of divine art and not a mere happening; he possesses free will and the ability to order his own actions. As such, he is a responsible being. He's no mere chance excrescence tossed up haphazardly by physical and chemical forces, shaped by accidental variations in his environment. To the contrary, man is endowed with a portion of the divine creativity, giving him the power to dynamically transform himself, and his environment as well, according to his needs and his vision of what ought to be.

The other orders of creation—animals, birds, bees, fish, and so on—live by the dictates of their instincts. But our species has no such

infallible inner guidelines as our fellow creatures possess; our guidelines are formulated in the moral code, as summed up in the Ten
Commandments.

Ethical relativism is a popular attitude today; it is a wrong answer
to such questions as: Is there a moral code? Are there moral laws? Let
me summarize briefly the argument that our universe has a built-in
moral order by showing that there is a striking parallel between the
laws of physical nature and moral laws.

The laws of science translate into words the observed causal regu-
larities in the world of physical nature, i.e., the realm of things which
can be measured, weighed, and counted. This is one sector of reality.
Reality also exhibits a moral dimension, where things are valued or
disdained on a scale of ethics ranging from good to evil. Biological
survival depends on conforming our actions to the laws of nature;
ignorance is no excuse. Social survival, the enhancement of individual
life in society, depends on willing obedience to the moral code that
condemns murder, theft, false witness, and the rest. Transgressors lead
us toward social decay and cultural disorder.

Your individual *physical* survival depends on several factors. If you
want to go on living you need so many cubic feet of air per hour, or
you suffocate. You need a minimum number of calories per day, or you
starve. If you lack certain vitamins and minerals specific diseases will
appear. There is a temperature range within which human life is possible: too low and you freeze, too high and you roast. These are some
of the requirements you must meet for individual bodily survival. They
are not statutory requirements, nor are they mere custom. They are
laws of this physical universe, which one can deny only at his peril.

Establishing a Moral Order

It is just as obvious that our survival as a community of men,
women, and children depends on meeting certain *moral* requirements:
a set of rules built into the nature of things which must be obeyed if
we are to survive as a society—especially as a social order characterized
by personal freedom, private property, and social cooperation under
the division of labor.

Moses did not invent the Ten Commandments. Moses intuited
certain features of this created world that tell us what we must do to
survive as a human community, and he wrote out the code: Don't

murder, don't steal, don't assault, don't bear false witness, don't covet. Similar codes may be found in every high culture.

It would be impossible to have *any* kind of a society where most people are constantly on the prowl for opportunities to murder, assault, lie, and steal. A good society is possible only if most people most of the time do not engage in criminal actions. A good society is one where most people most of the time tell the truth, keep their word, fulfill their contracts, don't covet their neighbor's goods, and occasionally lend a helping hand. No society will ever eliminate crime, but any society where more than a tiny fraction of the people exercises criminal tendencies is on the skids. To affirm a moral order is to say, in effect, that this universe has a deep prejudice against murder, a strong bias in favor of private property, and hates a lie.

The history of humankind in Western civilization was shaped and tempered by biblical ideas and values, and the attitudes inspired by these teachings. There was much backsliding, of course; but in the fullness of time scriptural ideas about freedom, private property, and the work ethic found expression in Western custom, law, government, and the economy—especially in our own nation. We prospered to the degree that we practiced the freedom we professed; we became ever more productive of goods and services. The general level of economic well-being rose to the point where many became rich enough so that biblical statements about the wealthy began to haunt the collective conscience.

The Bible does warn against the false gods of wealth and power, but it legitimizes the normal human desire for a modicum of economic well-being—which is not at all the same as *idolizing* wealth and/or power. As a matter of fact, the Bible gives anyone who seeks it out a general recipe for a free and prosperous commonwealth. It tells us that we are created with the capacity to choose; we are put on an earth which is the Lord's and given stewardship responsibilities over its resources. We are ordered to work, charged with rendering equal justice to all, and to love mercy. A people which puts these ideas into practice is bound to become better off than a people which ignores them. These commands laid the foundation for the economic well-being of Western society.

Western civilization, which used to be called "Christendom," did not prosper at the expense of the relatively poor Third World. This unhappy sector of the globe is poor because it is unproductive; and it is unproductive because its nations lack the institutions of freedom that enabled us to achieve prosperity.

During recent years a small library of books and study guides has poured off the presses of American church organizations (and from secular publishers as well) with titles something like "Rich Christians (or Americans) in a Hungry World." The allegation is that *our* prosperity is the cause of *their* poverty; in other words, the Third World has been made poor by the very same economic procedures—"capitalism"—that have made Western nations prosperous! Therefore—the argument runs—our earnings should be taxed away from us and our goods should be handed over to Third World countries—as a matter of social justice! The false premise is that the wealth we have labored to produce has been gained at their expense. Sending them our goods, then, is but to restore to the Third World what rightfully belongs to it! What perverse ignorance of the way the world works!

Nations of the West were founded on biblical principles of justice, freedom, and a work ethic, which led naturally to a rise in the general level of prosperity. Our wealth could not have come from the impoverished Third World where there was a scarcity of goods. We prospered because of our productivity; we became productive because we were freer than any other nation. Freedom in a society enables people to produce more, consume more, enjoy more; and also to give away more—as we have done—to the needy in this land and in lands all over the world. The world has never before witnessed international philanthropy on such a scale.

No one has denied Third World nations access to the philosophical and religious credo which has inspired the American practices that make for economic and social well-being. Few nations have done more to make the literature of liberty available to all who wish it than American missionaries, educators, philanthropists, and technicians. But there is something in the creeds of Third World countries that hinders acceptance. However, when non-Christian parts of the world decide to emulate Western ideas of economic freedom they prosper. Look what happened to the economies of Taiwan, South Korea, Hong Kong, and Singapore when they turned the market economy loose!

Regarding the Poor

Ecclesiastical pronouncements on the economy are fond of the phrase "a preferential option for the poor." It is invoked as the rationale for governmental redistribution of wealth, that is, for a program of taxing earnings away from those who produce in order to subsidize selected groups and individuals. But it is a fact that reshuffling wealth by programs of tax and subsidy merely enriches some at the expense of others; the nation as a whole becomes poorer. Private enterprise capitalism is, in fact, the answer for anyone who really does have a preferential option for the poor. The free market economy, wherever it has been allowed to function, has elevated more poor people further out of poverty faster than any other system.

Another phrase, repeated like a mantra, is "the poor and oppressed." There is, of course, a connection between these two words; a person who is oppressed is poorer than he would be otherwise. Oppression is always political; oppression is the result of unjust laws. Correct the injustice by repealing unjust laws; establish political liberty and economic freedom. But even in the resulting free society, where people are *not* oppressed, there will still be some people who are relatively poor because of the limited demand for their services. Teachers and preachers are poor compared to rock musicians because the masses spend millions to have their ears assaulted by amplified sound, in preference to the good advice often available for free!

Ecclesiastical documents announce their concern for "the poor and oppressed," but the authors of these documents are completely blind to the forms oppression may take in our day. If there are unjust political interventions that deny people employment, this would seem to be a flagrant case of oppression. There are many such interventions. Minimum-wage laws, for instance, deny certain people access to employment, and these people are poorer than they would be otherwise; the entire nation is less well off because some people are not permitted to take a job. The same might be said of the laws that grant monopoly status to certain groups of people gathered as "unions"—U.A.W., Teamsters, and the like. The above-market wage rate they gain for union members results in unemployment for others both union and nonunion. It is not difficult to figure out why this is so. The general principle is that when something begins to cost more we tend to use less of it. So, when labor begins to cost more, fewer workers will be hired.

It would take several pages to list all of the alphabet agencies that regulate, control, and hinder productivity, making the entire nation less prosperous than it need be. Our country suffers under these oppressions, economically and otherwise, but not so severely as the oppressed people of other nations, especially Communist and Third World nations. Churchmen recommend, as a cure for Third World poverty, that we deprive the already over-taxed and hampered productive segment of our people of an even larger portion of their earnings, so as to turn more of our money over to Third World governments. This will further empower the very Third World politicians who are even now oppressing their people, enabling those autocrats to oppress them more efficiently!

The New Testament and the Rich

It is not difficult to rebut the manifestoes issued by various religious organizations. But then we turn to certain New Testament writings and are confronted by what seem to be condemnations of the rich. How, for example, shall we understand Jesus' remark, found in Luke 18:25 and Matthew 19:24: "It is easier for a camel to go through a needle's eye, than for a rich man to enter into the kingdom of God"?

Jesus' listeners were astonished when they heard these words. Worldly prosperity, many of them assumed, was a mark of God's favor. It seemed to follow that the man whom God favored with riches in this life was thereby guaranteed a spot in heaven in the next.

There is a grain of truth in this distorted popular mentality. Biblical religion holds that man is a created being, with the signature of his Creator written on each person's soul. This inner sacredness implies the ideal of liberty and justice in the relations between person and person. These free people are given dominion over the earth in order to subdue it, working "for the glory of the Creator and the relief of man's estate," as Francis Bacon put it. This is but another way of saying that those who follow the natural order of things—God's order—in ethics and economics will do better for themselves than those who violate this order. The faithful, we read in Job 36:11, " . . . if they obey and serve Him . . . shall spend their days in prosperity and their years in pleasures."

Perhaps Jesus had something else in mind as well. Palestine had been conquered by Rome. Roman overlords, wielding power and enriching themselves at the expense of the local population, would certainly supply many examples of "a rich man." Furthermore, there were those among the subject people who hired themselves out as publicans to serve the Romans by extorting taxes from their fellow Jews. "Publicans and sinners" is virtually one word in the Gospels!

In nearly every nation known to history, rulers have used their political power to seize the wealth produced by others for the gratification of themselves and their friends. Kings and courtiers in the days of slavery and serfdom consumed much of the wealth produced by farmers, artisans, and craftsmen. Today, politicians in Communist, socialist, and welfarist nations, democratically elected by "the people," share their power with a congeries of special interests, factions, and pressure groups who systematically prey on the economy, depriving people who do the world's work of over 40 percent of everything they earn.

Many a "rich man" lives on legal plunder, today as well as in times past. Frederic Bastiat's little book, *The Law,* familiarizes us with the procedure. The law is an instrument of justice, intended to secure each individual in his right to his life, his liberty, and his rightful property. Ownership is rightfully claimed as the fruit of honest toil and/or as the result of voluntary exchanges of goods and services. But the law, as Bastiat points out, is perverted from an instrument of justice into a device of plunder when it takes goods from lawful owners by legislative fiat and transfers them to groups of the politically powerful. Political plunder is a species of theft. The fact that it is legally sanctioned does not make it morally right; it is a violation of the commandment against theft.

The Israelites had fond memories of King Solomon. "All through his reign," we read in I Kings 4:25, "Judah and Israel continued at peace, every man under his own vine and fig tree, from Dan to Beersheba." A nice tribute to individual ownership and economic well-being! The Bible has high praise for honestly earned wealth, and it is exceedingly unlikely that Jesus, in the passage we have been considering, intended anything like a general condemnation of wealth, as such.

At this point someone might raise a legitimate question: "Did not Jesus say, in the Sermon on the Mount, 'Blessed are the poor'?" Well, yes and no. The Sermon on the Mount appears in two of the four Gospels, in Matthew and in Luke. In Luke 6:20 the Beatitude reads: "Blessed are the poor"; but in Matthew 5:3 it is: "Blessed are the poor *in spirit.*" There's a discrepancy here; how shall we interpret it?

The Beatitudes were spoken somewhere between 25 and 30 A.D. The Gospels of Matthew and Luke appeared some 50 or 60 years later.

Both authors had access to the Gospel of Mark, to fragments of other writings now lost, and to an oral tradition extending over the generations. We do not have the original manuscripts of the Gospels; what we have are copies of copies, and eventually translations of copies into various languages.

Scholars tell us that the Aramaic original of those two words, "the poor," is *am ha-aretz*—"people of the land." The *am ha-aretz*—at this stage in Israel's history—were outside the tribal system of Jewish society; they did not have the time or inclination to observe the niceties of priestly law, let alone its scribal elaborations. The work of the *am ha-aretz* brought them into contact with Gentiles and Gentile ways of life, which in the eyes of the orthodox was defiling. Their status is like that of the people on the bottom rung of the Hindu caste system—the *Sudras*. Jesus is reminding His hearers that these outcasts are equal in God's sight to anyone else in Israel, and because of their lowly station in the eyes of society, they may be more open to man's need of God than the proud people in the ranks above them. The New English Bible provides an interesting slant on this text; it translates "poor in spirit" as "those who know their need of God."

In short, Jesus is saying that all are equally precious in God's sight, including the lowly *am ha-aretz;* He is not praising indigence, as such.

Biblical Interpretation

The Bible is full of metaphor and symbolism and allegory. Literal interpretation usually falls short; proper interpretation demands a bit of finesse . . . as in the case of St. Paul's remark about money.

St. Paul declared that "The love of money is the root of all evil." (I Tim. 6:10) The word "money" in this context—scholars tell us—does not mean coins, or bonds, or a bank account. Paul uses the word "money" to symbolize the secular world's pursuit of wealth and power. We tend to become infatuated with "the world." It's the infatuation which is evil, for God's kingdom is not wholly of this world. We are the kind of creatures whose ultimate destiny is achieved only in another order of reality: "Here we have no continuing city" (Heb. 13:14). Accept this world with all its joys and delights; live it to the full; but remember—we are pilgrims, not settlers. In today's vernacular, Paul might be telling us: "Have a love affair with this world, but don't marry it!"

We know that there are numerous unlawful ways to get rich, and these deserve condemnation. But prosperity also comes to a man or woman as the fairly earned reward of honest effort and service. The Bible has nothing but praise for wealth thus gained. "Seest thou a man diligent in his business?" said the author of Proverbs (Prov. 22:29). "He shall stand before kings." Economic well-being is everyone's birthright, provided it is the result of honest effort. But we are warned against a false philosophy of material possessions.

This, I think, is the point of Jesus' parable of the rich man whose crops were so good that he had to build bigger barns. (Luke 12:17) This good fortune was the man's excuse for saying, "Soul, thou hast much goods laid up for many years; take thine ease, eat, drink, be merry."

There is a twofold point to this parable. The first is that nothing in life justifies us in resigning from life; we must never stop growing. It has been well said that we don't *grow* old, we *become* old by not growing. The second point is that a material windfall—like falling heir to a million dollars—may tempt a man into the error of quitting the struggle for the real goals in life. Jesus condemned the man who put his *trust* in riches, who "layeth up treasure for himself and is not rich toward God." He did not condemn material possessions as such; He taught stewardship, which is the responsible ownership and use of rightfully acquired material goods.

Life here is probative; our three score years and ten are a sort of test run. As St. Augustine put it, "We are here schooled for life eternal." And one of the important examination questions concerns our economic use of the planet's scarce resources and the proper management of our material possessions. These are the twin facets of Christian stewardship, and poor performance here will result in dire consequences. Jesus put it very strongly: "If, therefore, you have not been faithful in the use of worldly wealth, who will entrust to you the true riches?" (Luke 16:12)

What does it mean to be "faithful in the use of worldly wealth?" What else can it mean except the intelligent and responsible use of the planet's scarce resources to transform them by human effort and ingenuity into the consumable goods we humans require not only for survival, but also as a means for the finer things in life? In practice, this means free market capitalism—the free enterprise system—in the production, exchange, and utilization of our material wealth in the service of our chosen goals.

Churches and the Social Order

It was once the unwritten rule in polite society that two topics have no place in civilized conversation: religion and politics. It was ill-bred to discuss religion; it was gauche to talk politics. But times have changed. We live in a different and more open age. Now we discuss religion for political reasons, and we talk politics for religious reasons! The Bishops issue a Letter; the highest dignitaries of the various denominations pronounce on matters of government and business. The people behind these proclamations represent only a tiny minority of the total church membership, but they presume to speak for everyone. What they say is, in effect, the Socialist Party platform in ecclesiastical drag.

These ecclesiastical documents focus on an economic malaise, poverty; the poverty of the masses, especially the masses of the Third World. Churchmen profess to know the cause of this poverty. Third World poverty is caused by the wealth of the capitalistic nations; *they* are poor because we, in becoming wealthy, have pauperized them. Likewise, within our own nation the wealth of those who are better off is gained at the expense of those who are made worse off in the process. These are the typical allegations: the rich get richer by making the poor poorer.

Ecclesiastical myopia views the market economy—or capitalism— as an evil system which, by its very nature impoverishes the many as the means by which the few are enriched. The suggested cure for these differentials in wealth is to use government's power to tax to exact tribute from the rich, and then distribute the proceeds to the poor— minus the cost to the nation of these wealth transfers. Robin Hood robs the rich to pay the poor, but Robin takes his cut!

It is as if these churchmen had swallowed the current secular agenda to which they have merely added oil and unction; as if social reform were the end, religion the mere means; as if religion has little more to offer modern men and women beyond what they can get from contemporary liberalism or socialism. The Church has a more impor-

---

From the August 1986 issue of *The Freeman*.

tant role to play in human life, as I shall suggest in the course of this article.

One of my favorite modern theologians is the late William Ralph Inge. Inge was the Dean of St. Paul's Cathedral in London, the scholar's pulpit of the Church of England. Dean Inge wrote some notable books in theology, philosophy, and social theory, but he was also a newspaper columnist during the 1920s where his hard-nosed comments on the passing scene earned him the nickname, "the gloomy Dean."

Christian Socialism was strong within the church of England, with some churchmen going so far as to declare that for a Christian not to be a socialist was to be guilty of heresy. A popular slogan was "Christianity is the religion of which Socialism is the practice." Dean Inge would have none of this, so he waged a perpetual war of words against the socialists, especially against socialists of the Christian variety. "I do not like to see the clergy," he wrote, "who were monarchists under a strong monarchy, and oligarchs under the oligarchy, tumbling over each other in their eagerness to become court chaplains to King Demos. The black coated advocates of spoliation are not a nice lot!"

It was not that Dean Inge was a defender of the *status quo;* far from it. Inge was a severe critic of many features of the modern Western world. He argued that socialism is little more than a logical extension of many of the worst features of the modern temper, derived from the French Revolution, with its inveterate faith that man is a good animal by nature, but corrupted by his institutions; "Man is born free, but is everywhere in chains," as Rousseau put it. This being the case said the socialists, all we have to do is change our institutions in order to produce an improved society out of unimproved men and women.

Dean Inge foresaw a tendency within this mind-set toward "a reversion to a political and external religion, the very thing against which the Gospel waged relentless war." It is not that Christianity regards social progress as unimportant, Inge goes on to say; it is a question of how genuine improvement may occur. "The true answer," he wrote, "though it is not a very popular one, is that the advance of civilization is in truth a sort of by-product of Christianity, not its chief aim; but we can appeal to history to support us that [the advance of civilization] is most stable and genuine when it is the by-product of a lofty and unworldly idealism."

The Pull of Public Opinion

Churchmen in every age are tempted to adopt the protective coloration of their time; like all intellectuals, churchmen are verbalists and wordsmiths; they are powerfully swayed by the printed page, by catchwords, slick phrases, slogans, and bumper stickers. In consequence, they are pulled first this way then that by whatever currents of public opinion happen at the moment to exert the greatest power over their emotions and imagination. Today, it is the powerful gravitational pull of "environmental determinism."

I'm using the phrase as a label for the belief that the human species is nothing but what external conditions have made us, that we are the victims of circumstances, that our lives are determined by forces we can barely understand, let alone control. Random chemical and physical interactions produced mankind in the first place. Then this raw material—mankind as it comes from nature—is shaped into various forms by the particular society in which we find ourselves. The social class to which we belong determines, finally, what we are and how we view the world and ourselves. Environmental determinism exerts a powerful attraction today over intellectuals of all creeds. It is the ideology of Marxists and non-Marxists alike that men and women are the mere end products of nature and society—responsible men and women no longer—and that social engineering can construct a perfect society out of defective human units. Environmentalism has the cart before the horse; it is dehumanizing.

If there is disorder in our society it follows that there is disorder within our very selves, in our faulty thinking and erroneous beliefs, in our misplaced loyalties and misguided affections. Disharmony in our personal lives will result in conflict and frictions in society. This is why serious religion has traditionally focused on the inward and the spiritual, on the mind and conscience of individual persons, to make them responsible individuals. The premise is that only right beliefs rightly held can produce right action. The good society emerges only if there is a significant number of people of intellect and character; and the elevation of character is the perennial concern of genuine religion, in league with education and art.

But the modern world views the matter differently. The modern world assumes that the human species is the mere end product of external forces; a product, first of all, of physics and chemistry—our natural environment; and a product, secondly, of the particular society in which an individual happens to live. The basic assumption is that man's character is made for him, by others; no individual is really responsible for himself. It is only necessary, then, for "the others" to acquire political power and use it to create social structures designed to produce a new humanity. Transform external arrangements and— according to this ideology—it matters little if men and women remain unregenerate; they will behave correctly because their institutions have programmed them to act according to the blueprint. This is the modern heresy.

Christianity, rightly understood, stands for a society with such basic features as personal responsibility, equal justice under the law, and maximum freedom for every person—the kind of society envisioned by the eighteenth-century Whigs like Burke, Madison, and Jefferson. Such a social and political order as the Whigs had in mind lays down the conditions in a nation which permit the operation of one kind of an economic order only, the free market economy—later nicknamed capitalism—the thing described by Adam Smith.

The economic order which Adam Smith challenged was called Mercantilism. Mercantilism was the communism or socialism or planned economy of the seventeenth and eighteenth centuries. The nation was covered with a network of minute regulations controlling every stage of manufacture and exchange, and the controls were brutally enforced, as they must be in every planned economy; in a 73-year period in France, 1686 to 1759, approximately 16,000 people were put to death for some infraction of the government regulations over the economy.

Adam Smith set out to free the economy with what he referred to as his "liberal plan of liberty, equality, and justice" (p. 628). It is more than a coincidence that *The Wealth of Nations* and the Declaration of Independence appeared within a few months of each other, in the year 1776. The Declaration endorses the Whig political vision whose main features were voiced by Jefferson in his First Inaugural: "Equal and exact justice to all men, of whatever state or persuasion, religious or political; peace, commerce, and honest friendship with all nations— entangling alliances with none ... freedom of religion, freedom of the press, freedom of the person under the protection of the habeas corpus," and so on. This was the political and legal framework laid down by the Whig theorists, within which Adam Smith's free market economy, or capitalism, had the freedom necessary if it was to function—his "liberal plan of liberty, equality and justice."

Millions of people during the twentieth century have turned away from the traditional religious faiths of the West—Christianity and Judaism—to embrace some form of secular religion, such as communism or socialism. The prevailing world view in our time is not Theism—the belief that mind and spirit are rock-bottom realities in the universe; it is Materialism—the belief that basic reality is composed of nothing else but particles of matter: the 105 elements from actinium to zirconium.

Materialism is explicit wherever Marxism is the official creed, but it is implicit almost everywhere else. Begin with the Marxist premise of Dialectical Materialism—or any other variety of Materialism—and some form of totalitarianism logically follows. Such a society reduces human persons to minions of the state, to be used and used up in the utopian endeavor to bring about the classless society of the communist pipe dream. Christian doctrine, by contrast, makes the individual person central. His role in life is to serve the highest value he can conceive—God; the modest role of the political order is to provide maximum freedom for all persons in order that we, as created beings, may achieve our proper destiny.

The Theocratic Temptation

In the free society, church and state are independent of one another, as set forth in the First Amendment. But there is, historically, a perennial temptation for church and state to join forces and form a theocracy—an alliance which tends to divinize politics and depreciate genuine religion. We are moving in that direction.

The church has been allied with the state ever since the fourth century, and this church-state combination has often been less than Christian in its treatment of Christians, and others. Edward Gibbon, the eighteenth-century historian, is only one of the many scholars who have chastised the official church for its misdeeds. But listen to Gibbon when he refers to original Gospel Christianity; he speaks of " . . . those benevolent principles of Christianity, which inculcate the natural freedom of mankind" (Vol. I, p. 661).

The idea of Christian freedom came into sharp focus in the preaching of eighteenth-century clergymen in New England. F. P. Cole, an historian of the period, writes: "There is probably no group of men in history, living in a particular area at a given time, who can speak as forcibly on the subject of liberty as the Congregational ministers of New England between 1750 and 1785."

It was the custom of the New England clergy to preach twice a year on some theme having to do with the secular order, the Artillery Day Sermon and the Election Day Sermon. These scholarly sermons were published by the Massachusetts General Court, as the legislature was then called, and they have provided the raw material for many a doctoral dissertation. Let me offer a typical statement by one of the ablest of these preachers, Jonathan Mayhew of Boston, in 1752. "Having been initiated in youth in the doctrines of civil liberty, as they were taught by such men as Plato, Demosthenes, Cicero, and other renowned persons among the ancients; and such as Sydney and Milton, Locke and Hoadley among the moderns, I liked them; they seemed rational. And having learnt from the Holy Scriptures that wise, brave, and virtuous men were always friends of liberty,—that God gave the Israelites a king in His anger, because they had not the sense and virtue enough to be a free commonwealth,—and that 'where the spirit of the Lord is, there is liberty'—this made me conclude that freedom was a great blessing."

Religion and the Founders

Most of the men we refer to as our Founding Fathers were not active churchmen, for one reason or another, but they were men of strong religious convictions. Norman Cousins has compiled a 450-page anthology of the religious beliefs and ideas of eight of these men in their own words (*In God We Trust,* 1958). Those quoted are Franklin, Washington, Jefferson, Madison, the two Adamses, Hamilton, and Jay. There's also a section devoted to Tom Paine. A familiar statement of Jefferson pretty well summarizes the outlook of this remarkable group of men. "The God who gave us life, gave us liberty at the same time."

Tom Paine authored some influential political pamphlets, and he also wrote a great deal on the subject of religion, much of it critical—which is all right, because there is much about the ecclesiastical life of any period which deserves criticism. But when it was a matter of Christian liberty, Paine was on target. Cousins, for some reason, does not quote a surprising statement by Paine: "Wherefore, political as well as spiritual liberty, is the gift of God, through Christ" (from his essay "Thoughts on Defensive War").

What was the situation in the nineteenth century? Let me offer a few remarks by one of the keenest foreign observers ever to visit this nation, Alexis de Tocqueville. Tocqueville landed in New York in May 1831. Nine months and seven thousand miles later he returned to France and wrote his great book, *Democracy in America,* with special attention being given to religion and the churches. "The Americans combine the notions of Christianity and of liberty so intimately in their minds," he wrote, "that it is impossible to make them conceive the one without the other. . . . Religion in America takes no direct part in the government of society, but it must be regarded as the first of their political institutions. . . . They hold it to be indispensable to the maintenance of republican institutions."

"Despotism may govern without faith," he continues, "but liberty cannot . . . [for] how is it possible that society should escape destruction if the moral tie is not strengthened in proportion as the political tie is relaxed?"

Tocqueville observed that the clergy stayed away from politics. The clergy, he observed, "keep aloof from parties and public affairs . . . . In the United States religion exercises but little direct influence upon the laws and upon the details of public opinion; but [religion] directs the customs of the community, and, by regulating everyday life it regulates the state."

A Spotty Record

The history of the church during the past two thousand years is a spotty record, with many ups and some downs. There have been glorious epochs, and there have been periods which make for melancholy reading. Occasionally, the church has sanctioned tyrannous political rule; from time to time it has lent its support to persecutions, inquisitions, and crusades. As an arm of the state, or as a tool of the state, it has betrayed its sacred task while it pursued secular goals like wealth and power.

In the twentieth century segments of ecclesiastical officialdom and councils of churches demand legislation to transfer wealth from one group of citizens to another. They work for a collectivist economic order planned, controlled, and regulated by government. The intended aim is to overcome poverty and feed the hungry; the means is the planned economy, otherwise labeled socialism, collectivism, the new deal, or whatever. Whatever the label, the planned economy puts the nation in a straitjacket; the planned economy, however noble the intentions of the planners, is the road to serfdom, as F. A. Hayek demonstrated in a landmark book written some forty years ago.

A planned economy forcibly directs the lives of individual men and women, and to do so the state must deprive people of their earnings which they would otherwise use to direct their own lives. Nation after nation during the twentieth century has gone in for political planning of the economy and the results have been disastrous; where the planning has been strictly enforced, as in Communist nations, the result has been a nation ill housed, ill fed, and ill clothed. It is a sad paradox indeed that the secular program, promoted by church hierarchies to alleviate poverty, has caused poverty in every society which has tried it. The only way to alleviate poverty in a nation is to increase productivity; and increased productivity is generated only by an economy of free men and women. Freedom is an essential part of the church's business. Freedom is a blessing in itself, and it's a double blessing, for prosperity follows freedom.

The socialists, until recently, have claimed the high moral ground. Their boast is that only socialists—or liberals—really care about people. What nonsense! Every person of good will wants to see other people better off; better housed, better fed, better clothed, healthier, better educated, with finer medical care, and all the rest. The dispute between socialists and believers in the free economy is not so much over the goals as over the means by which these goals may be met. The socialist's means—his command economy—will not achieve the goals he says he wants to reach; socialism makes the nation worse off; poorer in material wealth, and poorer in every other respect as well.

There is another route for churchmen to take, a way that leads to more freedom for people in society, rather than less freedom. Freedom is at the heart of the gospel message, and the true genius of our religion was proudly proclaimed by our forebears, some of whose words I have quoted.

Man's will is uniquely free; that's the way God made us. We are free beings precisely in order that each person shall be responsible for his own life and therefore accountable for his actions. It is by acts of will, acts of choice, exercised daily over the course of a lifetime that each of us becomes the person we have the potential to be. Each person is by nature self-controlling; each person is in charge of his own life.

The free society, then, is our natural habitat: freedom in the relations of persons to each other accords with human nature. The tactic of freedom in the business and industrial sectors is the free market economy; the free-choice economic system corresponds to the freely choosing creature that each of us is.

Animals, unlike us humans, have a finely tuned set of instincts which infallibly guides each creature according to its species. We humans do not have such elaborate instinctual equipment; instead of instincts we are given a moral code, which we are free to obey or not. Anyone can figure out for himself that no kind of society is possible unless most people most of the time do not murder, steal, assault, or lie. Thus we have commandments that say Thou shalt not murder, Thou shalt not steal, Thou shalt not bear false witness, and so on. These and other commands compose the basic moral code which is the foundation of our law.

Because we are flawed creatures as well as free, we occasionally break the law, and so we need an umpire to interpret and, if necessary, enforce the rules. We refer to this umpire function as the political order—government, the police power, the law. And we have the courts, where honest differences of opinion may be examined and resolved.

The Productivity of Capitalism

The free market economy, or private property order, or capitalism—if you like—is, by common agreement, the most productive economic order. In fact, it's the only productive economic order. Socialism in a given country lives by exploiting the previous productive economy of that country, and when that gives out, socialist nations live on largess from capitalist nations.

The incredible productivity of capitalism is generally admitted, even by its critics; it's the way the wealth gets distributed that they complain about. What's wrong about capitalism, the critics charge, is that some people in our society have enormous incomes while other people have to get by on a mere pittance. Disparities in income show up most vividly in the sports and entertainment industries. Take basketball players, for instance. Basketball is a fun game which thousands play for pleasure and recreation. But many professional players make more money in a year than any six of us will make in a lifetime of hard work. Baseball is almost as grotesque, and then the players threaten to strike for more pay! A rock singer gives what is laughably called a concert and more money changes hands in one evening than the Seattle Symphony sees in a year. Supply your own examples. The question is: How can any person with even a modicum of intelligence and refinement condone such grotesqueries? How do we respond to such a critic?

Part of the answer is that in a free society—a social order characterized by equal freedom under the law—the marketplace becomes a showcase for popular folly, ignorance, superstition, bad taste, and stupidity. The market, in other words, is individual free choice in action, and no one is pleased with everyone else's choices. But our displeasure is a price we must learn to pay if we are to enjoy the blessings of liberty. We must stand firmly behind the processes of freedom, even though we can barely stand some of the products of freedom. So let's stop wringing our hands; let's try to be tolerant, and let's get on with our lifelong task of setting a better example of what freedom means.

Remember that no one is *forced* to pay over good money to watch a sporting event; no one *has* to listen to some hyperkinetic young man howl and gyrate in public places to the accompaniment of amplified sound. You and I might not pay money for such a performance, and if everyone were just like us, those who now make millions playing games would have to go back to sport for its own sake, just like the rest of us. And if a miraculous change in musical taste should occur, there'd be crowds attending Bach recitals every Sunday afternoon on your local church organ.

Turn from the sports and entertainment field to the business and industry sector. Here, too, there are wide variations in wages, income, and wealth. How does this come about?

Here's a person with a knack for manufacturing a better mousetrap, which turns out to be just what millions of consumers have been waiting for. They are willing to pay handsomely for this better mousetrap, and so the manufacturer becomes wealthy. His employees also benefit. Our entrepreneur's wealth is voluntarily conferred upon him by consumers who aren't forced to buy the product, but who find that these new mousetraps make their lives safer, better, and more enjoyable. Every step in this procedure—manufacturing, marketing, exchanging—is free and fair, and when this is the case the resulting distribution of rewards is also fair. It is only when someone profits and becomes rich because government gives him a subsidy or provides him with some advantage over his rivals and his customers that there is maldistribution and unfairness in the final result.

Setting a Good Example

Let me emphasize the fact that the free market economy rewards each participant according to the value willing consumers attach to his offering of goods and services. Why does a rock singer make millions while your fine church organist makes hundreds? The answer is obvious; crowds of people would rather pay a lot of money to hear rock than to listen to Bach for free. We may find this intellectual and esthetic wasteland repugnant to our refined sensibilities. But what an opportunity this situation presents to every teacher. I refer not only to full-time professors, preachers, and writers. Most anyone can be a teacher. Nearly everyone, in other words, has the capacity to convey a new idea to some other person, to instill a nobler sentiment, a superior value, a higher moral tone. More persuasive than any of these, we can set a good example.

It is a solid truth, I believe, that you cannot build a free society out of just any old kind of people. A free society is built around a nucleus of people of superior intellect and integrity who are, at the same time, cognizant of economic and political reality. You need people who love God and their neighbor; people of understanding and compassion; people with enduring family ties. Our schools and our churches should be producing people of this caliber, for it is the function of education and religion—in the broad sense of both terms—to make us better and wiser men and women. When we have a significant number of wise and good people living lives of a quality high enough to deserve a free society we'll *have* a free society. All the rest of us, riding on their coattails, will reap the rich blessings of liberty.

Human Nature and the Free Society

Is there anything in the basic makeup of the men and women we know, or those we read about in the press, or encounter in the pages of history texts, which encourages us to believe that the free society we strive for is a realistic possibility?

Edward Gibbon, the great historian of Rome's decline and fall, offered, as his considered judgment, the opinion that "History is little more than a register of the crimes, follies, and misfortunes of mankind." The bleakness of this assessment is redeemed somewhat by the inclusion of the words "little more." Human nature does have its dark underside which pulls us down below the norm and produces the crimes, follies, and misfortunes recorded by historians.

But there is more to our story than this; there is also a record of the geniuses in every field—including heroes and saints—who demonstrate the realized potential of our common humanity. And then there are the multitudes who are just plain, ordinary, decent, hardworking folks, uplifted on occasion by the magnetism of those who rise above the average, and sometimes seized by a madness of sorts when the criminal and depraved acquire a kind of glamour.

Every society takes on its unique characteristics from the people who compose it; we are the basic ingredients of our society. The human story is a checkered affair; some ups, many downs. Does a realistic appraisal of our history on this planet provide any warrant for believing that we human beings are capable of approximating a truly free society with its market economy?

I propose to deal with four features of human nature and conduct which give me confidence that in the constitution of ordinary men and women are the characteristics which incline them to strive for a freer life with their fellows. I shall list these four points and then discuss them.

1. There is a strong instinct in all men and women to be free to pursue their personal goals.

2. There is a universal need in each of us to call something our very own; an instinct for property.

From the October 1987 issue of *The Freeman*.

3. There is an upward thrust in human nature to live a life that is not simply more comfortable, but better in a moral sense. We really believe in fair play; we respond to the ideals of justice.

4. The market is everywhere; people in every part of the globe have sought to better their economic circumstances by barter and trade. The market is universal; but only occasionally does the market become institutionalized as the market economy.

First Point—Freedom

Every person has a deeply rooted urge to be free to pursue his chosen goals; it is impossible to imagine a person, who is determined to accomplish a certain task, inviting people to hinder or prevent him from getting his job done. Even a dictator as vicious as Stalin, one of whose aims was to extinguish personal freedom in a great nation, demanded complete freedom to pursue his evil goals. Anyone who tried to hinder him was shortly referred to in the past tense.

But despite the universal urge for full personal liberty, most people who have ever lived have been slaves, serfs, bondsmen, thralls, helots, Sudras, retainers, lackeys, vassals, liege men, and the like. Despite the fact that every person wants to be free to live on his own terms, most of the earth's people have lived wholly or in part on terms laid down by someone else. There are more of them today than ever before. A powerful instinct for individual liberty animates virtually every man and woman, but this universal urge to be free has been fully institutionalized only once in history—in the theory and practice of old-fashioned Whiggery and Classical Liberalism, rising and falling during the period, approximately from the American Revolution to the early twentieth century.

Second Point—Property

The sense of personal identity is aroused in us early in infancy; it suddenly dawns on each of us that "I am me!" The seeds of our lifelong personal uniqueness are planted early. As soon as we learn to think "me" we begin to think its inevitable corollary, "mine." Every child early on comes to regard certain toys as his own. Each of us grows into a property relationship with things in his environment long before he evolves a theory of property, that is, a theory of the correct relationship between ourselves and the things that belong to us. Your property is an extension of yourself, no one can live his life to the full unless he owns the things on which his life depends, things which he may use and dispose of in any peaceful way he chooses. Justice demands that every person have a right to acquire property, for every person's sense of self is powerfully linked to the things he owns.

Because property is right, theft is wrong. The belief that property is right is so nearly universal that even thieves believe it. The pick pocket who steals your wallet does not intend his action as a symbolic gesture against the idea of private property; he may be a crook, but he's no socialist! Every crook believes in the sanctity of private property—he doesn't want people stealing from him! His attitude toward other folks' property is, shall we say, somewhat liberated. And there's the rub. "Me" and "mine" is a natural instinct; it's the "thee" and "mine" that needs to be fortified by moral values, by manners, and by the law. Gradually, as we mature into moral beings, reciprocity—the idea of "do as you would be done by"—generates the belief that mutual respect for individual property rights is the cornerstone of the free society.

Since the dawn of history, getting hold of other people's property by war, plunder, piracy, pillage, and looting has been a way of life for a large segment of mankind. "Robbery is perhaps the oldest of labor saving devices," wrote Lewis Mumford fifty years ago, "and war vies with magic in its efforts to get something for nothing." And Ludwig von Mises points out that "All ownership derives from occupation and violence." (*Socialism*, p. 32. See also *Human Action*, p. 679.) English civilization emerged in the aftermath of the Norman Conquest; most modern nations have followed a similar pattern, including our own. A people or a tribe acquires its territory by successfully doing battle. It is only the slow progress of civilization and the development of the idea of the Rule of Law that generates the belief that every person's property should be regarded as inviolate by every other person.

A corollary of this is the belief that the primary task of a just legal system is to secure every person's right to that which is his own. We do this by stressing the sanctity of private property and, when moral deterrents to theft are not enough, we seek to discourage thievery by invoking a swift and sure justice designed to increase the risks of robbery and diminish any conceivable benefits.

Third Point—Justice

The practice of pillage is ancient, but so is mankind's concern for justice. Some fifteen hundred years before Christ, a legislator of ancient Israel wrote: "You shall not pervert justice, either by favoring the poor or by subservience to the great. You shall judge your fellow country-men with strict justice" (Lev. 19:15). Pericles, the Athenian statesman of the fifth century B.C., said in his great funeral oration: "If we look to the laws, they afford equal justice to all in their private differences." And Cicero, one of the last of the old Romans, in the century before our era: "Of all these things respecting which learned men dispute there is none more important than clearly to understand that we are born for justice, and that right is founded not in opinion but in na-ture."

Long before some unknown genius framed a theory of justice, men and women knew when they had been wronged, betrayed, let down, dealt with unfairly. The capacity to make moral judgments is built into human nature itself; and human nature is constituted as it is because our nature is derived from the ways things are in the universe.

We are "in play" with the universe as we try to keep in time with its music. We have, for example, categories of round and square be-cause these shapes and others are found in the nature existing outside us. The concepts of long and short would be meaningless to us were length not one characteristic of the way things are. We have a sense of beauty because we have seen lovely things and listened to melodious sounds. And by the same token, the distinction that mankind univer-sally makes between right and wrong or good and evil presupposes a moral dimension in this universe from which our personal categories derive.

As far back as we can trace man's story we find him drawing ethical distinctions, employing the categories of right and wrong. Jeane Kirkpatrick speaks of " . . . the irreducible human concern with moral-ity." Obviously, we would not expect universal agreement as to which actions should be classified as right and which wrong; but the classifi-cation would stand—nearly everyone has agreed that some things are right and others are wrong. It is a long trail that leads from these primitive beginnings to the insights of the moral geniuses of the race— the Hebrew Prophets, Jesus, Confucius, St. Francis—and to the refinements of moral theory of the great philosophers of ethics—Aristotle, Marcus Aurelius, Aquinas, Spinoza, Adam Smith, to name a few.

At this point some timid folk may fear that we are treading on dangerous ground here. Start with the philosophical distinction between right and wrong, they point out, and the next step is to divide people into the multitudes who are wrong, and the few of us who are right. A third step seems to follow: We who are right are commissioned to correct the evil ways of the rest of you. Hence, crusades against the infidel, suppression, prohibitions, and the like. A spoilsport like Carrie Nation goes around with her hatchet busting up saloons! Innocent pleasures and festive occasions come under attack. Reaction against such real or imagined sequences of events contributes to the widespread ethical relativism of our time. Right and wrong, we now hear it said, is a matter of taste, a matter of feeling; everyone is entitled to decide for himself what is right or wrong for him. In today's vernacular, we are told: "Do your own thing."

But when you discard ethical yardsticks, the weak doing their thing are at the mercy of the strong doing theirs, as the twentieth century attests. Ours is the age of ethical relativism and nihilism, and it's no coincidence that "we live in an age unique for the unrestrained use of brute force in international relations." The words are those of Pitirim Sorokin, from his four-volume study of war during the past 2,500 years. The most widespread, potent, evangelizing religion of our time is Communism, and Communist theory has no place for the traditional ethical yardsticks; in Marxist theory, right and wrong are whatever the party commands. In consequence, Communist policy during the first seventy years after the Russian Revolution has exacted a toll of more than a hundred million lives, and what it has not destroyed it has damaged.

These horrors do not faze the liberals who, when their attention is called to the facts, like to refer to Lenin's remark that you cannot make an omelet without breaking a few eggs. Human life is cheap in the twentieth century.

You can burn down the barn and get rid of the rats, and you can discard the idea of a moral order and get rid of the reformers. But at what price! If there are no ethical standards, moral relativism holds sway, right gives way to might, and disaster overtakes us in the ways made familiar in this century.

Traditional ethical theory maintains that right is right and wrong is wrong, Why? Because the universe has a built-in moral dimension, a moral law, often identified with God's will. In any event, this moral law is anchored in something deeper and more fundamental than private feelings, majority opinion, party dictates, or the will of some despot. The moral law is an important facet of the nature of things, and it is binding on all men and women.

Every one of us is fallible; no one can be certain that he has correctly read some deliverance of the moral law. So we shouldn't be surprised when some would-be reformer comes out of the woodwork and annoys us with his eccentric interpretations of the moral law. He may earnestly desire to do good, but he goes about it in the wrong way. But such a person is harmless, unless he comes to power. Moreover, if we solicit the counsel of the most ethically advanced men and women we find that they are unanimous in telling us that the right and the good can be advanced in three ways only: by reason, by persuasion, and above all by example.

Fourth Point—Economic Action

It is a fact of the human situation—regardless of the nature of the social order—that man does not find, ready-made in his natural environment, the wherewithal to feed, house, and clothe himself. There are only raw materials in nature, and most of these are not capable of satisfying human needs until someone works them over and transforms them into consumable goods.

Man has to work in order to survive. He learns to cooperate with nature, making use of natural forces to serve his ends. Work is built into the human situation; the things by which we live do not come into existence unless someone grows them, manufactures them, builds them, and moves them from place to place .

Work is irksome and things are scarce, so people must learn to economize and avoid waste. They invent labor-saving devices, they manufacture tools, they specialize and exchange the fruits of their specialization. They learn to get along with each other, our natural sociability reinforced by the discovery that the division of labor benefits all. Division of labor and voluntary exchange constitute the marketplace, which is the greatest labor-saving device of all.

"This division of labor, from which so many advantages are derived," wrote Adam Smith, "is not originally the effect of any human wisdom which foresees and intends that general opulence to which it gives occasion. It is the necessary, though very slow and gradual, consequence of a certain propensity in human nature ... the propensity to truck, barter, and exchange one thing for another.... It is common to all men, and to be found in no other race of animals."

It is natural for us human beings, as we seek to improve our circumstances, to bargain, swap, barter, and trade. This is the market in action: men and women trading goods and services in a noncoercive situation. The benefits of such activity are mutual and obvious, which is why the market is everywhere. The market has always existed, and it's in operation today all over the world. Virtually no tribes are so primitive, and no collectivism so totalitarian as to prevent people from engaging in voluntary exchanges for mutual advantage. But only rarely has the market ever got itself institutionalized as the market economy—the thing called capitalism.

What does it mean to say that something has been institutionalized? When practices which heretofore have been informal and sporadic become formalized, regular, habitual, and customary, they are said to be institutionalized. As institutions they operate by an established rule or principle; they draw support from the moral code and are buttressed by appropriate laws.

For example, education is institutionalized as the school; religion is institutionalized as the church. And the market—individuals trading, bartering, and swapping—is institutionalized as the market economy, or capitalism. This occurs when free-market practices are allied with appropriate moral, cultural, legal, and political structures. Has this ever happened? Yes, but probably only once. and in a few countries only, when free-market practices coalesced with the Whig social order in the eighteenth and nineteenth centuries. This was the social order Adam Smith referred to as his "liberal plan of equality, liberty and justice."

I have briefly set forth four convictions of mine—which I would put into the category of self-evident truths. First, every person has an unquenchable urge to be free to pursue his personal goals—but seldom translates this into the idea of "equal freedom." Second, every person has an instinct for private property—every "me" requires a "mine." Third, every person has moral sense; he knows when he has been dealt with unfairly or treated unjustly. When we become mature persons we strive for equity; we try to treat others as we would like to be treated. In the fourth place, it is a fact of common observation that people of every culture, and at every level from the most primitive to the most civilized, engage in trade and barter; the market is ubiquitous.

A Fifth Point—Political Plunder

And now for the bad news: Whenever a society moves above the level of desperate poverty, and has generated even a modicum of prosperity, some citizens set up institutions which enable them to live on the fruits of others' toil. The law, established to achieve justice between person and person, is perverted into an instrument of plunder. This is the central message of Frederic Bastiat's *The Law*.

Citizens of our own nation have gone far in this direction. A recent news item reports that 66 million Americans receive 129 million checks each month from the Department of Health and Human Services. Tens of millions of additional Americans derive their incomes in part or in full from money taxed from productive working people. These 80 or 90 million people constitute what Leonard Read used to call a plunderbund.

We are now a nation where almost everyone is trying to live at the expense of everyone else. We have written a form of theft into our statutes. Why? Because there's a little bit of larceny in our souls! Large chunks of the American electorate have discovered that living off government handouts is easier than working for a living and safer than stealing, so they create political parties in their own image: and they elect politicians who promise them an inside track to the public treasury.

Present-day Americans are not unique in this respect. The legal transfer of wealth from producers to beneficiaries goes on today in every nation, and something like this has occurred in virtually every society since the dawn of time.

The Roots of Plunder

How did this politico-economic pattern originate? The most plausible answer is that the system of plunder was installed in the aftermath of a conquest. A hardy band of warriors swoops down from the hills and overcomes the people of the plain. The victors enslave the vanquished, setting themselves up as a governing body over a permanent underclass. Time passes, intermarriage occurs, and gradually the former warriors go soft and a hardier tribe overcomes *them,* and history repeats itself.

Apart from whatever excitement some men feel in battle, and the gratification that some people get from being the boss and giving orders, there is an economic motive behind the conquest and the subsequent system of rule. There is a natural drive in human beings to live better while working less; or, better yet, to live well without working at all.

Now, no one can get something for nothing unless he wields political power or is a friend of those in power. If you have such power you don't have to go into the marketplace and try to woo customers; you *take* what you want. This is not considered theft because the legal system has been set up to facilitate this transfer of property from those who produced it to those in power.

Such is the political pattern exhibited by most nations known to history. This pattern can be viewed as an effort to answer three questions:

1. Who shall wield power?
2. For whose benefit shall this power be wielded?
3. At whose expense shall this power be wielded?

What we are describing here is the well-nigh universal arrangement by which nations have been governed over the centuries by kings, presidents, and potentates; by emperors and mikados; by shahs, czars, maharajahs, and pooh-bahs of all kinds. Their institution is usually called "government." The word "govern" is derived from the Latin *Gubernare,* to steer. So when a group of people is elevated above the generality of citizens—as a result of conquest, usually—to ride herd on them, rule them, regulate them, control them, and exact tribute from them, they are "governing."

This was the *modus operandi* in the governance of nations, everywhere, and in every century. Then came the Whig breakthrough in the eighteenth century. It was the polar opposite of "rule" in the old sense; it was a new vision of a society which aspired to achieve liberty and justice for all. It was the novel idea of a government that did not "govern," but sought instead to protect the life, liberty, and property of all persons alike. The keynote of Whiggery was the ideal of equality before the bar of justice: the Rule of Law.

It is an idea familiar to everyone that the same instrument may be put to radically different uses. The knife you use to slice the roast may be used to kill someone. The hand that now caresses may, next hour, deal someone a mortal blow. And the law, as Bastiat points out, may serve justice, or it may violate justice when it is employed as an instrument of plunder.

The law serves justice when it acts to restore the peace, broken when someone's rights were violated. But the law may misuse the power entrusted to it by itself violating someone's rights, for its own ends or to further the purposes of a third party.

The Whigs used the word "government" but gave it a radically new meaning; from now on its role was to be limited to the actions required to maintain justice between person and person. Government was no longer to intervene positively in people's lives to rule them, regulate them, or interfere with the peaceful actions of anyone.

Confusion is sown when two radically different functions are tagged with the same label; the agency designed to serve the ends of justice by securing each person's rights to life, liberty, and property may rightfully be called "government." But the institution set up to *impair* people's rights to the life, liberty, and property ought to bear some other name. Albert Jay Nock suggested that the law, when perverted into an instrument of plunder, be called The State. The functional distinction between the two institutions—government and state—is clear.

It is in the nature of government, we might say, to use lawful force against aggressors for the protection of peaceful people. Government does not initiate action; government is triggered into "re-action" by earlier criminal conduct which causes personal injury to innocent people or otherwise disrupts the peace of the community. The state, on the other hand, initiates action. The state initiates legalized violence against peaceful people in order to advantage some people at the expense of others, or to further some grandiose national plan, or to promote some impossible dream. To paste the same label on two such radically different actions is to promote misunderstanding.

The problem is ancient, as witness the testimony of St. Augustine, dating back to the fifth century A.D.:

Without justice, what are kingdoms but great robber bands? For what are robber bands themselves, but little kingdoms. The band itself is made up of men; it is ruled by the authority of a prince; it is knit together by the pact of the confederacy; the booty is divided by the law agreed on. If, by the admittance of abandoned men, this evil increases to such a degree that it holds places, fixes abodes, takes possession of cities, and subdues people, it assumes the more plainly the name of a kingdom.

The Whig Idea

The Whigs got the point. Whiggery was the eighteenth-century creed of such men as Edmund Burke and Adam Smith; on these shores it was embraced by the likes of Thomas Jefferson and James Madison. Whiggism became Liberalism after 1832, and this noble creed projected a pattern for the lawful ordering of a society which was radically different from every political pattern known to history prior to the eighteenth century. Since the eighteenth century many nations have gone from monarchy to republicanism to democracy to socialism, but this is merely to rearrange the furniture while the political plundering continues much as before.

Whiggism is a difficult philosophy to grasp, for old ways of thinking stand in the way—and so does the ingrained reluctance of many to give up the ages-old political racket which operates whenever the law is perverted into an instrument of plunder.

Jefferson and his friends had a solid grasp of the old Whig idea when they wrote that "all men are created equal," and that they are "endowed by their Creator with certain unalienable rights," and that governments have no other reason for being than to secure people in their God-given rights.

The Whig idea filtered down into the popular mentality and came out as a piece of folk wisdom wrongly attributed to Jefferson: "That government governs best which governs least." Close, but no cigar. Thoreau did better with his play on words: "That government governs best which 'governs' not at all," perhaps having in mind Aesop's fable about King Log versus King Stork.

The Whig idea, the American idea as voiced in the Declaration of Independence, viewed "government" as an instrument of justice, set up to interpret—and enforce when necessary—the previously agreed upon rules without which a free society cannot function. "Government," then, would be analogous to the umpire in the game of baseball. The umpire does not direct the game, nor does he side with either team; the umpire acts as an impartial arbiter who decides whether it's a strike or a ball, whether or not the runner is safe at first, and so on. In the nature of the case these decisions cannot be made by the players or by the fans; the game of baseball needs an independent functionary who sees to it that the game is played within the rules. Every society, likewise, needs a nonpartisan agency to act when there is a violation of the rules on which that society's very existence depends.

The uniquely Whig and American political breakthrough was the conception of a government that did not "govern," an umpire government limited to insuring that the rules upon which a society of free people is premised are maintained—and with the authority to penalize anyone who violates those rules.

We have moved a long distance away from a truly free society; and we're even further from the theory or philosophy which gave rise to the free society. The restoration of that philosophy begins with a candid exploration of the issues.

However, no clarification of the issues is sufficient by itself to rehabilitate the old ideals of freedom and justice. The next step must be adequate educational attention to the matters in question; and from there on we rely on informed moral choice.

Instinct and Ethics

Nearly everyone is a moralist these days, and a moralist in popular caricature is one who always views with alarm. Even the self-proclaimed immoralists of our time fall into this category, for they denounce as "intolerant" any and all who look askance at their weird "beat" deviations. Disagreements are sharp at all levels, among the viewers with alarm, but the primary breach is between those who hold that the ultimate sanction for ethical standards must be sought in a supernatural order, and—on the other hand—those who assert that within the social and natural orders we may find the ingredients for a viable ethic. The first position is theistic; the latter humanistic.

The humanists, if we may be permitted this term for the second group, admit that the moral code which prevailed in the West until two or three generations ago was widely believed to have had its origin and sanction in religion. But, as they view the matter, the transcendent dimension has such a weak hold upon modern man that to insist on a metaphysical source of moral values in these times is to weaken ethics by tying it to a dead horse. Moral values they assert, are autonomous if they are anything; let them therefore stand on their own feet. Detach ethics from religion, they urge, in order that men may be virtuous for the sake of happiness! Men should not do right in a vain effort to please some deity or because they believe that God has arbitrarily commanded certain actions and forbidden others

These nontraditionalists tout a "scientific" or "rational" ethic. The opposite of "rational" in this context is not "irrational"; it is "theistic," "customary," or "received." No one would admit that his own ethical system or moral code is irrational, and it is obvious to everyone who has checked into the matter that there have been and are ethicists of several schools who are powerful reasoners. Every philosopher relies on reason, and not only rationalists; however, reason does tell some men that reason is not the exclusive route to knowledge of the complex reality that environs us.

A distinction which arises at this point seems to elude many. It is a distinction between reason as a means for achieving a norm, and

From the December 1969 issue of *The Freeman*.

reason itself as the norm. Perhaps the point may be clarified by analogy. "How do you propose to go to Boston?" is a question which demands answers in two distinct categories. "By car" is one answer, which informs us that the means of transportation is not train, plane, foot, or horse. Having settled this point, we still need further information before the question can be regarded as answered. "By way of the Taconic Parkway north, to the western end of the Massachusetts Turnpike, then east." This gives us the route, so that we know that the car will not proceed up the Merritt Parkway or over the New England Thruway.

Now take the serious question, "How shall we validate ethical norms?" Those who answer, "By reason," are really uttering a mere truism. "We're going to think about it," they are saying. And everyone who thinks about these or any other matters is using his reason. This is our only means for figuring things out, and it is not a means belonging exclusively to rationalists; it is the common means employed by everyone who philosophizes. Using this means, we seek for answers to the question of how to validate ethical norms. This has to do with the realm where the sanctions may find anchorage, whether within nature and society, or in a realm beyond the natural and social orders. Reason is our tool for operating on the problem posed; it is not itself the answer.

Experts at Debate

There are dogmatists on both sides of this controversy, and the skilled among them can and do expose weaknesses in their opponent's position. The humanist might charge his opposition as follows: The moral code is an acquired characteristic; it has to be learned anew by each generation. It is difficult enough to establish this code theoretically, even if we treat it as self-evidently useful to society and necessary for harmony in human relationships. Why, then, compound these difficulties and force things out of focus by involving ethics with metaphysics? The uncertain, in this or any other area, is shored up by relating it to the certain; but when you hook ethics up with metaphysics, you relate it to the even more uncertain, to the dubious! We don't need a transcendent sanction in order to validate or prove a down-to-earth ethic.

To which the theist might respond: If you appeal to Nature to sanction human conduct, you haven't looked very far into Nature. Not even Kropotkin with his mutual aid theories denied the Darwinian struggle for existence; he merely desired to point out that it was not the whole story. But it is part of the story, and a large enough part so that we are justified in saying that Nature gives a mandate to the powerful, the fleet, the unscrupulous to live off the weaker, the slower, the innocent. And if you think to draw your ethical sanctions from society, whose society are you talking about? A society of headhunters? Nazi society? Communist society? The Great Society? As a matter of fact, if a significant number of people can be made to believe that moral conduct is merely that which is sanctioned by the society in which they live, then morality is subverted into merely customary behavior and mere legality. Furthermore, you are confusing sanctions with consequences. An ethical code resides somewhere behind the sanctions advanced to validate it, and the consequences cited to justify it. If the code is put into practice, the consequences may well be personal happiness, interpersonal harmony, and a prosperous society. But these results do not constitute a set of sanctions; the sanctions are on the other side of the code, in the realm of philosophy. Once we are intellectually convinced that our moral code is valid, then muster enough will power to practice it, then—and only then—do we get a bonus in the form of well-being in society. But you have the thing turned around! So much for the preliminary give and take.

A Way Through the Dilemma

Evidently, each side has a case which might be spelled out at length. Is it a deadlock, or do we have here an instance of an impasse due to the hardening of the categories on either side to the point where their usefulness as conceptual tools has been impaired? And, if this is so, is there a way between the horns of the dilemma? There might be such a breakthrough if we could—by adopting a new perspective—pose and develop a thesis which might avail itself of certain strong points in both positions. Here's such a thesis: The moral code plays a role in the life of man comparable to the role of instinct in the lower organisms, in that each functions to relate the inner nature of the respective organism to the full range of its environment.

The *Harper Encyclopedia of Science* says that "the scientific study of instinct has increased greatly in recent years, and the concept itself has regained an academic respectability it has not had since the time of Darwin." At the forefront of this research, much of it under field conditions, are Tinbergen, Lorenz, Thorne, and Barrends; Europeans all. "It now seems clear," the entry continues, "that instinct and intelligence are two quite different ways by which animals meet life's problems. Instincts are essentially prefabricated answers." In a word, an organism's instinctual equipment adapts it optimally to its normal environment. Animals—along with birds, insects, and fish—are equipped with a kind of internal servomechanism, or automatic pilot, which keeps them effortlessly on the beam. Instincts align the animal with the forces of life, or with the laws of its own nature. Organism and environment are thus kept "in play" with each other—except when environmental changes are so catastrophic that the automatic adjustment equipment fails, the organism perishes, and perhaps a species becomes extinct.

The very perfection of automatic, instinctual adjustment may prove the undoing of organisms relying on this device; when survival depends on a creative response to novel environmental changes, something other than instinct is needed. This is, of course, intelligence. Instinct is not a mere precursor of intelligence, nor is intelligence an outgrowth of instinct; they are radically different. In order for intelligence in man to have an opportunity to flourish, the instincts had to be suppressed.

The Absence of Instincts

Human beings are virtually without specific instincts. There is no servomechanism in men which automatically keeps the human organism or the species within the pattern laid down for human life. Men have to figure things out and, by enormous effort, learn to conform their actions to the relevant norms in the various sectors of life. This absence of instincts in man constitutes the ground for man's radical inner freedom, the freedom of his will. Animal lives are fixed to run in narrow, constricted channels; they obey the will of God willy-nilly. Men, however, vary enormously from each other at birth, and the differences widen as individuals mature each into his specialized individuality. And each person has the gift of a freedom so radical that he can deny the existence of the creative forces which produced him. This freedom of his makes it not only possible but mandatory that man take a hand in the fashioning of his own life. No man *creates* himself, but every man *makes* himself, using the created portions of his being as his resources. This is what it means to say that man is a responsible being.

A magnificent animal like Man o' War is not a natural horse; he is the product of generations of human breeders and trainers of horses. They are mainly responsible for his superiority, not he. Of all the orders of creation only man is a responsible being; everything else, every horse, dog, lion, tiger, and shark is what it is. Only man is, in any measure, responsible for what he is. Man makes himself, and therefore each person is morally responsible for himself. This is possible because man has escaped from the straitjacket of instinct.

Let me quote from a once well known Dreiser novel, *Sister Carrie,* which appeared in 1900. "Among the forces which sweep and play throughout the universe, untutored man is but a wisp in the wind. Our civilization is but a wisp in the wind, scarcely beast, in that it is no longer wholly guided by instinct; scarcely human, in that it is not yet wholly guided by reason. On the tiger no responsibility rests. We see him aligned by nature with the forces of life—he is born into their keeping and without thought he is protected. We see man far removed from the lairs of the jungles, his innate instincts dulled by too near approach to free will, his free will not sufficiently developed to replace his instincts and afford him perfect guidance. He is becoming too wise to hearken always to instincts and desire; he is still too weak to always prevail against them."

Dreiser makes full use of a novelist's liberties here, but his pointer is in the right direction. Something within the tiger causes it to obey the laws of its inner nature unconsciously and easily, and, by so doing, the beast is in harmony with outer nature as well. But man's case is radically different. Does he have a true nature deep within him, visible when the environmentally imposed camouflages are peeled off? And, if so, what are its mandates? Once man knows the laws of his own being, how shall he muster sufficient will power to obey them while avoiding distractions and temptations that emanate from other facets of his complex nature?

My thesis is that the role played by instinct in the lower order—keeping the organism on target—is assumed in man by the ethical code. Animals have instincts but no morals; men have morality but no instincts. An animal's instincts guarantee that he will neither disobey nor deviate from the law of his being; a fish does not seek the dry land, a robin does not try to burrow in the ground, a gibbon does not yearn to swing on the North Pole. But man fulfills the law of his being only with the utmost difficulty—if then—and the only means at his disposal to align him with the forces of life is his ethical code. It is this code, and this alone, which may provide him with a life-giving, life-enhancing regimen.

A Single Ethical Code

Let me anticipate two quibbles. Instinct is sometimes contrasted with intelligence, and it is the latter, some say, on which man must rely. Or reason, as Dreiser suggests above. This is a play on words. We rely on intelligence to improve transportation, but we actually ride in automobiles or airplanes, which are the end result of applying intelligence to the problem of getting from here to there. Similarly, it is intelligence that discovers, analyzes, frames, and selects the ethical code. Which brings up the second quibble. Why *the* ethical code ? Are there not many conflicting codes? Well, no—to be dogmatic! There is a hard core of similarity, almost identity, in every one of the world's developed moral codes. This is the *Tao,* the Way, referred to by the great ethical and religious teachers in all cultures. Without it, man ceases to be man. (For an expansion of this point the interested reader is referred to C. S. Lewis' *The Abolition of Man.*)

This begins to move us away from the humanistic ethics referred to earlier. Do we need to part company, and if so, by how much? The two most prominent schools of naturalistic ethics are the utilitarians and the pragmatists. It was John Stuart Mill who invented the name and argued the case for the former. He described it as "the creed which accepts as the foundation of morals, utility, or the Greatest Happiness Principle." It "holds that actions are right in proportion as they tend to promote happiness, wrong as they tend to produce the reverse of happiness. By happiness is intended pleasure, and the absence of pain; by unhappiness, pain, and the privation of pleasure."

Pleasure and happiness are desirable indeed, and we wish more of them for everyone. But to equate "pleasure producing" with "right" at the outset of a proposed ethical inquiry is to beg the question. There is undoubtedly a connection here, for doing the right thing has a high degree of correlation with happiness, but the connection is along the lines of the intelligence-automobile illustration above. It is as if the utilitarian were asked, "What is the temperature of this room?" and he answered, "I feel chilly." Now there is some relation between this question and the answer, but the answer is not directly responsive to the question. It evades the question, implying that there is no way of finding out the temperature. There is no thermometer, perhaps. Mill and the utilitarians do not really get at the ethical question. They think they are talking about ethics when, in fact, they are discussing something else. Similarly, the pragmatists.

Why Does It Work?

The pragmatists are mainly concerned with workability; it's right if it works. Here is a map of the New England states. The pragmatist follows it and drives to Boston without getting lost. "Wherein lies the virtue of this map?" you ask him. "This map is good because it works; it got me to where I wanted to go." "Why," you pursue, "do you suppose this map got you to your destination?" "That," says our pragmatist, "is a metaphysical question of the sort I cannot be bothered with." So, we have to answer the question for him. The map "worked" because it was not just any old map; it was a map which corresponded to the terrain over which our pragmatist traveled.

An eminent British philosopher of a generation or two ago, W. R. Sorley, neatly wraps up and disposes of utility-workability theories. "It may be allowed," he writes, that the "relation between theory and practice does not necessitate the pragmatic explanation that the truth of the theory simply consists in its practical utility. The correspondence between theory and practice can also be explained on the view that the knowledge proves itself useful in its applications because it is true: the utility does not make it true; its truth is the ground of its utility. The former explanation is open to the fatal objection that it tends to discredit itself; for, according to it the truth of the view that truth consists in utility must consist in the utility of this view. It would be difficult to show any practical utility which the explanation possesses; but if we did succeed in showing such utility, it would be formulated in yet another proposition, whose truth again would have to consist in some practical end supposed to be served by it, and so on indefinitely. But if the truth of the proposition does not consist in or depend upon its utility, then we may hold that its utility depends upon its truth: it is useful because it expresses reality or real relations in the form of knowledge, and this brings them within the range, and possibly within the power, of the human mind."

Objective Moral Values

And now what about the weaknesses in the case for the theistic ethics, as that case is usually put? Fundamental to this position is the conviction that moral norms and standards are as much a part of the ultimate nature of things as the fact of the specific gravity of water. It might be convenient, at times, if water had other characteristics, but wishing won't alter the facts. Likewise, moral values. Honesty is right, and most of the time it may also be the best policy. But there are times when dishonesty would pay, where honesty makes us mighty uncomfortable; there is a conflict between what I want to do and what I know I ought to do. In order to maintain the integrity of the moral life, the ethicist champions the view that moral values are "out there," objective, as impervious to human tampering as any other fact of nature. Emphasis on their objectivity seems to imply that moral values are alien to human nature, and, if alien, hostile to man. If they are equated with God's will, God comes to seem an Oriental despot inflicting arbitrary and perverse rules upon his creatures for his pleasure and their frustration. This syndrome is, of course, a caricature.

Moral values are said to be objective in the sense that their validity is part of the system and order of the universe, of that same universe which is manifested also in persons. Neither is alien to the other, because both are part of the same reality. Sorley goes a step further! "The objective moral value is valid independently of me and my will, and yet it is some thing which satisfies my purpose and completes my nature." The ethical code may come into conflict with our superficial self on occasion, precisely because it takes its orders from our real self. Inner conflicts are a part of living, and we encounter them in all the ventures of life.

Take any sport played to win. It becomes a day and night preoccupation, with hours given over day after day for years to strenuous workouts. But this is only the visible part of the story. There is also a perpetual conflict with the impulse that wants to break training, to goof off, to lead a more normal life. Then there is the agony of the contest itself where the will to win takes over and pushes the athlete beyond his powers of conscious endurance in to collapse the moment after his victory. His deepest will had attached itself to a regimen for optimum functioning, overcoming the continuous static and rebellion from other facets of his personality. Similar experiences are encountered in the intellectual life, and in the moral life.

Check out the latter with a medieval theologian. Thomas Aquinas says: "If virtue were at odds with man's nature, it would not be an act of the man himself, but of some alien force subtracting from or going beyond the man's own identity." Go back to St. Paul. The Gentiles do not have the Mosaic law, he writes in his Epistle to the Romans, but "they show the work of a law written in their hearts." And Moses himself, as recorded in Deuteronomy, commends the keeping of God's commandments in order that there shall be flourishing life. "Choose life," he says. Where is this commandment, he asks rhetorically; is it up in heaven or beyond the sea? No, he declares, "the word is very nigh unto thee, in thy mouth and in thy heart, that thou mayest do it." What are we to understand Thomas, Paul, and Moses to be saying? Are they saying that to obey God's will for us is equivalent to following the laws of our own being? It's pretty close to that. And that is precisely what an animal's instincts do for him. The difference is that we are free to ignore or disobey the laws of our being, whereas no animal has that power.

Tested by Time, the Human Potential Emerges

In the course of several thousand generations of human beings a slow deposit has accumulated as the result of individuals here and there successfully realizing a portion of the human potential. The recipes they left behind, tested and winnowed over the centuries, form the hard core of the ethical code. This is not a prescription for a life of power-seeking, or one of money-making, a life devoted to fun and games or to fame. These things are not intrinsically evil, but an inordinate attachment to any one of them breaks training, so to speak. Proper use of them, on the other hand, is part of life's schooling process.

What are we being schooled for? A clear-cut positive answer to this question is impossible, for it outruns human experience. But a pretty clear hint comes through when we contemplate the alternatives. Wealth, pleasure, power, and even knowledge, when sought as ends in themselves, begin to send up signals that they are, in reality, only means to ends beyond themselves. The space scientists "build redundancy" into their capsules, more of everything than normal requirements would ever demand. Man, too, is overbuilt, in that each person has a wide range of potencies and a reservoir of untapped energy at his disposal, more than any of us ever use. Nor is man left on dead center with all this latent power. He has a chart containing the salient landmarks, and this chart is the ethical code. Let him begin to use this chart and the pieces fall into place, bits of the great design begin to emerge, the person fulfills his destiny. "The event is in the hands of God."

II. THE INDIVIDUAL IN SOCIETY

Battle for the Mind

The term *Weltanschauung* is nothing more than a highfalutin label for "world view." Everyone has a world view, although not everyone is fully conscious of it or aware of its implications. In other words, everyone conducts his life on the basis of some fundamental premises he takes for granted. The premises may not be explicitly stated, in which case they can be deduced from observations of the way a person habitually acts. Your *Weltanschauung is* analogous to the contact lenses you are wearing; you don't see the lenses while you are using them to see other things. The late Cornell philosopher E. A. Burtt put it well when he said: "In the last analysis it is the ultimate picture which an age forms of the nature of the world that is its most fundamental possession. It is the final controlling factor in all thinking whatever." That is why it is so important.

We are in the midst of a battle for men's minds. This is obvious at the level of the news, where we read and hear about a confrontation between Communism and what, for want of a better term, is labeled The Free World. The battle for the mind goes on at the level of official propaganda, and it is also fought out in the classroom, on the podium, from the pulpit, in books—wherever the intellect is engaged and ideas are wrestled with.

The Communists are pretty clear about their world view, Dialectical Materialism, and strongly motivated by it. The people of The Free World, on the other hand, are so unclear about their basic beliefs that little dedication is aroused. Once it was different. Two centuries ago the philosophy of freedom was in the ascendant and clear thinkers declared that "We hold these truths to be self evident." And they spelled them out in detail. The Free World today gives little more than lip service to its heritage, half-heartedly accepts a milk and water version of the opposition's world view. That makes for a lopsided contest, for the side that seems to be in focus and dynamic can always recruit fellow travelers from among the lackadaisical.

Two world views are in conflict: Materialism, intellectually insubstantial but passionately adhered to, versus non-Materialism, which

From the March 1985 issue of *The Freeman*.

generates only lukewarm devotion despite its intellectual and moral strengths. This essay exposes the weakness of the Materialist's case and demonstrates the strengths of the contrary world view.

Everyone, to repeat, entertains some picture of the entire scheme of things; everyone has a mental image of what the cosmic totality is like—in the final analysis. During the past couple of centuries the most popular world view has conceived the universe along the lines of a mechanism—an immense and intricate piece of clockwork, each cog and gear meshing with the others in a self contained system. If you like labels, this world view has been called Mechanism by some, Positivism by some, Materialism by others. Karl Marx adopted the belief that only matter is genuinely real, and he gave this doctrine enormous momentum. The Marxist version of this theory is called Dialectical Materialism, and Dialectical Materialism is the most widespread religion in the world today, numbering among its adherents millions who are not Marxists—except at the rock-bottom level of believing that matter is the fundamental reality in this universe.

I believe that Materialism is intellectually incoherent and demonstrably untrue in four essential areas. In the first place, this world view has no genuine place within it where mind, reason, and free will can find their rightful niche. Secondly, Materialism cannot accommodate the idea of inherent rights—immunities belonging to each person in virtue of his humanity. Thirdly, the idea of a moral order is incompatible with the notion that only material things are real. And finally, no one can achieve a proper view of himself as a person who accepts the Materialist teaching that he is merely a chance collocation of atoms, a by-product of physio-chemical interactions. Materialism is genuinely compatible with collectivism, but it is incompatible with the freedom philosophy. The free society and market economy need a world view which has a sound theory of mind, reason and free will; a logically grounded doctrine of inherent rights; a firmly based belief in the moral order; and an authentic under standing of personhood.

If we believe that only matter is genuinely real, we are logically committed to the corollary that mind is secondary, a derived thing dependent on that which is more basic than itself, namely matter. Mind, then, is not *sui generis;* it does not exist in its own right; it is not a primary ingredient of the cosmos. Mind, for the Materialist, is merely an epiphenomenon; it is matter in a late stage of development. Mind, intellect, consciousness, cognition, reason, rationality, will—are offshoots of matter; shadow, not substance. The really fundamental stuff of the universe—according to this theory—consists of the particles of matter which we can see, touch, count, weigh and measure.

The Reality of Matter Depends upon Reason

It is a peculiar quirk of the modern mentality to affirm without question the reality of matter, but to deny reality to mind. The catch is that it is only by using our mind that we know that matter exists! A rock does not know that stars exist; a tree is unaware of the oceans. Only we human beings know these and other things, and we know them by exercising our cognitive faculties upon the impressions gained through the senses. But our own mind is so close to us. It is so intimately a part of our very self, that we allow ourselves to be misled into downgrading our minds into something subservient to matter.

Matter is indisputably real; that is obvious. But the reality of the mental activity by which we come to know this is equally obvious; every attempt to prove otherwise must be self-defeating. Downgrade the mind, even by the tiniest degree, and you discredit any conclusion you presume to reach by the exercise of your mental powers. A rational case against reason is a contradiction in terms, for the more airtight your argument against reason the stronger the proof—contrary to your intention—of the efficacy of reason.

My proposition may be put in the form of Aristotle's Law of Identity: Mind is Mind. Mind is not a mere attribute of something sub-mental. Mind is a primordial ingredient of the universe at the most basic level. To reduce Mind to the non-mental is to declare that Mind is non-Mind, which is non-sense. Because Mind is Mind we human beings are able to understand, to make choices, to take charge of our own lives, and to order our lives in line with human purposes. If we believe anything less than this about ourselves we lower our capacity to resist those misguided authoritarians who would make us their creatures.

Our Declaration of Independence talks about "unalienable rights . . . endowed by the Creator," then goes on to say that governments are instituted to secure these rights. It appears to be one of those self-evident truths that no people would make a valiant effort to structure the laws of their society so as to protect each person's private domain and render justice for all, unless they first believe in individual rights—the idea that each person possesses an inviolable region at the core of his being. The old-fashioned Whig idea of the Founding Fathers was to limit the reach of the law to the task of securing and preserving freedom of individual action within the rules of the game, and the rules were designed to maximize liberty and opportunity for everyone, allowing everyone the elbow room each of us needs to pursue his personal goals. Only thus may each person's rights be secured.

The Nature of Rights

The word "liberal" today is the opposite of what the word meant when it first entered the vocabulary about two centuries ago, and a similar fate has befallen the word "rights." Formerly, rights signified individual freedom and personal immunity from arbitrary interference with peaceful action; the popular belief today is that "rights" are legal privileges entitling people to housing, medical care, education, equal pay, or whatever. How may we recover the sounder idea which was once the keystone of our political system?

There are three schools of thought as to the nature of rights. The popular "liberal" belief today is that society is the dispenser of rights, but this viewpoint depends on the verbal sleight of hand which confuses rights as immunities with "rights" as entitlements. If you define words to mean whatever suits your purpose, anything can be made to mean anything else. As Dr. Johnson said, if you call stones plums you can make plum pudding out of stones!

The second school of thought declares that nature is the source of rights. Let it be noted that rights, whatever they might be, are *not* material objects. Your liver, your brain, your heart *are* material objects; they have mass and extension, and can be weighed and measured. Likewise your body; when life has departed, your carcass can be reduced to $1.98 worth of chemicals! But your rights are like your ideas, in that neither your rights nor your ideas occupy space, nor can either be reduced to a chemical formula.

Now, nature is the material world; it's a marvelously intricate combination and recombination of the 105 chemical elements from actinium to zirconium. To speak of chemicals as the source of our rights makes as little sense as to speak of the chemical origin of mind and thought. Nor does it make much sense for the Materialist to speak of human nature as the source of man's rights, because his philosophy has first subordinated human nature itself to physical nature.

The world view of Materialism, I argued earlier, has no genuine place within it for Mind and thought; nor does it have a valid ground for the concept of rights—which is why it twists them into entitlement. There is a radical alternative to Materialism, but what shall we call this other world view? Call it whatever you like, but it's the religious or theistic world view in its affirmation of the reality of a non-material, mental, or spiritual dimension of the universe. Call it the sacred or divine order, if you like. Or refer to the *Mysterium Tremendum Fascinans* explored by Rudolph Otto in his seminal book *The Idea of the Holy*.

Our forebears were not afraid of using three-letter words in public so they used the term God for the creative Power. This Power also worked within—the word enthusiasm is derived from two Greek words meaning "the god within"—and thus each person participates in an order of reality beyond society and beyond nature. He is thereby endowed with an inner sanctum which is his alone, any trespass upon which is taboo. His rights are endowed by the creative Power.

The world view which declares that only material things are real, has no place for an independent moral order, and this leads to moral relativism. Theories of moral relativism have seeped into the popular mentality to emerge as slogans and bumper stickers such as "Whatever turns you on," "If it feels good, do it," "Do your own thing." The result is that the shrewd, the wily, the clever, the unscrupulous doing their thing have the rest of us over a barrel.

Moral Relativism

The *U.S. News and World Report* for October 8, 1984, has a story headlined "Nearly 1 in 3 Gets U.S. Benefits." It listed the eleven biggest programs from Social Security to infants' nutrition, involving 66 million people. Many of these recipients are into several programs, for 129,299,000 checks are mailed out from Washington regularly to these 66 million people. The report did not cover farm families, or union members, or the government bureaucrats, or those employed in schools paid for by taxpayers, or people in tariff protected industries, like those in Detroit who charge us thousands of dollars extra for the cars we buy. And there are others. We are now a nation where almost everyone is trying to live at the expense of everyone else. We have written a form of theft into our statutes. Why? Because there's a little larceny in our souls!

It's too easy, and too false, to blame the politicians. They're only our hired hit men, and in cases of this sort the principal is at least as guilty as his agent. Large chunks of the American electorate decided that living off government handouts is easier than working for a living and safer than stealing, so they created political parties in their own image and elected politicians who promise them an inside track to the public treasury.

Moralists in former periods inveighed against this sort of thing, but in the modern world they were no match for the theoreticians of Communism and socialism who convinced almost everyone that legal plundering was the wonderful wave of the future. Intellectuals today are not so sure, and many now side with the free society-market economy team. And it is our good fortune that many men and women in public life, people of integrity and intelligence, are fighting in their own way the same battle we are waging.

Reason to Believe in An Objective Moral Order

Is there an objective moral order? That is not possible within the world view of Materialism! Is it probable within a theistic world view? I think so. Your individual physical survival depends on several factors. You need so many cubic feet of air per hour, or you suffocate. You need a minimum number of calories per day, or you starve. If you lack certain vitamins and minerals, specific diseases appear. There is a temperature range within which human life is possible; too low and you freeze, too high and you roast. These are some of the requirements you must meet for individual bodily survival. They are not statutory requirements; nor are they mere custom. They are laws of this universe; they are built into the nature of things. This is obvious.

And it is just as obvious that there are certain requirements and rules built into the nature of things which must be met if we are to survive as a civilization characterized by personal freedom, private property, and social cooperation under the division of labor. It would be impossible to have any kind of a society where most people are constantly on the prowl for opportunities to murder, assault, lie, and steal. A good society is possible only if most people most of the time do *not* murder, assault, steal, and lie. A good society is one where most people most of the time tell the truth, keep their word, fulfill their contracts, don't covet their neighbor's goods, and occasionally lend a helping hand.

No society will ever eliminate crime completely, but any society where more than a tiny fraction of the population exercises criminal tendencies is on the skids. To affirm a moral order is to say, in effect, that this universe has a deep prejudice against murder, a strong bias in favor of private property, and hates a lie. We may not like living in a stringent universe which lays down a tough set of rules for individual and social survival. But let's face it; nobody has ever come up with a better alternative to living here and now.

Of course we know that this planetary home of ours is where we belong; and it's a pretty good place to be, even if at times it's a pretty tough test run. Each of us came into this world chock full of potentialities and with an immense capacity for learning. At birth we were, in effect, handed a do-it-yourself kit, a do-it yourself kit for the manufacture of a human being. And then we were given a life sentence in order to transform this raw material into a full-fledged mature adult. In the nature of the case this has to be an inside job, for each person is the custodian of the time, energies, and talents which are uniquely his own. Each individual is in charge of his own life, constructing, by the choices he makes hourly and daily, the person he has it in him to become. No outsider can take over this responsibility for us.

The collectivist promise that if we give them the power they will fashion a new social environment, which will create a new humanity, is a damnable lie—and I've chosen the word deliberately.

Becoming a human being is a full time job, and it's for life. But there is that perennial urge in the human psyche egging us on to bigger things, like the latest dream of empire, like a "brave new world," like one more desperate try at some newfangled model of the Tower of Babel. Every collapse of these megalomaniac dreams hurts, but it does provide some people with a clue that human fulfillment lies in a different direction; we have to begin from within. Gerald Heard used to say that we must grow as big inside as the whale has grown outside!

A cartoon shows a man paying the final installment on his psychiatrist's bill. As he hands over the money the former patient says to the doctor: "You call this a cure? When I came to you I was Napoleon;

now I'm nobody." We know that this former patient is on his way, but a gain of this sort feels at first like a loss!

Man is not God; he did not *create* himself, nor did he write the laws of his being; but men and women do *make* themselves. And as we seriously take ourselves in hand, we begin to discover who we are and what we may become. "That wonderful structure, Man," wrote Edmund Burke, "whose prerogative it is to be in a great degree a creature of his own working, and who, when made as he ought to be made, is destined to hold no trivial place in the creation."

No Continuing City:
The Paradox of a Christian Society

Benedict of Nursia pictured the ideal monastery as "a little state, which could serve as a model for the new Christian society." Those who respond to the call of monasticism and draw apart from secular society are to undertake a new community based upon the bond of fellowship set forth in The Rule of St. Benedict. The discipline of the Order was so rigorous as to make the Spartans appear hedonists by comparison. "The life of a monk," Benedict writes, "should be always as if Lent were being kept. But few have virtue enough for this," he adds sadly, "and so we urge that during Lent he shall utterly purify his life, and wipe out, in that holy season, the negligence of other times."

The "negligence" to which Benedict referred might crop up any time, for example, when it came a monk's turn to do kitchen work. Servers are urged to "wait on their brethren without grumbling or undue fatigue." As an inducement to good behavior they are awarded an extra portion of food. But what about wine? "God gives the ability to endure abstinence" to some; the others are rationed to a pint a day. Benedict yields this point reluctantly. "Indeed we read that wine is not suitable for monks at all," he writes. "But because, in our day, it is not possible to persuade the monks of this, let us agree at least as to the fact that we should not drink to excess, but sparingly."

No monk is permitted to call anything his own. "He should have nothing at all:" reads the Rule, "neither a book, nor tablets, nor a pen—nothing at all. For indeed it is not allowed to the monks to have bodies or wills in their own power." But the instinct for ownership sometimes broke through this prohibition, and the abbot is instructed to search each monk's bed frequently for concealed private property. "And if anything is found belonging to any one which he did not receive from the abbot, he shall be subjected to the most severe discipline."

Life within the walls outdoes nature in the harshness of its struggle for existence and only the most fit are permitted to enroll. "When any new comer applies for admission," reads the Rule, "an easy entrance

From the February 1978 issue of *The Freeman*.

shall not be granted him." He must persevere in knocking at the gate, and if he is "seen after four or five days to endure with patience the insults inflicted upon him, and the difficulty of entrance, and to persist in his demand, entrance shall be allowed him. . . . "

But the new man must then pass time in each of several decompression chambers lest he get the spiritual equivalent of "the bends." He stays a few days in the guest cell, then graduates to a novice's cell under the surveillance of an elder brother who tells him of "the harshness and roughness of the means through which God is approached. . . . " After two months of this the Rule is read to him. If he doesn't falter "again he shall be tried with every kind of endurance." Six months of this and the Rule is again read to him; four more months and another reading. And then, after "he shall promise to keep everything, and to obey all the commands that are laid upon him: Then he shall be received in the congregation; knowing that it is decreed, by the law of the Rule, that from that day he shall not be allowed to depart from the monastery, nor to free his neck from the yoke of the Rule, which, after such long deliberation, he was at liberty either to refuse or receive."

Even after this rigorous culling of the unfit the old Adam continued to reassert itself, in ways noted above, and even in physical violence among the monks. This is the implication of Rule LXX: "No one shall take it upon himself to strike another without orders."

Benedictine Influence

Such is the discipline of one earnest and successful effort to fashion a society of and for saints. It endures to this day. Benedictine monks converted England. The important Clunisian reformation of the tenth century stemmed from the Benedictine Abbey at Cluny, France. The Cistercian Order was a twelfth-century offshoot. The influence of these movements on Western culture was immense. "By degrees," says Newman, writing about Benedict, "the woody swamp became a hermitage, a religious house, a farm, an abbey, a seminary, a school of learning and a city."

Let us turn from the sixth century to the sixteenth, from the historical reality of the Benedictines to a literary artist's dream—to Rabelais' exuberant ideal construct of a society of gentlefolk, the Abbey of Thélème.

Gargantua is the hero of Rabelais' masterpiece. He is a mighty leader in battle—among other things—and with the help of friends emerged victorious from the Picrocholian War. His friends deserve a reward for their help, and what is a more suitable gift for a knight than a castle? This will hardly do for Friar John of the Funnels, however. Why not, in this case, find a suitable monastery and make Friar John its abbot? "But the monk gave him a very peremptory answer, that he would never take upon him the charge nor government of monks. 'For how shall I be able,' said he, 'to rule over others, that have not full power and command of myself? If you think,' continued John to Gargantua, 'that I have done you, or may hereafter do you any acceptable service, give me leave to found an abbey after my own mind and fancy.'" This was done, and we are given a Renaissance man's vision of a model community.

The Thelemites had but one rule: Do What Thou Wilt. "All their life was spent," writes Rabelais, "not in laws, statutes, or rules, but according to their own free will and pleasure." This did not mean that Rabelais countenanced a lax hedonism; it means that Rabelais had confidence in the gentleman and his code: "Because men that are free, well-born, well-bred, and conversant in honest companies, have naturally an instinct and spur that prompteth them unto virtuous actions and withdraws them from vice, which is called honor. Those same men, when by base subjection and constraint they are brought under and kept down, turn aside from that noble disposition by which formerly they were inclined to virtue, to shake off that bond of servitude wherein they are so tyrannously enslaved; for it is agreeable to the nature of man to long after things forbidden, and to desire what is denied us."

In order to get this kind of a person for his abbey, Rabelais practiced an exclusion almost as rigorous as that set forth in the Benediction Rule. The inscription on the great gate of Thélème warned off "... religious boobies, sots, imposters, ... bigots." Rabelais wanted no "attorneys, barristers, nor bridle-champing law-practitioners;" no "usurers, pelf-lickers, ... gold-graspers, coin-gripers.... Here enter not, unsociable wight, humorsome churl...."

But the red carpet is rolled out for others. "Here enter you, and welcome from our hearts, All noble sparks, endowed with gallant parts.... Here enter you, pure, honest, faithful, true, Expounders of the Scriptures, old and new; Whose glosses do not plain truth disguise.... Strange doctrines here must neither reap or sow, but Faith and Charity together grow." The net result is that at Thélème, "Sound bodies, lined with a good mind, Do here pursue with might, Grace, honor, praise, delight."

Mere Freedom—Only That

The vision is an enchanting one, and even Albert Jay Nock was moved to enthusiasm. "The lover of freedom," he writes in his essay on Rabelais, "the disbeliever in a dull and vicious mechanization of the human spirit, its debasement and vulgarization of life's abiding values, will nowhere find a more abundant consolation and encouragement than in this vision of the humanists. Nowhere, we believe, is there a more elevating, convincing, and wholly sound conception of human nature's possibilities when invested with no more than mere freedom—only that."

Let it be granted that the vision of Benedict of Nursia and the Rule it inspired reflected a saint's nature and met, to a significant degree, the needs of spiritual athletes for whom life is a period of probation only, and the delights of the world a snare for the soul. Rabelais, on the other hand, although consciously within the Christian heritage, was most at home in that wing of it which embodied those elements of Christianity which have been called the last creative achievement of classical culture. As a humanist, he projected the vision of an ideal society which reflected the new awareness of what a marvelous creature man is at his best—"how like a god"—inhabiting a world only a little less wonderful than himself.

Thus we have, in theory, taken care of those constructed along heroic lines—the saints and the gentlefolk. What about the rest of us, who are neither saints nor heroes, and who have been forced to concede that the gentleman's code—while it works well on the tennis court or in the drawing room—does not fully meet the demands of life on all its levels? What about the run-of-the-mine citizen? It was possible to discount him in classical political theory, whose most enduring expositor, Aristotle, could not conceive of a civilization without slavery. But Christian social theory cannot take this way out. As every man is precious in God's sight, so every man must signify in any Christian sociology, and he must signify in terms of the Christian understanding of man—a creature who is out of joint with his true nature, who has to negotiate a fallen world, and who must await another order of reality to attain his own fulfillment.

I take it to be a distinguishing feature of Christian sociology that it is non-ideological and anti-utopian. I would call a social theory "ideological" which views man in terms of only one of his aspects; which takes account only of man's material needs; or regards him as a purely spiritual being; or stresses his rationality, or his instincts, or whatever, at the expense of his wholeness. It is obvious that man is a creature of many facets, but violence is done if the wholeness of man's nature is ignored or denied.

Social Heredity

A social theory is "utopian" to the extent that it assumes that man's felicity is attainable in time and within history by a simple reliance on the natural harmonies, when these are uncorrupted by the artificial institutions of civilization. "Man is born free," cried Rousseau, "and is everywhere in chains"—fastened on him by the societies he has fashioned. Actually, society is man's native habitat. Society is as natural to man as water to a fish—neither organism could survive without its natural environment. As a creature of his genes man is a mere anthropoid; his "social heredity"—absorbed and learned one generation from another—makes him human.

Harmony, according to the utopians, is to be attained in one or the other of two directions; by anarchism or collectivism. That is to say, we might achieve an ideal society if the arrangements between people were the result of freely contracted relationships based on each man's rational calculation of his own self-interest or advantage. Or, on the other hand, social harmony might be attained by the political imposition of a rational plan from the top down which put every man through his paces, according to the superior wisdom of a ruling elite.

In contrast to the position of the utopians—whose dubious premises and faulty reasoning can be used equally well to justify either anarchism or collectivism—man, as he is understood in Christian thought, has his citizenship in two realms, not one after the other, but concurrently. The natural sensory world engages him, obviously. It is an essential part of his environment which he shares with the animals;

but man is the only animal who participates also in a non-spatial, non-temporal environment. This means that society has a more than natural and social significance; it is part of the cosmic scheme.

Our economic needs could not be met if we tackled them individually; and fellowship with others is a demand of our natures. But society has a significance beyond the meeting of our creaturely need for bread and our social need for fellowship; by a just ordering of social life we are, as Augustine put it, "schooled for life eternal."

City of God

V.A. Demant, the contemporary Anglican theologian, writes, "Perhaps, only because man is not in the Kingdom of God has he to make civilization, but the effort is made because of the pull of his *Patria* in the Eternal World impels him to make a frame of life which upholds him when he is *in via* on earth." This point is, of course, the theme of Augustine's *City of God*, and I quote from Book XIX. "Even the heavenly city, therefore, while in its state of pilgrimage, avails itself of the peace of earth, and, so far as it can without injuring faith and godliness, desires and maintains a common agreement among men regarding the acquisition of the necessaries of life, and makes this earthly peace bear upon the peace of heaven; for this alone can truly be called and esteemed the peace of the reasonable creatures, consisting as it does in the perfectly ordered and harmonious enjoyment of God and of one another in God."

Christian social theory is at odds with most secular social theory, but this is not the only difficulty; it has intramural problems as well. Yielding to those who demand a Single, Simple Formula, Christian social theory may become a parody of itself in one or the other of two directions—material or spiritual. Although Marxian Communism is a purely secular scheme of salvation on the social level alone, and within time, there are some who have seen no incompatibility between Communism and Christianity. A more common parody of the full-bodied Christian position is that which vaporizes it into a cloying spirituality. The former seeks to resolve social problems without reference to man's spiritual nature and needs; the latter stresses the inner life as if there could be a healthy spirituality apart from a righteous ordering of human relations. When things are right the inner, spiritual life of individuals is "in play" with the structures of their social life. Josef Pieper has said that the Western culture of Christendom might be character- ized as "theologically grounded worldliness."

A Bedrock of Faith

If man is more than a natural and social being it follows that the problems emerging on these levels cannot be resolved, or even under- stood, on these levels alone. The dislocations that bedevil us on the political and economic level cannot be cured at that level because they stem from a malady rooted on the spiritual level; they are surface manifestations of a distortion of our beliefs and our system of values. Our society was originally founded on the bedrock of a spiritual faith, and today we must again probe beneath the surface to that same bed- rock. But the purpose of going down to bedrock is not to stay there; it is to build from there!

Every Christian believes in spiritual values, but not necessarily in the kind that are vacuum packaged; not in the kind that become the private jewel of some connoisseur for his solitary ecstasy. The path between altar and marketplace has always been a two-way street. Jesus' summary of the law was twofold: love God and love your neighbor, balancing ethical expenditure by spiritual income. It conveys some- thing like a half truth and a whole error to label man a spiritual being. He is, in fact, a spiritual being who eats, feels the cold, and needs shelter; a being whose nature demands fellowship with his own kind. True spirituality cannot exist apart from sound thinking, just dealing, and efforts to improve the quality of human relationships.

We have gone through a period when large numbers of people shared a belief that we could solve just about every human problem by political action. This is, of course, absurd. But it is a sorry reaction to this absurdity to subtract one's weight and influence from such healthy forces as are now at work in social and political life. This mood of retreat and resignation is a dubious kind of spirituality. In reality it is a new "failure of nerve," and a critic has written caustically about those so afflicted: "Having abandoned genuine thought about prob- lems—especially the new problems that cannot yield to old formulae and incantations—they luxuriate in the feeling of greater purity and spirituality than their fellows."

The Ancient City

If we reduce spirituality to a kind of private fancy it is easy for us to think of religion and politics as two distinct spheres, as separate as church and state. Such a view would have been incomprehensible to the ancient Greeks. The classic study of the religious and civil institutions of ancient Greece and Rome is *The Ancient City* by Fustel de Coulanges. "The foundation of a city," he writes, "was always a religious act ... A city was like a little church, all complete, which had its gods, its dogmas, and its worship.... Neither interest, nor agreement, nor habit creates the social bond; it is this holy communion piously accomplished in the presence of the gods of the city." It was a social system "where the state was a religious community, the king a pontiff, the magistrate a priest, and the law a sacred formula; where patriotism was piety, and exile excommunication; where individual liberty was unknown; where man was enslaved to the state through his soul, his body, and his property." Christianity, on the other hand, "taught that only a part of man belonged to society.... The mind once freed, the greatest difficulty was overcome, and liberty was compatible with social order."

It is risky to generalize thus about a complex civilization like Greece which underwent several changes of character over the centuries, so let us use Socrates as a type case. Ernest Barker, in his *Political Thought of Plato and Aristotle,* writes "The laws of his country were to him [Socrates] a sacred thing.... For him there was no rule of natural justice outside the law ... what is just is simply what is commanded in the laws." Barker goes on to say that "To a State like the ancient State—both church and State in one—any new religious beliefs, or disbeliefs, resulting in the formation of hostile groups of opinion, were in reality dangerous." The ancient society, in other words, represents the fusing of religion and politics into a unitary state, leaving little elbow room for the exercise of individual initiative.

"The victory of Christianity," writes Fustel, "marks the end of ancient society.... It was not the domestic religion of any family, the national religion of any city, or of any race. It belonged neither to a caste nor to a corporation. From its first appearance it called to itself the whole human race." Such a religion was bound to have momentous political consequences. Christianity created a new kind of individualism. After some fifteen centuries of its influence, "The Englishman ... ," G. G. Coulton writes, "could carry his own atmosphere with him everywhere; he was self-sufficient *avec sa Bible et son Anglaise.*"

Encounter and Tension

The enlargement of the idea of God, from a family, urban or tribal deity into a Being with universal attributes, developed the kind of religious institution—a church—which must forever confront political institutions in an atmosphere of encounter and tension. The history of Europe is in large measure polarized between the two powers; sword and scepter, crown and miter, Empire and Papacy. Such a dualism is fatal to the idea of the monolithic state. The effect of this polarity is to decentralize power and disperse authority. There is no other way to deal with the root problem of politics—the governance of power. In addition to the division of authority between Empire and Papacy, power was further fragmentized among numerous kings, counts, and lesser officials.

In practice, then, during much of the history of Europe, power got itself deadlocked; with the result that there was widespread practice of what might be called "interstitial liberties" by the people. Men were free in the spacious nooks, crannies, and crevices of European society long before the law moved up to recognize specific freedoms. We had to wait till the seventeenth and eighteenth centuries for a developed philosophy of freedom.[1]

But just about as that occurred, Christianity as conscious faith lost its hold on men's minds and loyalties, and we began to slide back toward a kind of pseudo-theocracy, or "totalitarian democracy," which, in modern Communism and fascism, amalgamates religion with politics and succeeds in debasing both. Politics, in the collectivized state, is a sheer power struggle with no concern for the ends of justice and freedom. Religion, in the collectivized state, must be forced into state service as an opiate of the people. Omnipotent government cannot abide a universal religion; it must construct its own domesticated variety of secularized religion.

And thus we complete one of those enormous spirals of history. Religion, ethics, and politics are once again wrapped up in one package, as they so largely were in Greek speculation. The individual Greek could hardly conceive of ends for his life outside his *Polis.* Aristotle's remark that "man is a political animal" might be translated "man is a creature found only in city-states."

Beyond Society

With modern men it is different. Our pilgrimage has brought us to a different turn on the spiral of history and we know that we have a potential that projects us beyond society. We have acquired a sophistication which will not permit us to be reabsorbed into our societies without inner tension and conflict. This is one result of our centuries of encounter with Christianity. We may be anti- or non-Christian but nevertheless its effects have leaked into our lives to shape the modern psyche in the region of the values and premises we take for granted. Our mood is mostly Christian, whatever creed or philosophy we profess.

This may sound like a call for a religious revival, and, in a sense, it is just that. But a mere revival of religion is not what we need, unless the religion which is revived understands that man exists for ends beyond society and beyond history—Augustine's two cities again. Nor will this sort of a revival be accomplished by mere exhortation. Perhaps it will not happen at all so long as men expect to wring utopian results out of any kind of political or economic action.

There are political implications in the concept of spiritual liberty; the practice of justice is urged upon us as a religious imperative, and the relevance of the Christian religion to American institutions has been spelled out many times. But where does economics fit in? At first glance, economics appears to deal solely with the provisioning of our material and creaturely needs and to have no religious significance. This is a misreading of the situation, I believe, so let me say a few words about economics.

Economic Activity Fundamental to Human Existence

Economic activity is fundamental to human existence. A Robinson Crusoe could get along without politicking, but if he did not work he would die of hunger and exposure. Emerging from economic activity are the concepts of rights to property and claims to service around which many political battles are fought. Economics, on the surface, deals with prices, production, and the operations of the market as determined by the buying habits of every one of us.

In reality, however, economics is concerned with the conservation and stewardship of the earth's scarce goods: human energy, time, material resources, and natural forces. These goods-in-short-supply are our birthright as creatures of this planet. Use them wisely, as natural piety dictates and common sense confirms—that is providently and economically—and human well-being is the result. Ignore the realities in this area, as we have done in our time, and a host of evils follows. We might be able to live with economic ills if we didn't think we could cure them with political nostrums, but our political efforts aimed at mopping up the consequences of economic mistakes head us in the direction of the Total State.

Every collectivist ideology—from the Welfare State idea to totalitarian Communism—is strung on a framework of economic error. People are prisoners of their beliefs, and so long as they cherish a wrong understanding of economics they will be appealed to by one form of collectivism or another. But when they embrace sound economics, collectivism will cease to be a menace.

All creatures take the world pretty much as they find it, save man. Man alone has the gifts which enable him to entertain an idea and then transform his environment in accordance with it. He is equipped with needs which the world as it is cannot satisfy. Thus he is compelled to alter and rearrange the natural order by employing his energy on raw materials so as to put them into consumable form. Before he can do much of anything else, man must manufacture, grow, and transport. His creaturely needs man shares with the animals, but he alone employs economic means to satisfy them. This is an enormous leap upward, for by relying on the economic means man becomes so efficient at satisfying his bodily hungers that he gains a measure of independence from them. And when they are assuaged, he feels the tug of hungers no animal ever feels: for truth, for beauty, for meaning, for God.

A Means to All Our Ends

Whatever may be man's capacities in the upper reaches of his nature—to think, dream, pray, or create—it is certain that he will attain to none of these unless he survives. And he cannot survive for long unless he engages in economic activity. At the lowest level economic action achieves merely economic ends: food, clothing, and shelter. But when these matters are efficiently in hand, economic action is a means to all our ends, not only to more refined economic goods but to the highest goods of the mind and spirit. Add flying buttresses and spires to four walls and a roof, and a mere shelter for the body develops into a cathedral to house the spirit of man.

There are two schools of thought which incline to dismiss economics, but neither has much excuse for being except as a protest against the errors and one-sidedness of the other. On the one hand are the economic determinists, who argue as if man were merely a soulless appendage to his material needs. For them, the modes of production at any given time decree the nature of man's institutions, his philosophies, and even his religions. Economics, under this dispensation, will lose its independence and become a mere tool of the State.

On the opposite side of the fence is a school of thought which appears to regard it as a cosmic calamity that each soul is sullied by connection with a body which must be fed and kept warm. Spiritual purity will not be attained until there is deliverance from this incubus, but until that happy day let us try to forget that man has creaturely needs which only the products of human labor can satisfy. Nothing in this scheme disposes men to pay any attention to economics! But there is a third way.

The mainstream of the Judeo-Christian tradition is characterized by a robust earthiness which makes it as alien to the materialism of the first of the above alternatives as to the disembodied spirituality of the second. Soul and body are not at war with each other, but are parts of our total human nature. It is the whole man who needs to be saved, not just the soul. Creaturely needs are, therefore, legitimate; and being legitimate they sanction the economic activities by which alone they can be met. They cannot be met by political action. The market economy presupposes a moral order, and it needs a framework of law to punish breaches of the rules. But granted this institutional framework economic activities are self-starting and internally regulated. Political action which goes deeper into economic life than maintaining the Rule of Law commits the injustice of giving economic advantage to some at the expense of others.

Christianity is a religion of world and life affirmation. It includes the dimension of eternity but it is not "other worldly." It can therefore extend diplomatic recognition to the temporal order and respect the integrity of its political and economic rules while insisting at the same time that ultimate felicity is not to be attained by any conceivable improvement of that order. Utopia is not within its purview.

Contemporary social and scientific theory is now at least open-ended toward this idea, having shed the utopian expectancy of last century. Theories about people and things are no longer expected to hang together with the neatness of a proposition in Euclidean geometry. The rationalist may demand that life conform to his verbal formulations of it, but reality refuses to be thus coerced. Anyone can draw up a blueprint for an ideal society composed of bloodless abstractions who are expected to perform like puppets. But when we deal with man in all his concreteness, the rules must be tempered with artistry. In religious terminology, this artistry is the practice of the traditional religious virtues of mercy, compassion, and charity.

---

1. The history of the Eastern Church and Empire is another story. Christopher Dawson writes: "The Byzantine Church became so closely bound up with the Byzantine Empire that it formed a single social organism which could not be divided without being destroyed. . . ." (*The Making of Europe,* p. 57)

The Person and His Society

Every person pursues his individual goals in the context of some society. The norms, customs, habits, and fashions of that society seem at times to hinder him, but at the same time they are a sustaining presence. Likewise the laws of his nation. Man is said to be a political animal, in the sense that society is his native habitat. But he's also a political animal in one further respect; people create governments in their own image. This is obvious in a democratic system.

It is self-evident that the politicians elected to public office are men who embody the consensus. The successful candidates are those who most persuasively promise what voters believe government should deliver; politicians operate on that slippery spectrum bounded, on the one hand, by what voters expect and demand of government, and by what they will put up with from government, on the other. A nation tends to get the government it deserves, in the sense that pressure groups will eventually organize to make wrongful demands upon government, unless the nation's "aristocracy of virtue and talent"—men with the ability to teach what expectations and demands are legitimate—are heeded.

When educators, philosophers, and men of letters fail to properly nourish the intellect, the conscience, and the imagination of significant segments of a society, they betray a sacred trust as teachers of mankind, and in the wake of their defection a secular religiousness becomes the popular faith. Leviathan—the omnipotent State—is the god of this faith. Men serve Leviathan in the confident expectation that he will provide his votaries with ease, comfort, security, and prosperity. The modern world does indeed provide more of these things for more people than earlier periods, but it also exacts a toll in the form of perpetual warfare, social unrest, hardening of the arteries, softening of the brain, and a troubled spirit.

We Are the Enemy

When we attempt to assess the modern malaise we are tempted to say: "An enemy hath done this thing." But the truth of the matter is

From the January 1981 issue of *The Freeman*.

that we have done it to ourselves—the actively guilty, the passively guilty, the ignorant, the stupid, and all the innocent bystanders—we are all in this thing together.

Every society has its characteristic pecking order, and ours is no exception. Certain men, certain ideas, certain life styles are at the top of the pecking order; the masses admire and seek to emulate these men, ideas and life styles. If these ideas and styles are not life-enhancing, there is frustration and thwarting at the deep levels of human nature and a whole society is sidetracked. The Remnant who keep the faith are superfluous; society has no use for their services. Such a society will necessarily get Leviathan—a government which matches its warped and ill-favored nature. Edmund Burke puts the matter plainly in a letter to constituents in Bristol: "Believe me, it is a great truth, that there never was, for any long time, a corrupt representative of a virtuous people; or a mean, sluggish, careless people that ever had a good government of any form."

Civilizations rise and fall, nations come and go. Why this occurs is the subject of learned speculation and debate. There is little unanimity among scholars, who disagree among themselves even as to the yardsticks by which decline and progress might be measured. But even though the overall movement of a civilization is difficult to detect, there are two trends in the modern world in all progressive countries, where the facts are clear; the first has to do with politics, the second with economics.

The thrust of eighteenth-century Whiggery and of Classical Liberalism was to pry various sectors of life out from under the yoke of the State, to free them from political controls. The aim was to shrink government to a limited, constabulary function. The twentieth century has reversed this trend, with a vengeance. The theory of the free society has come under increasing attack, and totalitarian governments have emerged in nation after nation.

As Classical Liberalism expanded the voluntary sector of society the economic controls of the Mercantilist era were removed from business, industry, and agriculture. Adam Smith demonstrated that—within the framework of the Rule of Law, which Liberalism supplied—the economic order was subtly regulated by the buying habits of consumers; and the free economy began to emerge within Western nations. Freedom in economic transactions was never fully achieved in any nation, but we made greater progress in that direction in the

United States than elsewhere, and we paid lip service to the ideal of the market economy. But ideals change.

National Planning

The new freedom did not bring about utopia, or a paradise on earth, and in the aftermath of this disappointment, a new scheme captured the imagination of the intellectuals—nation-wide planning for the achievement of national purposes and goals. The New Deal marked a major change in the popular attitude toward the free economy; efforts to frame the rules necessary for attaining competition in the marketplace gave way to the urge to put the marketplace under bureaucratic regulation. The free economy was to be phased out, step by step.

I am a believer in the free society and in the free economy. The free society is to my taste because I like its variety, I like the diversity it encourages, I like the spontaneity it permits. I also like the free economy. I like it because it is more productive than any alternative; people eat better, have more things, are more secure in their possessions. Freedom works, and therefore I resist the collectivizing trends of the twentieth century which would transform people into creatures of the State. But my belief in freedom is grounded, ultimately, on my reading of the nature of the human person.

Man, I believe, is a created being; there is a sacred essence in him. Man is on this planet in consequence of a mighty plan—of whose outlines we may gain faint intimations—and his life is used to further a vast purpose—of which we are given an occasional clue. If man is indeed a created being, and the members of a society act upon their belief that such is their nature, they will begin to frame political theories consonant with their convictions. They will erect political structures designed to safeguard the sacred essence in each person; the law will attempt to maximize each person's opportunity to realize his earthly goals.

Believing that God wills men to be free, such a society will regard any trespass on the true liberty of even the lowliest individual to be a thwarting of some intent of the Creator. The deep conviction that each human being is a person and not a thing will generate ideas of equal, inherent rights; and this central dogma will exert pressure on personal attitude and conduct, on government and law, on every level of the free society, to bring all into harmony with the key belief that man is a created being.

But suppose man is not a created being. Suppose the human being is not a person, but a thing. If the universe is simply brute fact, mindless and meaningless; reducible in the final analysis to mass and motion—then man is a thing just like any other item in the catalogue of the planet's inhabitants.

The Materialistic Concept of Human Beings

Suppose we assume—as do many of our contemporaries—that man is the chance product of the random movement of material particles. Man's haphazard appearance on a fifth-rate planet is, then, a fluke; he just happened to occur, as the accidental by-product of physical and chemical forces. He's merely a part of nature, like every other species on the planet. Except that the human species is more foolish than the rest, loves to be bamboozled, and has such a gift for make-believe that its continued existence is problematic!

When we confront a strange object we try to size it up, so we'll know better how to deal with it. If it's a person, we get onto a person-to-person basis; but if it's a thing, we treat it like a thing. We make a crucial decision here, and the way we decide depends upon our basic philosophy, our understanding of the fundamental nature of the universe.

If we have embraced some variety of Materialism as our philosophy then we must eventually come to the logical conclusion that human beings are things, and once we conclude this we'll begin to treat people as things. People then come to be regarded as units of the State, as objects to be manipulated, as pawns in a political game to be used up in some national plan, as guinea pigs for experiments in genetic engineering, as robots programmed for utopia. Shades of 1984!

I am prepared to argue that we get the free society only after the consensus has firm convictions about the sacredness of persons, and that we get the free economy only after we have the free society. Now, when we reflect on the nature of persons we involve ourselves in some pretty deep philosophical and theological questions, and some of our contemporaries are impatient with such speculation. They believe that the intellectual opponents of the free market can be devastated by straightforward economic arguments, and once we have the free market everybody will be doing his own thing and we'll get the free society as a matter of course. Things are not this simple; if they were, freedom in human affairs would be the rule; voluntary transactions and unhampered exchange would then mark the economic life of all nations. The reverse is true: freedom has always been in jeopardy, and the liberties which expanded during the Classical Liberal Era are now contracting everywhere.

The Conditions of Freedom

There is a deep-rooted urge in each person to be unhampered in the pursuit of his own life goals, but this individual instinct for freedom has only rarely in history been institutionalized as the free society. Likewise, each person has a deeply rooted desire to conserve his energy and improve his material well-being; trade and barter are as old as mankind. But despite the economizing urge the free economy seldom appears on this planet.

The free society and the free economy did emerge in the eighteenth century and freedom expanded during the nineteenth. An excellent literature came into being to expound and defend political and economic freedom, despite which freedom retreated during the twentieth century because there was a leak at the philosophical level, where we deal with the nature of personhood and the meaning of life.

The economizing spirit is concerned to save energy and resources; it strives ceaselessly to diminish inputs and maximize outputs. Which is to say that economics is the drive to get more for less. Now, unless this more-for-less impulse is counterbalanced by non-economic forces it develops into a something-for-nothing mentality. And when the something-for-nothing mentality takes over the free economy dies of auto-intoxication.

The advice to "do your own thing" has been repeated so often as to be an incantation, and if freedom could be had by casting a spell then the free society would be a shoo-in. But the free society cannot be sustained by magic, and lacking a philosophy of personhood, the advice to "do your own thing" is an invitation to disaster. The weak doing their thing are at the mercy of the strong doing theirs, and the unscrupulous have the upper hand over the rest.

I belong to a bicycle club and have two friends with whom I ride. Joe is a weightlifter, a powerful man, and a "square." Fred is a middle-aged retiree with strong affinities for the youthful life styles of today. We three were in a resort town for a bike rally, and in addition to cyclists there were many young people whose sartorial and tonsorial disarray proclaimed their devotion to individual liberty. The three of us stopped for refreshments at a soft drink stand and watched the passers-by. A pair of especially unkempt and unwashed young men strolled by, and Joe—the muscular "square"—muttered, half under his breath, "I'd like to wring their necks!" Fred, a gentle and sympathetic soul, said, "But, Joe, they're only doing their thing." To which my obvious retort was, "Yes, Fred, but Joe's thing is wringing hippies' necks!"

The Rule of Law

Classical Liberalism was built around the idea of the Rule of Law equal justice for all, and thus it erected certain guidelines and standards, whose observation maximized each man's liberty in society. And it framed these rules because each person is a sacrosanct individual, free in virtue of his very nature. When convictions about the sacredness and mystery of personhood are energized, then men will seek to erect institutional safeguards around each individual, and we move toward the free society. But if the prevailing philosophy has a faulty doctrine of personhood, then people lose that sense of their true humanness which would lead them to strive for an ordered liberty, and we lapse into the closed society.

Modern thought, the ideology which has prevailed during the past two centuries, has many facets and some undeniable strengths. But it has one glaring defect: it has no adequate doctrine of personhood. This ideology is reductionist in tendency, whenever it contemplates the Self. It reduces men to animals and animals to machines. It defines thought as subvocal activity, dismisses reason as rationalization, explains mind as a mere reflex of activity among the brain cells, and invokes the conditioned reflex to account for every variety of behavior.

I am painting with a broad brush in order to highlight a drift or tendency in modern thought, "a mean, sluggish, careless" streak in the realm of ideas. When a thinker uses a finely tuned instrument—his mind—to reach the conclusion that thought cannot be trusted, we have evidence of corruption in philosophy. Let me illustrate.

Philosopher-Kings

There are philosophers of considerable and deserved reputation who have dreamed up world views in which human beings figure as creatures of a lesser stature than persons. Be it noted, however, that the philosopher guilty of devaluating personhood generously exempts himself from the strictures he applies to others! Given his blind spot, he concludes that it is only other people, the mass of mankind, who fall within the scheme of manipulable objects; the philosopher who regards us as unpersons finds another category for himself. He's the philosopher-king!

Bertrand Russell, in a celebrated essay entitled "A Free Man's Worship," declares that "Man is the product of causes which had no prevision of the end they were achieving; his origin, his growth, his hopes and fears, his loves, and his beliefs, are but the outcome of accidental collocations of atoms." In short, we are—along with our beliefs—merely the end result of a chance arrangement of material particles.

It follows, on Lord Russell's own showing, that his opinion that such is the case is itself only a reflex of an "accidental collocation of atoms." What point is there in publishing this opinion unless its author regards it as being closer to the truth than alternative views? But can the designation true or false be applied to an "accidental collocation of atoms" or any product thereof? By the internal showing of Russell's statement, his own beliefs are below the idea level; they are subreason. Furthermore, the publishing of these words bespeaks a wish on the author's part to persuade other people of the validity of his position. But why bother to offer enlightenment to creatures whose beliefs are nothing but the chance result of blind forces?

Bertrand Russell was immensely gifted as a philosopher and mathematician, but his philosophy is deficient in its attempts to account for selfhood; it has no adequate place for persons. And if Russell is deficient here, how much more deficient are the lesser men who instruct us in the meaning of life!

Philosophical Entrapment

The widespread irrationalism of the present day represents the dead end of a philosophy which developed a world view wherein was no proper niche for the creator of that world view—the philosopher himself! It takes a brilliant and ingenious mind to arrive at such a paradoxical conclusion which so blatantly denied the obvious. Any fool knows that white is white and black, black; so does the wise man. But in between the fool and the wise man are those who are able to argue with perverse brilliance that white is a kind of black.

C. A. Campbell, emeritus professor of philosophy at Glasgow University, makes a sound observation: "As history amply testifies, it is from powerful, original and ingenious thinkers that the queerest aberrations of philosophic theory often emanate. Indeed it may be said to *require* a thinker exceptionally endowed in these respects if the more paradoxical type of theory is to be expounded in a way which will make it seem tenable even to its author—let alone to the general philosophic public."

To be a man is to search for meaning. Philosophy begins in wonder, and we can't help wondering what life is all about, and how human life fits into the total scheme of things. We try to decipher the mysteries of the universe, hoping to obtain a few clues to help us play our roles in life with zest and joy. We wonder if human values and ideals find reinforcement in the nature of things, and if the values that concern us most deeply—love and honor, truth, beauty and goodness—are realities. Or are they merely illusions we cling to for comfort in an otherwise cheerless existence?

We consult the philosophers, and all too many of them are mired in the cults of unreason, meaninglessness, and absurdity. Man is a cosmic accident, they assure us; the universe is a moral and aesthetic blank, completely alien to us. We cannot trust our own thought processes, they say, as they simultaneously downgrade mind and insist that we accept their theories! Well, they can't have it both ways! Of course, if matter is the ultimate reality, mind is discredited. But if this discredited instrument is all we have to rely on, how can we put any confidence in its findings? If untrustworthy reason tells us that we cannot trust reason, then we have no logical ground for accepting the conclusion that reason is untrustworthy!

Well, I don't trust the reasoning of people who champion the irrational, and I do know that our reasoning powers may be—like anything else—misused. But when human thought is guided by the rules of logic, undertaken in good faith, and tested by experience and tradition, it is an instrument capable of expanding the domain of truth.

Reason is not infallible, but it is infinitely more to be trusted than nonreason!

A Religious World View

Deep down within us we know with solid assurance that we really do belong on this planet; that we are the key component of the total richness. We know this, but we need reminding—as in these words from the gifted and unorthodox thinker Anthony M. Ludovici:

> The profound and cultivated man of wanton spirits, whose sense of self is the outcome of healthy impulses springing from the abundant energy and serenity of his being, not only affirms his own self and the universe with every breath he takes, but, by the intimate knowledge he acquires of life through the intensity of his own vitality, he feels deeply at one with everything else that lives. The intensity of his feeling of life helps him to perceive, behind the external differences of living phenomena, that quality and power which unites him to them. The luxuriant profligacy of nature finds a reflection in his soul, but it also finds an answering note in his feelings. Profound enough not to be deceived by surfaces, he feels the dark mystery behind himself and the rest of life, and what is more important, guesses at the truth that he himself cannot, any more than the daisy or the antelope, stand alone, or dispense with the power which is enveloped in that dark mystery. (*Man: An Indictment,* p. 204)

These are the authentic accents of a religious world view, and a citizenry in whom this vision lives will invest each person with a sacredness, a protected private domain, a body of rights and immunities. The law, then, is established to secure these prerogatives of the person, and government is limited to those functions which maximize liberty and justice for all. This is Jefferson's "Equal and exact justice to all men, of whatever state or persuasion." This is the free society, and it is not an autonomous social order, suspended in midair, it is based necessarily on a religious foundation.

Freedom in the Market When Options Are Open

Even less autonomous is the free market. Freedom of action in the economic sphere does not beget itself, but a society which maximizes liberty for all persons equally has freedom in economic transactions as well. The free economy, in other words, is simply the label attached to human behavior in the marketplace when our options are open, as they should be.

"The heavens themselves, the planets and this centre observe degree, priority and place." Shakespeare was right; there is an overarching Order and Pattern built into the nature of things. Everything has its rightful place in that Order, and each thing after its own kind manifests its peculiar nature—except man.

Man does not simply and naturally manifest his own nature; he is open-ended! Unlike the other orders of creation, man is not infallibly guided by instinct—he is free. Not being locked into a behavior pattern, he has to establish contact with his deeper self, and then properly interpret and carry out its mandates. Only then may he learn to express his true being by conforming himself and all his works to the universal Pattern.

Plato, in the *Laws,* refers to an ancient saying that God, who holds in his hands beginning, end and middle of all that is, moves through the cycle of nature, straight to His end. And Plato adds:

> Justice always follows Him and punishes those who fall short of the divine law. To that Law, he who would be happy holds fast and follows it in all humility and order; but he who is lifted up with pride or money or honour or beauty, who has a soul hot with folly and youth and insolence, and thinks that he has no need of a guide or ruler, but is able of himself to be the guide of others, he, I say, is deserted of God; and being thus deserted he takes to himself others who are like him, and jumps about, throwing all things into confusion, and many think he is a great man. But in a short time he pays the penalty of justice and is utterly destroyed and his family and state with him. (*Laws,* IV, 716)

We are the architects of our own Leviathan. Whenever a people goes slack, whenever the mean, sluggish, and careless are moved up to the top of the pecking order, then we get an unlovely society to match our own ill nature. But this need not be. The way we express our nature is not fixed in one mode only; we are free to change the pattern of our lives. There is a right way, a way that is good for man, a way that meets the needs and demands of human nature and the human condition, a way that fulfills the law of our being. Walking in that way, men and women find their proper happiness in a free and prosperous commonwealth.

Our Disordered Lives

The colonists had won a war and, desiring to set up a republican form of government, they installed a Constitution designed to limit the public authority and thus maximize personal liberty.

Now that they were free, what did these early Americans do with their newly won liberty? For one thing, they worked. They had to provide their own food, clothing, and shelter, so work was a necessity of survival. Moreover, these people remembered the poverty endured by their ancestors in Europe and how life was demeaned thereby. Now that these Americans were free to enjoy the fruits of their toil they became more productive, and with the gradual increase of wealth came a new sense of human dignity which accompanies modest economic success. The Puritan Ethic was sound when it endorsed work, thrift, and frugality. This ethic fitted in well with the burgeoning interest in the new science of economics, masterfully set forth in 1776 by Adam Smith. It is significant that more than twenty-five hundred copies of *Wealth of Nations* were sold in this country within five years of its appearance. Obviously, the book addressed itself to a real need.

Economic activity is fundamental to human existence. A Robinson Crusoe could get along without politicking, but if he did not work he would die of hunger and exposure. Emerging from economic activity are the concepts of rights to property and claims to service around which many political battles are fought. Economics, on the surface, deals with prices, production, and the operations of the market as determined by the buying habits of every one of us. In reality, however, economics is concerned with the conservation and stewardship of the earth's scarce goods; human energy, time, material resources, and natural forces.

These goods-in-short-supply are our birthright as creatures of this planet. Use them wisely, as natural piety dictates and common sense confirms—that is providently and economically—and human well-being is the result. Ignore the realities in this area, as we have done in our time, and a host of evils follows. We might be able to live with economic ills if we didn't think we could cure them with political

From the July 1973 issue of *The Freeman*.

nostrums, but our political efforts aimed at mopping up the consequences of economic mistakes head us in the direction of the Total State. Every collectivist ideology—from the welfare state idea to totalitarian Communism—is strung on a framework of economic error. People are prisoners of their beliefs, and so long as they cherish a wrong understanding of economics they will be appealed to by one form of collectivism or another. But when they embrace sound economics, collectivism will cease to be a menace.

Man's Nature

All creatures take the world pretty much as they find it, save man. Man alone has the gifts which enable him to entertain an idea and then transform his environment in accordance with it. He is equipped with needs which the world as it is cannot satisfy. Thus he is compelled to alter and rearrange the natural order by employing his energy on raw materials so as to put them into consumable form. Before he can do much of anything else, man must manufacture, grow, and transport. His creaturely needs man shares with the animals, but he alone employs economic means to satisfy them. This is an enormous leap upward, for by relying on the economic means man becomes so efficient at satisfying his bodily hungers that he gains a measure of independence from them. And when they are assuaged, he feels the tug of hungers no animal ever feels: for truth, for beauty, for meaning, for God.

Whatever may be man's capacities in the upper reaches of his nature—to think, dream, pray, or create—it is certain that he will attain to none of these unless he survives. And he cannot survive for long unless he engages in economic activity. At the lowest level, economic action achieves merely economic ends: food, clothing, and shelter. But when these matters are efficiently in hand, economic action is a means to all our ends, not only to more refined economic goods but to the highest goods of the mind and spirit. Add flying buttresses and spires to four walls and a roof, and a mere shelter for the body develops into a cathedral to house the spirit of man. Economics is not one means among many, Hayek has pointed out, it is the means to all our ends.

Material Progress

The freer a nation's economy the more prosperous are its citizens. The wealth of Uncle Sam became the envy of the world. America's greatness is not, of course, to be measured by monetary income and material well-being; but it is interesting to note how well Americans have done economically with the resources available to them.

The United States is only one-sixteenth of the land surface of the world, and Americans are only about one-fifteenth of the world's population. Nevertheless, Americans own three-quarters of all the television sets. Americans consume about two-thirds of all the petroleum products in the world, one-half of all the coffee, two-thirds of all the silk. An American factory worker can buy four suits of clothes with a month's wages; his counterpart in a totalitarian country can buy half a suit with a month's wages. An American can buy six pairs of shoes with the results of a week's work; his totalitarian counterpart can buy one shoe. These figures prove only one thing. They demonstrate with what dramatic success Americans have waged the great war on poverty.

There was general progress during the nineteenth century; the American Dream appeared to be in the process of realization. The War Between the States shed brothers' blood and dealt the nation a staggering blow, but the country's spiritual and political leadership had enough vitality to begin the long job of putting the pieces together again. There were several periods of economic dislocation during the nineteenth century, but the masses of Americans tightened their belts and took the hardships in stride. The prevailing mood, as the nation entered the twentieth century was optimistic, but this mood was badly shaken by World War I. There was a lot of cynicism in the literature of the twenties and a few voices began to propagandize for the Planned State. Then came the shattering experience of the Great Depression and large numbers of Americans lost faith in themselves and in their institutions. They felt powerless before the forces leading them toward the war they entered in 1941.

Given their "druthers," most people choose freedom; they would have settled—anytime during the 1929–1941 period—for a resumption of the old ways and the prospect of a steady job. But there was almost no one to tell them that economic stagnation and war are not marketplace phenomena; these are consequences of political interference with the free market. The economy which collapsed in 1929 and continued stricken during the thirties was a politically rigged economy; it bore little resemblance to the classical model of the free market!

The Voice of Socialism

This message was drowned out in the thirties by the confident, strident voices of Socialists, Communists, and Social Planners. The prescriptions of these folk were heeded, in large measure, and their remedies applied. The welfare state was given carte blanche in the 1930s and has had the field virtually to itself for the past forty years. What are the consequences? Examine any sector of the nation you choose and the survey turns up a shambles. Dissension tears apart our churches; influential church bodies support revolution; churchmen embrace one weird theology after another. On the campuses there is not only a breakdown of educational theory, there are student riots, burnings, and bombings. Never have Americans been so divided against each other; never has America stood so low in the eyes of the world.

It is an ominous portent for a nation when significant numbers of its people carry the political dialogue out into the street, forsaking the painstaking, two-way process of argumentation and discussion for the more spectacular device of demonstration. Thus the marches, the sit-ins, kneel-ins, pray-ins, wade-ins, and the like. Public order exists only because the overwhelming majority of people voluntarily obey the rules of the game. The law does not create public order; law is the creature of that order. Order creates an instrument, the law, to punish those occasional breaches of propriety which occur because men are not angels. No society comes into existence, nor can a society endure, unless most of the people can be trusted most of the time to play fair and deal justly with their fellows.

Every free society develops its customary style of political life as a reflection of its peculiar ethos and, according to its own lights, gives to every faction in the society a voice to match its merits. A free society devises political machinery for the orderly succession in office, and cannot long endure chaos in this sphere.

Not a Tyrant's Rule

Our situation in 1973 is not like that of a conquered country, pinned down by a tyrant's heel. A suppressed people is denied access to the political levers by which orderly changes in society are effected. They cannot plead their case across the abyss which separates them from their conquerors, and thus they are impelled to protest by actions which smack of guerrilla warfare. How different here! The channels of political communication in the United States were never more open than today, but never has the country witnessed more protest marches, demonstrations, and riots. The ends the demonstrators hope to accomplish by taking to the streets—recognition, economic improvement—were not being thwarted by the strongest political currents flowing during the past generation; to the contrary, new ground was being gained with each passing year, and the trend was continuing. There was undeniable progress, but it was not being accomplished fast enough by regular political means, seconded by moral and educational movements; so they took to the streets to speed up the action.

Then there are the cop-outs, the denizens of the counterculture, the drug people, the vagabonds, the experimenters with new life styles.

What went wrong? What will bring us back into the mainstream of the American tradition?

The Decline of Religion

The past two centuries—the period during which the American experiment got started, rose to heights of prosperity, then lost its sense of direction—coincides with the general decline of religious belief. The decline I refer to is not something to be gleaned from statistics. There are millions of people who attend church every Sunday; there are a great many devout Christians and pious Jews in Europe and America; there are philosophers who can demonstrate by close reasoning that God is; and there is in the average man a sense that he is taking part in events of a more than mundane significance. But the God reached at the conclusion of a chain of reasoning is not the same God as The One in Whom our being is rooted—although it is with the philosopher's God that the recovery of religious faith must begin. Hold fast to that which can be proved; then faith, when it comes, is a gift of grace.

While religion has gotten onto rather shaky ground in modern times, the philosophy of Materialism has gained ascendancy almost everywhere. It is the typical faith of the laboratory and the marketplace. Science has taken on a magic radiance during the past two centuries, appearing to deliver what religion had only promised; and the world view dictated by science was widely assumed to be Materialism. Scientists, for the purposes of their work, visualized the universe as an intricate, interlocking piece of clockwork. Every event is the effect of a mechanical cause, and a thing is "understood" when broken down and analyzed into its antecedents. Science takes on messianic significance in what Karl Marx referred to as his "Scientific Socialism," and the philosophy of dialectic Materialism on which Communism is based rigorously excludes God and regards religion as the enemy.

Religion was a compelling force in the formation of American ideals and institutions. From the religious heritage of Christendom came our understanding of human nature and destiny—the belief that God has called men to His service while in the body to perform their duties as citizens, their tasks as employers and employees, as well as in their homes, their churches, and their play. The central doctrine of our political theory is the idea that each person possesses inherent, God-given rights, whose protection is government's primary job.

But if man is not a created being, if man instead is simply the end product of material and social forces—as the strict environmentalists believe—then there is not a spark of the divine within him. If there is no God there are no God-given rights in a person, which all other persons are bound to respect. And if there are no rights natural to man as such, then men will not strive to limit government to the public domain. To the contrary, the powers and functions of government will be extended and some men will come to regard other men simply as objects to be manipulated: "We who wield power will create the environment to mould men to our specifications and thus bring a new humanity into being." At the first Creation God made man in His own image; the second Creation proposes to improve on the first!

The philosophy of Materialism cannot allow the idea of inherent rights, nor does it countenance the idea of a soul, or mind, as a genuine reality. Materialism is the theory that bits of matter alone are ultimately real, and when one reflects on this position it is evident that Materialism is self-refuting. If only matter is real, the *theory* that only matter is real is fanciful! A theory, or an idea, or a belief is certainly nonmaterial;

and the fact that we can have an *idea* of matter demonstrates that there is more to the universe than matter!

The Reality of Ideas

Ideas are real! An idea does not occupy space, nor is it in time; it will not submit to chemical analysis, nor can it be weighed or measured. But it begs the question to assume that these are the only tests for genuine reality. If we deny reality to an idea or a thought, then neither can we vouch for the truth of an idea or thought. The Materialist actually denies the validity of thought when he doubts the reality of an idea; and, to be candid, he must admit that he cannot trust the reasoning which purports to lead him to Materialism!

The tragedy is that religion has weakly succumbed to this ideology, and the idea of rights derived from the Creator has been replaced by the notion of privileges granted by the State. This has had a profoundly disturbing effect on American political institutions.

The second ill consequence following upon the decay of religious belief affects the individual person by diminishing his life goals. It is the Christian position that man is made to serve a transcendent end, in other words, to seek first the Kingdom. The ancient promise is that if we put this first thing in first place the other necessary things will come in sequence. But under the rule of Materialism men are limited to the pursuit of earthly goals which, in practice, boil down to two; the pursuit of power and the pursuit of wealth.

The relentless pursuit of power destroys the idea of limited, Constitutional government; the ruthless pursuit of wealth destroys the market economy. If a people acknowledge the Ten Commandments, seek freedom and justice, practice love of God and of neighbor, and then employ a modicum of intelligence in their economic and political arrangements, they will restrain government and release productive energy; they will have a free and productive commonwealth on these terms, and on no others. For it is almost a truism that disorder in society is but a reflection of disorder in the souls of men. Earmarks of today's inner disorder are widespread: uncertainty about the meaning of life, loss of proper goals, confusion as to what it all signifies, a loss of hope, and an enfeeblement of resolution.

As the religious man understands the universe, this natural world is grounded in a spiritual reality, which we cannot sense, but whose reality may be corroborated by intuition, reason, or revelation. When man loses contact with this divine order he will transfer his loyalty to worldly objects, and a part of him will be crippled as a result. The full embodiment of the Gospel vision is beyond the capacity of any generation of men. But the City of Man may be a proving ground for the City of God, and a portion of that vision has worked its way into the law, customs and conventions of Christendom. This ideal once inspired our free institutions, and its original inspiration can be rekindled. Until that rekindling occurs the promise of America remains unfulfilled.

What Is Life's Meaning?

Each of us is thrust into life and saddled with the task of discovering what this life of ours is all about. The first thing we discover is that the life-meaning we seek is not something which will simply drift toward us while we passively wait; we have to work for it. It is only as active participants in life that we begin to discover clues as to the meaning of our earthly pilgrimage.

The full meaning is, of course, denied us. Mortal man, with his finite understanding, can do no more here than "see as through a glass darkly." But the part we can and do see is at least enough so that we know what our next step should be. Take the right step and it leads to another. Look back over our trail and a definite pattern is decipherable.

We human beings did not invent ourselves. Our fumbling efforts to discover the laws of our being—the rules for our proper operation—contribute toward making human life the painful thing it is. But this pain of ours is a peculiar pain; joy is mingled with the pain—the joy that comes from knowing that each one of us participates in the very process of creation itself. Every other creature but man obeys the Laws of God, which are the Laws of Life, willy-nilly—almost mechanically. But God solicits the cooperation of man. We have free will, and we may refuse to cooperate; or, we may exercise our power of choice and thus begin to realize the tremendous potential that lies latent in each one of us.

Life challenges us to grow, and it provides abundant occasions and opportunities to test our nerve. Every test is just a little beyond our capacity; so, in one sense, we fail. But in the very act of striving lies our success, for new powers emerge out of our shortcomings; and the hardships we overcome on each level of life spur us to rise higher.

Zero Population Growth versus the Free Society

One of the great entertainers of our time is Victor Borge. It is somewhat ironic that Borge achieved his fame as a comedian, although he was also a concert pianist. In one of his comedy routines, Victor Borge told stories of his uncle, who was a very bright man. Borge's uncle was so smart that he invented a cure . . . for which there was no known disease!

Every time some population expert mounts his podium to address the world and says to us: "There are too many of you out there," I think of Victor Borge's uncle. The population expert views with alarm a "problem" which is largely nonexistent—where it actually does exist it is less acute than other problems—and his proffered solution, Zero Population Growth, would cure nothing.

The problem, as visualized by proponents of ZPG, is too many people. We are menaced by "the population bomb," "the population threat," "the fertility explosion," a plague of people. The human race has always had to contend against the Four Horsemen of the Apocalypse: Conquest, War, Famine, and Death. To which we now add a fifth horseman, People! "The gravest issue the world faces over the decades ahead . . . short of thermonuclear war itself . . . is . . . population growth." The words I have just quoted are those of Robert S. McNamara, President of the World Bank, from an address delivered at the Massachusetts Institute of Technology, April 28, 1977.

"Indeed, in many ways," Mr. McNamara continues, "rampant population growth is an even more dangerous and subtle threat to the world than thermonuclear war, for it is intrinsically less subject to rational safeguards, and less amenable to organized control.

"The population growth of the planet is not in the exclusive control of a few governments, but rather in the hands of literally hundreds of millions of individual parents who will ultimately determine the outcome."

Mr. McNamara has harsh words for "societies that procrastinate while dangerous population pressures mount." No government, obviously, "can afford to let population pressures grow so dangerously

From the October 1977 issue of *The Freeman*.

large that social frustrations finally erupt into irrational violence and civil disintegration," and so governments must intervene to "improve access to modern means of fertility controls." In practice, this means that governments must provide "a broad selection of the current contraceptives ... as well as sterilization, and—where the society desires it—abortion."

Mr. McNamara is not an extremist; compared to other ZPG'ers, his statement of the issues is calm and his advocacy of further governmental interventions and controls is the typical "liberal" panacea; the "liberal" confronts something he doesn't like and his stereotyped response is: "There ought to be a law."

There have been studies of population trends ever since Thomas Robert Malthus penned his celebrated *Essay* in 1798. Malthus feared that population would always impinge on subsistence; no matter how great the increase in the production of foodstuffs, population would increase at a faster rate, and mankind therefore faced perpetual misery. Malthus looked through the wrong end of the telescope, and so his prophecy makes a certain amount of sense as history. Look backward over the centuries when this planet housed a mere few hundred million people, and it is true that most people went hungry most of the time, only to perish during the periodically recurring famines.

What Is Overpopulation?

If you define overpopulation as more people on the planet than a given area can sustain, then the world until modern times has nearly always suffered from overpopulation! Before the Europeans came to this continent this land mass was inhabited by less than a million Indians. Food was nearly always in short supply and starvation was a constant threat. There was an imbalance between food supply and the number of mouths requiring to be fed; such an imbalance is the only meaningful definition of overpopulation. Pre-Columbian America was overpopulated.

But then some important developments occurred in western nations as political liberty flowered in the eighteenth century. Serfs and slaves became free men with a right to enjoy the fruits of their labor— so they produced more. It was a period marked by science, inventions, and technology—with progressive increases in agricultural and industrial production as a consequence. Wages doubled, redoubled, and doubled again. The entrepreneur—the man able to combine capital, labor, and resources to best satisfy consumers—was accorded status and prestige. Work acquired a new dignity, thrift was praised, increasing prosperity and material well-being were enjoyed by the multitudes. The immense productivity of the American people during the past two centuries has resulted in a situation where famine is no longer a threat in this land, and where well over 200 million people live well on the same acreage that once barely sustained a million. We feed the world with our surplus, proving Malthus a lousy prophet!

Demographic Hysteria

Scholars have been studying population trends for the better part of two centuries; students who specialized in the subject began calling themselves "demographers" about a hundred years ago. But this scholarly discipline, demography, began to go hysterical about a generation ago, largely because of the so-called baby boom which came along in the aftermath of World War II. That boom lasted just long enough to cause a spate of prognostications about a planet in the year 2000 with standing room only. The baby boom burst, birth rates began to decline; and so the alarmists had to change their tune: the birth rate is not declining fast enough!

Mr. McNamara, in the speech cited earlier, tells us that a "significant decline in fertility ... has occurred in 77 of the 88 countries for which estimates are available." The world-wide fertility rate has fallen off nearly 13 percent over the past two decades. But a 13 percent decline in the birth rate is not enough to satisfy Mr. McNamara, who declares that "Unless governments, through appropriate policy action, can accelerate the reduction in fertility, the global population may not stabilize below 11 billion. That would be a world none of us would want to live in." Eleven billion people is just over twice the number of people now inhabiting the globe. How does Mr. McNamara know that none of us would want to live in such a world?

Mr. Colin Clark, for one, would not mind living with 11 billion people, nor, indeed, with many more. Colin Clark is a celebrated economist and one of the world's leading statisticians. *Fortune* magazine, in its December 1960 issue, published an article by Colin Clark entitled "Do Population and Freedom Grow Together?" His thesis was that economic progress and political freedom are often stimulated by population growth. Estimating the number of people this planet can sustain—if we use our intelligence—he made this startling statement:

> Today the best agriculturalists in Europe—the Dutch—produce a very good and varied diet on the equivalent of two-thirds of an acre of land per person. If all the land suitable for agriculture throughout the world were cultivated in this manner assuming at the same time that the whole world eats as well as the most prosperous countries do now, provision could be made for 28 billion people, or ten times the world's 1960 population. If we take Japanese instead of Dutch standards of cultivation and of diet—after all, the Japanese are quite a healthy people—the world could provide for three or four times as many again.

The Intelligence Factor

The critical factor for a nation is not the number of people it contains, nor even its population density: the critical factor is the amount of intelligence the people bring to bear on their institutions, especially in the way they organize agriculture and industry. Take the unhappy country of India, for example; poverty is everywhere and misery weighs down the spirit. Why is India in such parlous condition? Is it her "teeming masses"?

There are indeed a lot of people in that subcontinent, nearly 700 million of them; but the territory is vast. India's population density is just about one-half that of the Netherlands, and we never speak of the teeming masses of Holland. England has fifty more people per square kilometer than India, Japan has 117 more people per square kilometer than India.

India has the people and she has the resources; what she lacks are the institutions that make for productivity and prosperity. Her people suffer terribly in consequence, not because there are so many of them, but because—for religious reasons—they do not choose to establish the political and economic conditions which make for material progress. That's why India's situation is so heartbreaking; the problem is not India's "teeming masses."

I have stressed the alarmist and hysterical note typically struck in the writings of the proponents of Zero Population Growth—those who speak of people as a plague, a threat, an impending disaster. These writers prophesy that people are driven to breed senselessly and prolifi-cally—unless governmental controls are imposed to prevent this calam-ity.

I have cited a tiny bit of the evidence on the other side. merely to cast some doubt on the ZPG thesis that there is a demographic crisis which provides a new rationale for governmental intrusion into affairs once regarded as most private and personal—a couple's decision as to the size of their future family. Mr. McNamara is horrified that this decision is in the hands of "literally hundreds of millions of parents." He thinks it should be turned over to the same people who operate the Post Office!

Built-in Safeguards

On the parallel question—as to the optimum number of people who shall walk the face of the earth—every one of us is aware that quality is more important than quantity and we do not like unhealthy urban concentrations of people. The very last thing any of us would want to see is a globalized New York City! But then, we're in no danger of such a thing happening. Living organisms are not at the mercy of some imagined demonic force causing them to multiply be-yond their subsistence. There are built-in safeguards in nature and society to prevent such an eventuality.

A "Believe It or Not" cartoon points out that if all the progeny of a single pair of oysters were to live and go on reproducing for a year there'd be a mass of oysters three times the size of the earth. Or something like that. But as a matter of fact, nature does not behave that way. I offer you a passage from a 1968 book by Arthur Koestler, *The Ghost in the Machine:*

> In recent years biologists have discovered that every ani-mal species which they studied—from flower beetles through rabbits to baboons—is equipped with instinctive behaviour patterns which put a brake on excessive breeding, and keep the population-density in a given territory fairly constant, even when food is plentiful. When the density exceeds a certain limit, crowding produces stress-symptoms which affect the

hormonal balance; rabbits and deer begin to die off from "adrenal stress" without any sign of epidemic disease; the females of rats stop caring for their young, which perish, and abnormal sexual behaviour makes its appearance. Thus the ecological equilibrium in a given area is maintained not only by the relative distribution but also by a kind of intraspecific feedback mechanism which adjusts the rate of breeding so as to keep the population at a stable level.

I realize that human beings are not geared into nature's rhythms by instinct, in the same manner as the other orders of creation. Our species is unique. With a portion of our being we transcend nature; we possess reason and free will. By the responsible exercise of our rational faculties and our power of choice, we have the ability to arrive at a decision after reflecting on the evidence. It is by taking thought that we human beings make our accommodation to the demands of nature and the requirements of our society. This is what it means to be a free and responsible human being; to be inner-directed and self-directed in the pursuit of our life goals is a mark of a free person.

The Road to Tyranny

This brings us to what I regard as the crux of the population controversy. The evidence does not sustain the doomsday thesis that the planet will soon have standing room only; but suppose it did. The dire prophecies of the proponents of ZPG about "the population bomb" will never eventuate, but if we do believe these people and accept their remedy, we'll be saddled with a monstrous and tyrannical government. Farewell to freedom, then, as the bureaucracy mushrooms, spawning a multitude of snoopers, spies, and enforcers. Citizens would be tested, tagged, ticketed. There'd be dissent and the suppression of dissenters; there'd be rebellions to put down. Mr. McNamara tells us that we would not like living on a planet with 11 billion people, and I would tell Mr. McNamara that the government he would invoke would be Brave New World and 1984 combined—impossible to live with! It would crush the individual.

Many people are concerned today, and rightly concerned, with the Soviet dissidents. We believe that the rights of these individuals are being violated, that something in each of these persons, which does not belong to the State, is being appropriated by the State. What that something is in each person may be called by different names—a portion of divinity in him, his soul, his sacred prerogatives, his rights. Whatever you choose to call this inner being of persons, which belongs to them simply because they are persons, we believe it should be held inviolate. The Soviet philosophy views the matter differently; the Soviet citizen is a product of the Soviet State and therefore he belongs to the State. The State owns him. Some Jews who wished to emigrate to Israel had to buy themselves from the Soviet State, the purchase price being the estimated cost to the State of their manufacture from child into citizen. The Soviet citizen lives to serve the State.

We take the opposite view, that the State or the government exists to serve citizens—in very limited ways. Governments are instituted to secure individuals in the rights which are theirs because the Creator so endowed them. "The God who gave us life," declared Jefferson, "gave us liberty at the same time." The government of a free people must not itself invade the rights of any person, and the law provides penalties for anyone who transgresses the rights of another.

The Rule of Law

The essential function of the government of a free society, in harmony with the moral code, is to use lawful force against criminals in order that peaceful citizens may go about their business. The use of lawful force against lawbreakers for the protection of law-abiding citizens is the earmark of a properly limited government. Standing in utter contrast is a government's use of tyrannical force against peaceful citizens—whatever the excuse or rationalization. It's the contrast between the rule of law and oppression.

People should not be forced into conformity with any social blueprint; their private plans should not be overridden in the interests of some national plan or social goal. Government, the public power, should never be used for private advantage; it should not be used to protect people from themselves. Well, then, what should the law do to peaceful, innocent citizens? It should let them alone!

And this is precisely what the ZPG people do not intend; they do not intend to let anyone alone!

The idea of the intrinsic value, merit, or sacredness of the individual human person has suffered a drastic devaluation in the modern world. The human being once thought of himself as God's special creation, a favorite of the Almighty. But the religious vision of the totality—call it Theism—gave way to the world view of Materialism.

According to the Materialist there is nothing in the universe that shares man's values or responds to his aspirations. Man is a waif in an alien universe, buffeted by forces he cannot comprehend, doomed at last to complete his pointless journey with as little distinction as he began it, his proudest achievements reduced to dust and forgotten. The mood of our time is begotten by this world view, and the mood is a compound of sadness, resignation, rebellion, defiance, and despair. The mood is anti-life, and especially anti-human life.

A Sense of Life

Only a society harboring a deep undercurrent of hostility to human life and its continuance could treat abortion casually, as a mere matter of personal preference. And the idea of Zero Population Growth could not possibly make any headway in a society with healthy values, where people experienced a genuine lust for life, appreciated the vast promise in every newborn child, loved life for its joys, took its pains in stride, and experienced life as a venture in destiny.

A profound sense of life is not be found within the world view of Materialism, or Secularism, or Humanism—choose your own label. We can recapture a profound sense of life only within the religious world vision of Theism. Faith in man can be rebuilt only around faith in God. Easy to say the words; what do they mean?

To believe in God is to act on the premise that a Creative Intelligence is at work in the universe; fulfilling its purposes through nature, in history, and above all by means of persons. This is the basic theistic premise and some primary implications are to be drawn from it: the totality is a coherent whole, i.e., a *universe;* history has meaning; human life has a purpose; individuals count. To say "God exists" is to affirm that the whole show makes sense.

To reject God, on the other hand, is to deny that any Creative Intelligence manifests itself in nature, history or persons. To deny God is to affirm that everything which exists is the mere end result of blind forces operating on dead matter over immense time. Accept *this* premise and it follows that there's no meaning to the whole; there's no cosmic purpose for human life, i.e., no discoverable pattern in the nature of things which offers man a clue as to how he should conduct his affairs.

No person can believe in the human enterprise, or find a purpose for his own life, if he rejects the belief that the cosmos makes sense. When people cannot make sense out of things, they come to feel that they are at the mercy of fate. In our day fate takes the form of material forces or historical trends which use people and use them up. Persons cease to believe that they are free beings, capable of making the significant choices which shape their own future. Having accepted the notion that human beings are the mere chance end products of natural forces—like everything else in nature—they lose heart; they lose faith in their own capacity to think, to understand, to plan, to project their dreams and realize them. I take it as axiomatic that external disorder and social strife is a reflection of disorder in the mind and soul. The calamities of today grew out of the bad ideas and misplaced affections of yesterday, for people tend to act out their ideas. As we believe so will we become. As we are within, so will our society be: for it is in the nature of the human condition as such that man forever seeks a harmony within himself, that is, an ordered soul; and secondly, he works for an outer order of society.

The critical question then is not the number of people who shall inhabit the earth; the critical question has to do with our understanding of human nature and destiny, the purpose of life, and the meaning of it all. If we are sound at this point, then we can deal nobly with the issues of life. And with God's help, we might make it.

Defending Freedom and the Free Society

Countless generations of men have lived in unfree societies, but many men dreamed of freedom and hoped for the day when their children would be free. Gradually the West developed a philosophy of freedom, a rationale for individual immunity against governmental power. This intellectual movement gathered strength in the eighteenth and nineteenth centuries; Liberalism, as it was called, became the major social force in country after country. As the twentieth century dawned it appeared that the ideals of the free society were safely installed in the thinking of the West and progressively realized in practice in the major countries. But then something happened. In country after country, the highway of Liberalism turned into the road to serfdom. We made an about face in this country, but those who led off in a new direction didn't even bother to change the labels. They still call themselves Liberals, but the program of Liberalism in 1993 is radically opposed to the ideals of a free society. It is merely a pragmatized version of old-line socialism.

We sense that all is not well with our society, nor with our world. Our traditional rights and liberties, once taken for granted, are in jeopardy; they are undermined by dubious theories, and often overridden in practice. Under constant attack are such things as individual liberty, limited government, the private property concept, and the free market way of doing business. Taken together these items are the essential elements of the free society.

This essay is an effort to get to the roots of the present situation, to determine, if possible, some of the causes; and to suggest, in the light of this analysis, the nature of the remedy. The dislocations which meet the eye most immediately appear on the economic and political levels, but they stem—if the analysis of this paper is correct—from aberrations at the deeper levels of ethics and religion. Believing that no remedy can be successful that does not go at least as deep as the disease, it is suggested that sound economic and political theory, while imperative and good as far as it goes, does not go far enough by itself to make the case for liberty. It is further suggested that the typical

From the January 1993 issue of *The Freeman*.

111

added arguments from ethics are in fact substitutes for a genuine ethical theory. The difficulties that confront any effort to construct or revive an ethical consensus are alluded to, leading to an awareness of the need for reconstruction in the area of philosophy or theology. The case for liberty, in short, needs to be watertight. If there is an open seam at any level it may prove to be the gap through which liberty will be lost, for "Nature always seeks out the hidden flaw."

Liberty Lost

Given a choice, most people today, will choose liberty—other things being equal. People don't give up their liberties except under some delusion, such as the delusion that the surrender of a little liberty will strengthen the guarantee of economic security. There never has been a serious anti-liberty philosophy and platform as such, whose principles people have examined, accepted, and then put into practice. Things haven't happened this way. But although we haven't chosen statism, statism is what we are getting: Speaking now not of conquered countries where liberty has been suppressed but of nations like our own where the old legal forms have been preserved, we may say that the steady attrition of liberty in the modern world is not the consequence of a direct assault by open and avowed anti-libertarians. No, the steady decline of liberty among people who sincerely prefer liberty if given a choice is the unforeseen and unwanted by-product of something else.

Liberty Regained

Many people are concerned with the plight of liberty and are working toward its restoration. The tremendous upsurge of interest in the libertarian-conservative philosophy since 1950 is sufficient witness to that fact. The libertarian-conservative camp is unanimous in its opposition to every variety of collectivism and statism, but at this point the unanimity begins to break down. Libertarians and conservatives differ among themselves in their estimate of what it takes to challenge the prevailing ideologies successfully. There are four possible levels or stages of the anti-collectivist, pro-freedom argument: the economic, the political, the ethical, and the religious. Do we need to use all four? Or is one or two sufficient? Opinions differ in the libertarian-conservative camp. Let us examine some of the arguments advanced at each level, beginning with the economic.

It is enough to expound free market economics, say some. Socialism is nothing more than economic heresy and all we have to do is demonstrate the greater productive efficiency of the free market and the socialists will retire in confusion. Freedom works, they say, and as proof point to America's superiority in computers, telephones, bathtubs, and farm products. The improvement of his material circumstance is man's chief end, and the only thing that makes a man a Communist or a collectivist is his ignorance of the conditions which must prevail if a society is to be prosperous.

Most of those who stress economic arguments add considerations drawn from political philosophy. Socialism is not only unproductive economically, but the operational imperatives of a socialist society make government the sole employer. Society is run by command, by directives from the top down, the way an army is run. The individual citizen must do as he is told, or starve. There is no independent economic base to sustain political resistance, so the population in a socialized society is necessarily reduced to serfdom. This is an inevitable consequence of a managed economy, a development which is fatal to such political goods as the Rule of Law, respect for the rights and dignity of the individual, and the idea of private ownership protected by law.

Some libertarians and conservatives agree with the urgent need to argue the case on economic and political grounds, but believe that it must be carried a stage further—into ethics. There is not, they would argue, one ethical code for politicians and another for people—there is just one set of ethical norms which is binding on rulers and ruled alike. A socialized society is poor in economic goods, and its citizens are, politically, reduced to serfs. These are social consequences of the moral violations which are built-in features of every variety of collectivism and statism. The moral violations which this argument has in mind are not simply the obvious sins of totalitarian regimes; the lying for political advantage, the murders for convenience, the concentration camps, and so on. These are included, of course, but this argument is mainly directed at the more subtle moral violations inherent in the operations of the welfare state.

The welfare state in America, whether run by Democrats or Republicans, is based on the redistributionist principle: "Votes and taxes for all, subsidies for a few." In actual practice, the welfare state deprives all citizens of a percentage of their earnings in order to redistribute this money to its favorites—after taking out a healthy cut to cover its own costs. Such a Robin Hood operation would be both illegal and immoral if private citizens engaged in it; and although any government can, by definition, make its actions legal, it cannot make them moral. Every variety of collectivism, therefore, is charged with ethical viola-tions, in addition to practicing economic and political lunacy.

"Social Utility" Trap

It is at this point that a major rift begins to appear in the freedom camp. Some libertarians challenge the validity of ethical arguments. The universe, they assert, displays no recognizable ethical dimension. Says one of them: "Nature is alien to the idea of right and wrong. . . . It is the social system which determines what should be deemed right and what wrong. . . . The only point that matters is social utility." Well, all sorts of habits and customs, from primitive ritual cannibalism to using the proper soup spoon, serve the ends of "social utility," and if social utility is "the only point that matters" I doubt that the case for liberty can be made convincing, however skillful our economic reason-ing.

Those who discount ethical and religious arguments get off the bus here. These sturdy fighters for freedom have made their choice of weapons and they are drawn exclusively from the arsenal of economic and political theory. But even among those who would use ethical arguments there is great difference of opinion. "Whose ethics?" they ask, or "What theory of ethics?" One group steers clear of religion, regarding it as a strictly private matter with little or no relevance to the free society. A second group regards religion as hostile to the free society. I propose to deal first with this position.

These anti-religionists employ what they label ethical arguments, as well as arguments drawn from economic and political theory, but when it comes to religion, they draw the line. They want nothing to do with this God stuff! God's existence is, in their eyes, improbable, but this is not all; religious belief is actually harmful! The title of a lecture in a series sponsored by this group is "The Destructiveness of the God Idea." They proudly proclaim themselves atheists.

There are numerous conceptions of God, and every one of us is a-theist-ic with reference to one or more of them. Most self-styled atheists are a-theist-ic with respect to a childish version of the deity. This is about on a par with not believing in the moon because some people say it is made of green cheese! In history there have been men of incomparable intellectual attainments who have been theists, who would not have been theists if they had had to believe in such a concept of the deity as the typical atheist rejects. And the same is true of contemporary theists. There are popular and degrading notions of God, but the argument is not confined to the limitations imposed by superstition!

Competing Ethical Codes

Now let me return to the first group of ethicists; those who lean heavily on ethical arguments but steer clear of the religious area. These people generally understand that in economics, liberty means reliance on the uncoerced buying habits of consumers as a guide to making economic decisions; "the market," in short. In politics, liberty implies limited government. This means that governmental action, circum-scribed by a written constitution, is designed to protect the lives, the liberties, and the property of all citizens alike. But it also means that both government and constitution must operate within the framework imposed by an ethical code. In terms of this ethical code, political invasions of personal liberty and property are morally wrong. If an act is wrong when done by private citizens, it is just as wrong when done by public officials.

Such a statement as this assumes that private citizens and public officials acknowledge and try to live by the same ethical code. They may, or again, they may not. There is not just one ethical code in 1993; there are several competing and conflicting codes even in this country. Today, however, there is general confusion in the area of our moral values, and some contend that "right" and "wrong" are not meaning-ful terms. Ethical relativism is widely accepted, and this creed main-tains that something which may be right in one time or place may be wrong in another time or place.

A century ago in this country the ethical code could pretty much be taken for granted; people's notion of what things were right and what things were wrong were, for the most part, deductions from a common source. We derived our ethical consensus from the prevailing religion of the West, Christianity. This ethical consensus was recognizably different, even a century ago, from the ethical consensus of Hindu society, which sanctioned the division of society into inferior and superior castes, and put millions of outcastes outside the category of human beings. It differed in important ways from the ethical consensus which had prevailed in Greece and Rome. W.E.H. Lecky's famous book, *History of European Morals* (1869), was a dispassionate account of the transformation wrought in the moral ideals of the ancient world by the introduction of Christianity.

But, although there was a nineteenth-century ethical consensus, fateful developments were pending in the realm of religion and ethics. Friedrich Nietzsche told his contemporaries, in effect: You have given up the Christian God and this means that you cannot long retain your ethical code which is bound up with this faith. Let's get back to the ethical code of the ancient Greeks! Nietzsche urged what he called "a trans-valuation of all values." Karl Marx was telling us during this period that the productive efforts of a society are the main thing; ethical, intellectual, and spiritual things are mere superstructure. The moral values of the nineteenth century, therefore, were capitalist ethics; get rid of capitalist production and capitalist ethics would follow it down the drain, to be replaced by Communist ethics. And Communist ethics, as spelled out by Lenin, are an inversion of Christian ethics. Whatever advances the Party is right and good. Lying and murder are endorsed as ethical practices if they further the cause of the Communist Party.

The ethical confusion has worsened in our own day, and become more complicated. And so an awareness grows that the kind of an ethical code *we* would endorse is by no means obvious to a lot of people; therefore, if this code is again to become an active principle in the lives of people it needs some attention.

The Lack of an Ethical Consensus

Our traditional ethical code is the end result of a particular historical development. This code is something people have learned; they have imbibed it from Western culture. It is not, in other words, a biological set of guidelines with which people come equipped at birth, as they have two hands, two feet, one head, and so on. Recognition of this fact turns up in odd places. John Dewey, himself no Christian, spent some time in China after World War I, and in 1922 he made this pertinent observation: "Until I had lived in a country where Christianity is relatively little known and has had relatively very few generations of influence upon the character of people, I had always assumed, as natural reactions which one could expect of any normal human being in a given situation, reactions which I now discover you only find among the people that have been exposed many generations to the influence of the Christian ethic." In other words, our traditional ethical code is one we have learned over the centuries in a Christian culture. We were educated into it century after century, until the past several generations, during which time we have been slowly educated out of it. The assumption that we can take our ethical code for granted and use it to confound the collectivists presupposes a situation that does not exist; it presupposes an ethical consensus, when it is precisely the absence of such a consensus which has helped create the vacuum into which collectivism has seeped!

As the French philosopher André Malraux tells us, we are living in the first agnostic civilization. Until the past two or three generations, men believed that their moral ideals reflected the nature of the universe. But if the universe is a complete moral blank, completely alien to notions of right and wrong, then all moral codes are merely homemade rules for convenience. A rule against murder is on the same level as a rule against driving on the left hand side of the street; there is no intrinsic difference between the two. A libertarian writer defends the integrity of scientific and economic laws as the only constants in the universe. These, he writes, "must not be confused with man-made laws of the country and with man-made moral precepts." It follows, therefore, that if men do not happen to like the ethical code they are living under they can write themselves a new one, just as easily as they can change from summer to winter clothing.

To sum up the matter: We can no longer take our traditional ethical code for granted. The foundation it was based upon has been neglected, and an ethical code, by its nature, is a set of inferences and deductions from something more fundamental than itself. We may behave decently out of habit, but ethical theory—by its very nature—must be grounded in a theology, or cosmology, if you prefer. A belief in the impossibility of ethics because the universe is a moral blank is an instance of the truism that every code for conduct is a deduction from a judgment based on faith as to the nature of things.

We hear it said frequently that individual man, in the totalitarian countries, is made for the state; but here, the state is made for man. If we say that the state is made for man, the implication is that we have come to some tentative conclusions as to what man is made for. We must have asked, and found some sorts of answers, to questions such as the following: What is the end and goal of human life? What is the purpose and meaning of individual life? What is my nature, and my destiny? Within what framework of meaning does the universe make sense? These are theological and religious questions, and when they are seriously pondered some sorts of answers are bound to come.

That things are senseless and individual life without meaning is one sort of an answer. Once this answer is given, it will start to generate an appropriate ethical code. This is a sort of salvage effort to which the works of the late Albert Camus were devoted. "I proclaim that I believe in nothing," he writes, "and that everything is absurd." The only appropriate response to this act of faith is rebellion, arising "from the spectacle of the irrational coupled with an unjust and incomprehensible condition." This is one reading of the universe and the human condition, together with an appropriate recommended code of conduct. It is, therefore, a religion, although the number of its adherents do not appear in any census. In passing, one might remark that it is a curious kind of "incomprehensible condition" from which a man can apprehend enough to write several books about it! Communism is another contemporary religion. Its universe is a materialistic one, but the universe contains a dynamic force—the mode of production— which is working toward the fulfillment of history in a classless society. And there is an appropriate code of conduct enjoined upon all good Communists.

Choosing Christianity

There is a third option which makes considerable sense to me, and that is Christianity. Such a statement comes as no surprise, and you are probably telling yourself that I, as a professional religionist, have a vested interest in offering just such a conclusion. Permit me, therefore, to digress and sound an autobiographical note. If anyone had told me during my high school years, or up to my senior year in college that I'd wind up as a minister, I'd have taken it as a personal affront! As things turned out, however, I did find myself in theological school after college, but before the first year had gone by I had decided that the ministry was not for me. I was skeptical about theological matters and decided to go into the field of psychology. In theological controversy it seemed to me there were good arguments in favor of all the basic doctrines, and good arguments against. How, then, does one tip the balance in one direction or another? On the level of doctrinal theory it was difficult for me to say. To make a long story short, I finally returned to theological studies, got my degree, and—full of misgivings—was foisted upon an innocent and unsuspecting congregation.

During these years I held to a parallel set of interests in economics and political science. I was a libertarian before I ever heard the word, based on an acquaintance with the thinking of the Classic Liberals and a prejudice in favor of freedom. But my social thinking was in one compartment and my religion was in another. Unbeknownst to me, however, these two things were on a collision course, and it was fated that one day they should bump into each other. They did, and lots of things began to fall into place. I became aware of what Christianity had meant to Western civilization and to the framing of America's institutions, and before long I had the ingredients to tip my theological balance in the direction of firmer religious convictions. I also knew why Classic Liberalism failed, although it had played its own game with its own deck—it lacked the religious dimension which alone makes life meaningful to individuals and provides a foundation for ethics.

People were freer in the nineteenth century than men had ever been before. This period was the heyday of Liberalism, but it also happened to be the twilight of religion. Large numbers of people became uncertain about the ends for which life should be lived. Lacking a sense of purpose and destiny they were afflicted by the feeling that life has little or no meaning, that the individual doesn't matter nor his life count. Just when people had the most freedom they lost touch with the things which make freedom really worth having. Freedom had once been affirmed as a necessary condition for man if he were to achieve his true end, but when the religious dimension dropped out of life the advocates of freedom got themselves into a "promising contest" with the collectivists as to which could outpromise the other when it came to delivering the maximum quantity of material things. As was to be expected, the collectivists outpromised their opponents, although their actual performance must for ever fall short. Liberty, in other words, is recognized for the precious thing it really is when significant numbers of people know that they must have it in order to work out their eternal destiny.

There are two things I am not saying. I am not saying that we have to cook up or feign an interest in religion merely to accomplish political or economic ends. Such efforts would be fruitless, but even if they were effective I'd oppose them. Secondly, I am not saying that men who, for reasons of their own, cannot embrace religion and ethics, cannot therefore be effective champions of free market economics and limited government. There are technical areas in political theory, and especially in economics, where a lot more enlightenment is needed, and where there is no impingement on the domains of ethics and religion. Non-religious libertarians may be invaluable here. Even so, they cannot touch all bases. The man who is a socialist for religious or ethical reasons won't be shaken in his convictions by economic and political arguments alone; his religious and ethical misconceptions must be met on their own ground.

Utilitarianism

At this point I shall be reminded that economists, after Adam Smith to the present day, do tend typically to hold some variety of the ethical theory known as Utilitarianism, which dates back to Jeremy Bentham and John Stuart Mill in the early and middle part of the nineteenth century. But as Mill himself pointed out, the creed has a long history, dating from Epicurus in the third century B.C.

Utilitarianism states its principles in various ways, but invariably it emphasizes two cardinal points—maximum satisfaction and minimum effort. Man, in terms of this theory, acts only to maximize his happiness, pleasures, satisfactions or comfort, and he seeks to do this with a minimum expenditure of energy. Utilitarianism has little or nothing to say about the spiritual, ethical or cultural framework within which its "maximum economy-maximum satisfaction" principle operates. It minimizes or denies life's spiritual dimension, it uses the word "good" in a non-ethical sense, i.e., equivalent to "happiness producing," and it asserts that men are bound together in societies solely on the basis of a rational calculation of the private advantage to be gained by social cooperation under the division of labor.

The Utilitarian proposition that each man invariably tends to achieve his ends with a minimum of effort says nothing about the means he may or will use. The "maximum economy" principle, when it first took over as a conscious maxim of human behavior—in nineteenth-century England—operated within the value system or ethical code persons happened to have at the time. The ethical code in the West during the period of the appearance and gradual acceptance of the "maximum economy" principle—during the past century—was largely a product of the religious heritage of Europe. This ethical legacy assured that although men would tend to take the line of least effort in the attaining of their ends, they would at the same time use only those means which are compatible with the moral norms enjoined by their religion. Moral norms are restraints on certain actions, and if the "maximum economy" principle is fervently accepted it must go to work on the restraints embodied in the ethical code whenever they interfere with the line of least resistance between a man's aims and their realization. The "maximum economy" principle, by its very nature, necessarily sacrifices means to ends, and in the circumstances of the modern world Utilitarianism begins to undermine the old ethical norms wherever these impede an individual's attainment of his economic ends.

Robbery, it has been observed, is the first labor-saving device. If a man accepts, without qualification, the precept "Get more for less" as his categorical imperative, what will he do when a combination of circumstances presents him with a relatively safe opportunity to steal? His ethical compunctions against theft have already been dulled, and the use of theft as a means of acquiring economic goods is one of the possible logical conclusions that may be drawn from the "greatest economy" principle. Theft is, of course, forbidden in many of the world's ethical codes, and conformity to these codes over the millennia has bred a reluctance to steal in most men. Thievery there has been aplenty despite the bans, but it has been accompanied by a guilty conscience. The "maximum economy" principle, when first accepted, is applied to productive labor within the framework of the code. But if the idea of "Get more for less" is a principle, why not apply it across the board?

There are two impediments to a man's acquisition of economic goods: First, there is the effort required to produce them, and second, there is the prohibition against stealing them. The former is in the nature of things, but the latter comes to be regarded as merely a man-made rule. The "greatest economy" principle goes to work on the first impediment—productive effort—by inventing labor saving devices; it goes to work on the second impediment—the moral code—by collectivizing it. It reduces the commandment against theft to a matter of social expediency.

Society is admonished against theft on the grounds that a society in which property is not secure is a poor society. But this truism offers no guidance to the individual who finds himself in a situation where he can steal with relative impunity. To the extent that he is emancipated from "outmoded" taboos and follows the line of least resistance, he will steal whenever he thinks he can get away with it, and to make theft easier and safer he will start writing a form of theft into his statutes: "Votes and taxes for all, subsidies for us." Utilitarianism, in short, has no logical stopping place short of collectivism. Utilitarian collectivism is not a contradiction in terms, although particular Utilitarians, restrained by other principles, may stop short of collectivism.

Utilitarianism purports to be a theory of ethics; man ought to act, it declares, so as to augment the quantity of satisfactions. It is usually linked to a theory of motivation which sweepingly declares that every human action aims at improving the well-being of the acting agent: "acting is necessarily always selfish." Capitalism, it is asserted, is based on this deterministic psychology. The militant atheist group mentioned earlier adopts what it calls a morality of self-interest. "Morality is a rational science," we read in their literature, "with man's life as its standard, [and] self-interest as its motor." "Capitalism," the author continues, "expects, and by its nature demands that every man act in the name of his rational self-interest." Let us examine this unqualified assertion. Capitalism, or the market economy, begins to work automatically in a society where there is a preponderance of fair play and an evenhanded justice in operation. Lacking these essential conditions capitalism cannot be made to work. Here's a person with more shrewdness than ability; he has little energy and fewer scruples. On the market, the verdict of his peers is that his services aren't worth very much; so he consults his rational self-interest—unimpeded by old-fashioned ethics—and learns that his shrewdness and lack of scruples admirably equip him to operate a racket. He starts one, and becomes wealthy and famous. Would anyone care to try to convince an Ivan Boesky, for instance, that it is really to his own self-interest to play the game fairly even though this would put him behind the wheel of a bakery truck at $160.00 per week? How can the anti-capitalistic men-tality, if it is true to itself, and acts in its own self-interest, project a capitalist society? The answer is, it can't.

Some accidents of history shattered our society's ethical and reli-gious framework just at the time when free market economists came forth armed with insights into human behavior in the areas of produc-tion and trade. But because men respond one way in one sector of life it cannot be inferred that they respond the same way everywhere, nor that they should. Oddly enough, it is precisely free market economists themselves who best embody this truism. Free market economists in these days find a poor market for their services. There is, on the other hand, a great public demand for the tripe palmed off as the new eco-nomics by the "social scientists."

Resisting all such market demands the free market economists stand by their principles even though this means that, with motives impugned, they are lonely voices, victims of academic and professional discrimination. Why do they not yield to pressure of popular demand, as they themselves advocate should be done in the realms of produc-tion, trade, and entertainment? Does the market demand ridiculous spike-heeled shoes and mismatched clothes? Then give the public what it wants, say the free market economists; in the realm of material things, the majority is always right. Are there complaints about the high salaries of rock wailers and Hollywood sex symbols, coupled with laments about the low estate of the legitimate theater? Yes, but not from free market economists who conceal any disgust they may feel and merely say, "Let the public be served." But when it comes to the realm of ideas the economists, to their enormous credit, ignore the market—public and majority pressures—and do not trim or hedge or yield an inch on their convictions. In other words, they operate with one set of principles in the realm of material things—"Give the public what it wants"—but they invoke another set of principles when they enter the realm of economic ideas—"Resist public pressure on behalf of intellect and conscience." Oddly enough, however, there is nothing in their philosophy to legitimize the second set of principles. They know by a kind of instinct or intuition that ideas or opinions which have a price tag attached—as if they were marketable commodities like any other—aren't worth much, and neither is the person who hawks them. But instincts and intuitions, however civilized and humane, are largely uncommunicable.

Conduct, however exemplary, cannot make its point when it is tied to a philosophy which alleges that the game of life has no rules; therefore, seek private advantage, maximize personal satisfactions. No matter how such ingredients as these are combined they won't result in a philosophy of liberty. This needs something else, namely, a frame work of values which makes possible a different approach. The restoration of our ethical consensus and the repair of our value system brings us to arguments on the religious level. The traditional arguments in this area won't be given a fair shake by our contemporaries unless there is a contemporary approach to them which really confronts us with them. Perhaps there is such an approach.

The City of God and the City of Man

Christianity introduced a concept into the thought of the West which is alien to the thinking of Plato and Aristotle, the two major thinkers of the ancient world. This new concept has been called, after Augustine, the idea of the two cities: the City of God and the City of Man. Man, it is asserted, holds his citizenship papers in two realms, the earthly and the heavenly. He is to negotiate this life as best he can, seeking as much justice and such happiness as this world permits, but in full awareness that his ultimate felicity may be attained only in another order of existence.

This concept would have been largely incomprehensible to the Greeks. Man, for Aristotle, was a political animal who might find complete fulfillment in the closed society of the Greek city-state. A standard work on this aspect of Grecian life is Ernest Barker' s *Political Thought of Plato and Aristotle* (1906, 1959), and a few sentences from this book convey the flavor of the Greek outlook. Summarizing Aristotle, Barker writes: "The good of the individual is the same as the good of the society. . . . The notion of the individual is not prominent, and the conception of rights seems hardly to have been attained." Speaking of Socrates, Barker writes, "For him there was no rule of natural justice outside the law; law is justice, he held, and what is just is simply what is commanded in the laws." Ethics and politics are one, and there is no distinction between Church and State. The city-state, "being itself both Church and State . . . had both to repress original sin—the function to which medieval theory restricted the State, and to show the way to righteousness—a duty which medieval theory vindicated for the Church."

After the decay of ancient society and the polarization of Church and State, the distinction between spiritual and secular power in Europe and America for the past nineteen centuries guaranteed that there would always be some separation and dispersal of power within the nation. But with the dropping of the religious dimension from modern life we return to the unitary state in both theory and practice. This was obvious to Barker early this century as he foresaw the rise of the welfare state: "It seems to be expected of the State that it shall clothe and feed, as well as teach its citizens, and that it shall not only punish drunkenness, but also create temperance. We seem to be returning to the old Greek conception of the State as a positive maker of goodness; and in our collectivism, as elsewhere, we appear to be harking 'back to Aristotle.'"

Christianity introduced another concept into Western thought which has had an effect upon our thinking about government, the concept of the Fall. Christian thought distinguishes between the created world as it came from the hand of God, and the fallen world known to history; between the world of primal innocence we posit, and the world marred by evil, which we know. It follows from this original premise that Christian thought is non-behaviorist; it is based on the idea that the true inwardness of a thing—its real nature—cannot be fully known by merely observing its outward behavior. Things are distorted in the historical and natural order, unable to manifest their true being. Man especially is askew. He is created in the image of God, but now he is flawed by Sin.

Some political implications may be drawn from these premises: It has been a characteristic note in Christian sociology, from the earliest centuries, to regard government not as an original element of the created world but as a reflection of man's corrupted nature in our fallen world. Government, in other words, is a consequence of sin; it appears only after the fall. Government is an effect of which human error and evil are the causes. Government, at best, is competent to punish injustice, but it cannot promote virtue. In other words, the Christian rationale for government is incompatible with the total state required by collectivism. When the Christian rationale for government is understood and spelled out, the only political role compatible with it is the modest function of defending the peace of society by curbing peace breakers. When government is limited to repressing criminal and destructive actions, men are free to act constructively and creatively up to the full limit of their individual capacities.

We arrive at a similar conclusion by contemplating the second half of the Great Commandment, where we are enjoined to love our neighbor as ourselves. The bonds that should unite people, it is here implied, are those of unyielding good will, understanding, and compassion. But in collectivist theory, on the other hand, people are to be put through their paces by command and coercion. This is the nature of the means which must be, and are being, employed in even the most well-intentioned welfare state. In practice, every collectivized order careens toward a police state whose own citizens are its first victims. The love commandment of the Gospels, brought down to the political level, implies justice and parity and freedom. There is no way to twist these basic premises into a sanctioning of the operational imperatives of a collectivist society.

The argument from liberty to Christianity has now been sketched in outline. Those who would limit the defense of liberty to a discussion of free market economics, with an assist from political theory, have a genuine role to perform, as far as they go. And if they cannot bring themselves to accept the truth of ethics and religion, integrity demands that they refuse to pretend otherwise. Their economic arguments are much needed, and thus they are invaluable allies in this sector. But liberty has not been lost on this level alone, and it cannot be won back on this level alone.

We are confronted, not only by highly developed and sophisticated arguments for socialism and Communism, but by fully collectivized nations.

Before there was ever a collectivist nation, there was a collectivist program. Before there was ever a collectivist program, there was a collectivist philosophy. Before there was ever a collectivist philosophy, there were collectivist axioms and premises, with appropriate attitudes toward life, and an appropriate mood.

The roots of collectivism go this deep, right down to our basic attitude toward the universe and our primordial demands on life. This is the level of a man's fundamental orientation of his life, the level at which religion begins to do its work. We must get squared away here, otherwise our thinking on the other levels will be distorted. But with a proper religious orientation—at this fundamental level of basic attitudes and mood—we can work out a philosophy of freedom.

When we have worked out the philosophy of freedom, we can advance a program based upon it.

And when we have a freedom philosophy and program we will eventually get a free society. This sounds like a laborious route to take, and it is. But life doesn't serve up many short cuts.

Equal: But Not the Same

The real American revolution of two hundred years ago took place in the minds of people; it was a philosophical revolution which evolved a new temper and state of mind. There were some daring assumptions about the nature of the human person, with his Creator-endowed rights, as set forth in the catalog of self-evident truths contained in the Declaration of Independence. The acceptance of these novel truths about the human person led logically to a new conception of government, a theory of right political action radically different from all previous theories of the purposes of government in human affairs.

Government, according to the Declaration, is instituted for one purpose only—to secure every person in his God-given rights. Period. No longer was the State to exercise the positive function of ordering, regulating, controlling, directing, or dominating the citizens. The new idea was to limit government to a negative role in society; government's task is to protect life, liberty, and property by using lawful force against aggressive and criminal actions. Government would discipline the anti-social, but otherwise let people alone. The law was to apply equally to all; justice was to be impartial and even-handed.

Along with the words Life, Liberty, and Property, the word Equality has a prominent place in the political vocabulary of American thought.

Our Declaration of Independence reads: "We hold these truths to be self-evident, that all men are created equal." Note well that the men who prepared this document did not say that all men *are* equal; they did not say that all men are born equal or *should be* equal, or are *becoming* equal. These several propositions are obviously untrue. The Declaration said: "*created* equal." Now, the created part of a man is his soul or mind or psyche. Man's body is compounded of the same chemical and physical elements which go into the makeup of the earth's crust, but there is a mental and spiritual essence in man which sets him apart from the natural order. Man alone among the creatures of earth is created in God's image—meaning that man has free will, the capacity to order his own actions, and so become the kind of person God intends him to be.

From the April 1988 issue of *The Freeman*.

128

The political theory enunciated in the Declaration is based upon certain assumptions about human nature and destiny which were ingredients of the religion professed by our forebears. It was an article of faith in the religious tradition of Christendom—a culture compounded of Hebraic, Greek, and Roman elements—that man is a created being. To say that man is a created being is to affirm that man is a work of divine art and not a mere accidental by-product of physical and chemical forces. Man is God's property, said John Locke, because He made us and the product belongs to the producer. As an owner, God cares for that which belongs to Him. Therefore the soul of each person is precious in God's sight, whatever the person's outward circumstances. "God is no respecter of persons." (Acts 10:34) He " . . . makes His sun to rise on good and bad alike, and sends the rain on the honest and dishonest." (Matthew 5:45) Equality before the law is the practical application of this understanding of the nature of the human person. Equal justice means that a nation's laws apply, across the board, to all sorts and conditions of men, regardless of race, creed, color, position, pedigree, income, whatever. In the eyes of the law, all are alike.

But right there the likeness ends; human beings are different and unequal in every other way; they are male and female, in the first place—and they are tall and short, thick and thin, weak and strong, rich as well as poor, and so on. They are equal in one respect only; they are on the same footing before the law. Equality before the law is the same thing as political liberty viewed from a different perspective; it is also justice—a regime under which no man and no order of men is granted a political license issued by the State to use other men as their tools or have any other legal advantage over them. Given such a framework in a society, the economic order will automatically be free market, or capitalistic. (We are speaking now of the idea of equality in a political context. Later I shall deal with the opposing concept of economic equality, which is incompatible with limited government and the free market.)

Political Equality

Political equality is the system of liberty, and its leading features are set forth in Jefferson's First Inaugural Address: "Equal and exact justice to all men, of whatever state or persuasion, religious or political;

peace, commerce, and honest friendship with all nations,—entangling alliances with none ... freedom of religion, freedom of the press; freedom of person under the protection of the habeas corpus" and so on.

The idea of political equality—equal justice before the law—is a relatively new one. It did not exist in the ancient world. Aristotle opened his famous work entitled *Politics* with an attempted justification of slavery, concluding his argument with these words: "It is clear, then, that some men are by nature free, and others slaves, and that for these latter slavery is both expedient and right."

Plato conceived the vision of a society constructed like a pyramid. A few men are at the top wielding unlimited power; then descending levels of power—the men on each level being bossed by those above and bossing, in turn, those below. On the bottom are the slaves, who outnumber all the rest of society. Plato knew that those in the lower ranks would be discontented with their subservient position, so he proposed a myth to condition them with—in his words—a "noble lie," or an "opportune falsehood." "While all of you in the city are brothers, we will say in our tale, yet God in fashioning those of you who are fitted to hold rule mingled gold in their generation ... but in the helpers silver, and iron and brass in the farmers and other craftsmen." You know darn well that fraudulent theories of this sort are invented by men who suspect gold in their own makeup!

Hinduism, with its system of castes, provides a contemporary example of a system of privilege. Men are born into a given caste, and that's where they stay; that's where their ancestors were, and that's where their descendants will be. There is no ladder leading from one level in this society to any of the others. Hinduism justifies these divisions between men by the doctrine of reincarnation, arguing that some are suffering now for misdemeanors committed during a previous existence, while others are being rewarded now for earlier virtue. This outlook breeds fatalism and social stagnation. The eminent Hindu philosopher and statesman S. Radhakrishnan defends the caste system with a metaphor. He likens society to a lamp and says, "When the wick is aglow at the tip the whole lamp is said to be burning."

Politics—it must be emphasized—rests upon certain assumptions in basic philosophy. We of the West make different philosophical assumptions than do Greek and Hindu philosophers, for we have a different religious heritage than they. The fountain source of the religious heritage of Christendom is, of course, the Bible. The Bible was the textbook of liberty for our forebears, who loved to quote such texts as "Where the spirit of the Lord is, there is liberty," (2 Cor. 3:17) and, "You shall know the truth, and the truth shall make you free." (John 8:32) And they turned often to the Old Testament prophets with their emphasis on justice and individual worth.

Let me quote a few lines from an unsigned editorial appearing in the magazine *Fortune* some years ago:

> The United States is not Christian in any formal sense, its churches are not full on Sundays and its citizens transgress the precepts freely. But it is Christian in the sense of absorption. The basic teachings of Christianity are in its bloodstream. The central doctrine of our political system—the inviolability of the individual—is the doctrine inherited from 1900 years of Christian insistence upon the immorality of the soul.

It takes a while, centuries sometimes, for a new idea about man to seep into the habits, laws, and institutions of a people and shape their culture. It was not until the eighteenth century that Adam Smith came along and spelled out a system of economics premised on the freely choosing man. Smith referred to his system as "the liberal plan of equality, liberty and justice." The European society of Smith's day was, by contrast, a system of privilege; it was an aristocratic order.

The Rise of Aristocracy

England's aristocratic order did not rise by accident; it was imposed by a conqueror. England's social structure may be traced back to the battle of Hastings in 1066 and the Norman invasion of England. William of Normandy had a claim, of sorts, to the British throne, a claim which he validated by conquering the island. Having established his overlordship of England he parceled out pieces of the island to his followers as payment for their services. In the words of historian Arthur Bryant, "William the Conqueror kept a fifth of the land for himself and gave one-quarter to the Church. The remainder, save for an insignificant fraction, was given to 170 Norman and French followers—nearly half to ten men."[1] In other words, 55 percent of the territory of England was divided among 170 men, ten of whom got the lion's share, or 27 percent among them, while 160 men got the rest. This redistribution of England's territory was, of course, at the expense of the Anglo-Saxon residents who were displaced to make room for the new owners. The new owners of England from William on down were the rulers of England; ownership was the complement of their rulership, and the wealth they accumulated sprang from their power and their feudal privileges and dues.

Norman overlordship was a system of privilege. That is to say, the Norman rulers did not obtain their wealth by satisfying consumer demand. Under the system of liberty, by contrast, where the economic arrangements are free market or capitalistic, the only way to make money is to please the customers. Under the various systems of privilege you make money by pleasing the politicians, those who hold power. Either that, or you wield power yourself.

This was a fine system—from the Norman viewpoint; but the Anglo-Saxon reduced to serfdom viewed the matter quite differently. It was obvious to the serf and the peasant that the reason why they had so little land was because the Normans had so much and, because wealth flowed from holdings of land, the Anglo-Saxons reasoned correctly that they were poor because the Normans were rich! It is always so under a system of privilege, where those who wield the political power use that power to enrich themselves economically, at the expense of other people. It makes little difference whether the outward trappings of privilege are monarchical, or democratic, or bear the earmarks of 1984; in a system of privilege, *political power is a means of obtaining economic advantage*.

When our forebears wrote that "all men are created equal," they threw down a challenge to all systems of privilege. They believed that the law should keep the peace—as peacekeeping is spelled out in the old-fashioned Whig-Classical Liberal tradition, as liberty and justice for all. This preserves a free field and no favor—which is the real meaning of laissez faire —within which peaceful economic competition will occur. The term laissez faire never meant the absence of rules; it doesn't imply a free-for-all. Government, under laissez faire, does not intervene positively to manage the affairs of men; it merely acts to deter and redress injury—as injury is spelled out in the laws. This is the system of liberty championed by present-day exponents of the freedom philosophy—whether they call themselves Libertarians, or Conservatives, or Whigs, or whatever.

The Wealth of Nations

Adam Smith's "liberal plan of equality, liberty and justice" was never practiced fully in any nation, but what was the result of a partial application of the ideas of *The Wealth of Nations*? The results of abolishing political privilege in Europe and starting to organize a no privilege society with political liberty and a market economy were so beneficial that even the enemies of liberty pause to pay tribute.

R. H. Tawney, one of the most gifted of the English Fabians, was an ardent socialist and egalitarian. His most famous work is *Religion and the Rise of Capitalism,* but in 1931 he wrote a book entitled *Equality,* arguing, in effect, that no one should have two cars as long as any man was unable to afford even one. He wished to take from those who have and give to those who have not, in order to achieve economic equality. But he acknowledged that there was an earlier idea of equality—equal treatment under the law. Here is what Tawney writes about the beneficial results of the movement toward political liberty and the free economy in the early decades of the nineteenth century, the movement known as Classical Liberalism:

> Few principles have so splendid a record of humanitarian achievement .... Slavery and serfdom had survived the exhortations of the Christian Church, the reforms of enlightened despots, and the protests of humanitarian philosophers from Seneca to Voltaire. Before the new spirit, and the practical exigencies of which it was the expression, they disappeared, except from dark backwaters, in three generations.... It turned [the peasant] from a beast of burden into a human being. It determined that, when science should be invoked to increase the output of the soil, its cultivator, not an absentee owner, should reap the fruits. The principle which released him he described as equality, the destruction of privilege.[2]

Smith's "liberal plan of equality, liberty, and justice" means the practice of political liberty. Now, when people are free politically and legally equal, there will still be economic inequalities. There will continue to be rich and poor, as there have been wealth differentials in every society since history began. But now there's this difference: in the free economy the wealthy will be chosen by the daily balloting of their peers in the marketplace, and the wealthy won't necessarily be the powerful, nor will the poor necessarily be the weak.

Variation is a fact of life; individuals differ one from another. Some are tall and some are short; some are swift and some are slow; some are bright and others are not so bright. The talents of some lie along musical lines, others are athletes, a few are mathematical wizards. Some people in every age are highly endowed with a knack for making money; whatever the circumstances, these people have more worldly goods than others.

Rich and poor are relative terms, but every society reveals a population distribution ranging from opulence to indigence. This occurs under monarchies, and it occurs in primitive tribes which measure a man's wealth by cattle and wives; it occurs in Communist states where, as Milovan Djilas pointed out in a famous book, a "new class" emerges out of the classless society, and the "new class" enjoys privileges denied the masses.

Under the system of liberty, the free market will reward men in differing degrees so that some men will make a great deal of money while others, such as teachers and preachers, have to get by on a very modest income. But under the system of liberty even those in lower income brackets enjoy a relatively high standard of living, and, furthermore, the practice of the Rule of Law guarantees that there'll be no persecution for deviant intellectual and religious beliefs. The government does not try to manage the economy or control the lives of the citizens; it keeps out of people's way—unless rights are violated.

Under conditions of political equality—which is the system of liberty, with the Rule of Law and the market economy—a man's income depends upon his success at pleasing consumers, at which game some people are much more successful than others. A certain American entertainer earned millions of dollars last year by gyrating and howling in public places. He didn't get any of my money, and except for the fact that I believe in liberty, I might have paid a substantial sum to keep him permanently tranquilized! On a somewhat higher level, there are talented people who are sensitive to consumer demand, and so they produce the kinds of goods or render the kinds of services that people will be able and willing to buy. They'll make a bundle, in virtue of their ability to attract customers in free market competition.

Our own country's past affords the best example of the enormous multiplication of wealth—broadly shared—which results from the release of human creativity under a system of liberty. But reintroduce a system of privilege, and dreams of prosperity fade.

Helping the Poor

The big domestic issue is poverty. Ever since New Deal days in the 1930s, governments have legislated various welfare schemes designed ostensibly to help "the poor," spending trillions of dollars in these efforts. And the big issue is still poverty! It's only the relative prosperity of the private sector, working against politically imposed obstructions, which has provided the funds to fuel the futile political programs touted as the remedy for economic distress. These are false remedies. The truth of the matter is that only economic action can produce the goods and services whose lack is indigence and destitution. Misguided political programs actually manufacture poverty by hampering productivity. Should we trust further government interventions to correct the very conditions government has caused by its earlier interventions?

Poverty may be measured in various ways, but whatever else it is, poverty means a lack of the things which sustain life at the basic level, or not enough of the things which make life pleasant and enjoyable. A genuinely poor person in the United States lives in a shabby room, dresses in hand-me-down clothing, and eats meals running heavily to starchy food, with little meat and fruit. A person who is this poor would be better off if he enjoyed a larger and finer house, had several extra suits, and ate tastier and more nourishing food. After improving the situation at the level of necessities he'd move ahead to the amenities: to recreation, a second car, air-conditioning, and so on. The point to note is that people move away from poverty and toward prosperity only as they command more economic goods, more of the things which are manufactured, grown, transported, or otherwise produced.

Poverty is overcome by production, and in no other way. Therefore, if we are seriously concerned with the alleviation of poverty, our concern for increased production must be equally serious. This is simple logic. But look around us in this great land today and try to find anyone for whom increased productivity is a major goal. There are some able production men in industry, but many established businesses have learned to live comfortably with restrictive legislation, government contracts, the foreign aid program, and our international commitments. The competitive instinct burns low, and the entrepreneur who is willing to submit to the uncertainties of the market is a rare bird. And then there are the farmers. Agricultural production has taken a great leap forward in recent years, but no thanks to those farmers who latch onto the government's farm program and accept payment for keeping land and equipment idle. Union leaders claim to work for the betterment of the membership, but no one has ever accused unions of a burning desire to be more productive on the job. Politicians are not interested in increased industrial or agricultural production, which is why government welfare programs manufacture poverty, and the economic well-being of the nation as a whole sinks below the level of prosperity a free market economy would achieve.

Confirmation of this point comes from a *New York Times Magazine* article by the celebrated economist Thomas Sowell: "To be blunt, the poor are a gold mine. By the time they are studied, advised, experimented with and administered, the poor have helped many a middle class liberal to achieve affluence with government money. The total amount of money the government spends on its anti-poverty efforts is three times what would be required to lift every man, woman, and child in America above the poverty line by simply sending money to the poor."

An overall increase in the output of goods and services is the only way to upgrade the general welfare, but there is no clamor on behalf of increased productivity. The clamor is for redistribution, for political interventions which exact tribute from the haves and bestow largesse on the have-nots. Present-day politics is based on the redistributionist principle: taxes for all, subsidies for the few.

I'm arguing on behalf of a philosophy of government which understands the primary function of the Law as the defense of the life, liberty, and property of all persons alike. Such a political establishment leads to the kind of society in which bread and butter issues are handled by the market. So now, a few words about the nature of the market.

The market is not a magic instrumentality which comes up automatically with the right answer for every sort of question. The market is a sort of popularity contest; the market tells us what people like well enough to buy; it's an index of their preferences. Thus, the market provides a very valuable piece of information, but it's far from the whole story. It's important for a manufacturer to project an accurate guess as to where the hemline will be next season, or what people will look for when the new car models are unveiled. But a similar fingering of the popular pulse is an abomination in the intellectual and moral realms—unless one is a liberal intellectual! I refer to the proclivity of the current crop of liberal opinion molders to ask: "What's going to be the fashion in ideas next season?" One glaring example of this—a former professor of mine was a leading clerical spokesman for involving the United States in World War II; but when the climate of opinion changed he became a co-chairman of SANE. This man has a good market in the intellectual realm, but of course he opposes the market in the economic realm!

The market is not some entity; the market is only a word describing people freely exchanging goods and services in the absence of force and fraud. The market is the only device available for serving our creaturely needs while conserving scarce resources. But the market is no gauge of the validity of ideas. The market measures the popularity of an idea or a book or a system of thought, but not its truth or worth. Mises and Hayek are, for my money, far better thinkers and economists than Samuelson and Galbraith; but the market for the services of the latter pair is enormously greater than the popular demand for Mises and Hayek. Likewise in aesthetic questions. An entertainer's popularity is no index of his musicianship, and a best-selling novel may fall far short of the category of literature.

The Market as Mirror

The market is simply a mirror of popular preferences and public taste; but if we don't like what the mirror reveals we won't improve the situation by throwing rocks at the glass! There is a great deal more to life than pleasing the customer, but if the integrity of the market is not respected, consumer choice is impaired and some people are given a license to foist their values on others. Permit this kind of poison to infect economic relationships and our ability to resist it elsewhere is seriously weakened.

We are throwing rocks at the mirror whenever we undertake programs of social leveling, aimed at economic equality. The government promises to aid the poor by redistributing the wealth. This, of course, is a power play, and it is the poor—generally the weakest members of a society—who are hurt first and most in any power struggle. Furthermore—and this is an important point—economic inequalities cannot be overcome by coercive redistribution without increasing political inequalities. Every form of political redistribution widens power differentials in society; officeholders have more power, citizens have less; political contests become more intense, because the control and dispersal of great amounts of wealth are at stake.

Every alternative to the market economy—call it socialism or communism or fascism or whatever—concentrates power over the life and livelihood of the many into the hands of the few who constitute the State. The principle of equality before the law is discarded—the Rule of Law is incompatible with any form of the planned economy—and, as in the George Orwell satire, some people become more equal than others. We head back toward the Old Regime—the system of privilege.

Those who have assumed or seized power to take from the "haves" and give to the "have-nots" will eventually realize that they are operating a dumb racket. The "have-nots" who may be on the receiving end at the beginning are generally not society's best and brightest, not the kind of people the power brokers like to hobnob with. The politically powerful who operate the transfer system will—when the light dawns—continue to plunder the "haves" but will then divvy up their take between themselves and the beautiful people who possess enough sensibility to realize the rightness of running a society for the benefit of such as they! The poor are squeezed out; they are worse off than before. And the nation is saddled with the "democratic despotism" predicted by Alexis de Tocqueville as far back as 1835.

Those of you who are fans of Lewis Carroll will remember his poem, "The Hunting of the Snark." Hunters pursued this strange beast, but every time they thought they had their quarry the snark turned out to be a quite different beast—a boojum! Every time a determined group of people have concentrated power in a central government to carry out *their* program, the power they have set up gets out of hand. The classic example of this is the French Revolution, which turned and devoured those who had started it. It is not so much that power corrupts, as that power obeys its own laws. Our forebears in the old-fashioned Whig-Classical Liberal tradition were aware of this, so they sought to disperse and contain power. They chose liberty. They chose liberty in full awareness that in a free society the natural differences among human beings would show up in various ways; some would be economically better off than others. But in a free society there would be no political inequality; everyone would be equal before the law.

The alternative to the free economy is a servile state, where a ruling class enforces an equality of poverty on the masses, and lives at the expense of the producers. To embark on a program of economic leveling, then, is like trying to repeal the law of gravity; it'll never work, and the energy we waste trying to make it work defeats our efforts to attain the reasonable goals which are within our capacity to achieve.

---

1. *Story of England,* Arthur Bryant, Vol. I, p. 154.
2. *Equality,* R. H. Tawney, pp. 120–121.

Six Ideas to Keep Us Human

Most people live lives of quiet desperation, Henry David Thoreau told us. If there was truth in that observation, in the pleasant, spacious old New England of Thoreau's day, how much more truth is packed into those words in these melancholy days! Events have gotten out of hand and the world lurches into chaos.

Things have fallen apart faster than any of us would have dared predict, and we are seized by pangs of guilt and self-doubt. So many promising experiments have gone sour, from the New Freedom of Woodrow Wilson to the latest ukase of the present administration. The statesmen of this era talked peace and sought to outlaw war, but they let the twentieth century break down into the bloodiest period of all the twenty-five hundred years of warfare studied by Pitirim Sorokin. "We live," wrote this great scholar, "in an age unique for the unrestrained use of brute force in international relations."

The threat of protracted international conflict is bad enough, but there is also the well-founded fear of domestic violence and crime. And even if we are lucky enough to escape actual robbery, we know that inflation is steadily draining our wealth. We've seen the race issue go from integration to Black Nationalism; we've witnessed the emergence of the sex and drug cult, the rise of astrology, witchcraft, and voodooism; V.D. has reached epidemic proportions among the young; and then there is abortion, homosexuality, the campus crisis, the environmental crisis, the inner crisis in man himself. For is it not true, as Yeats says in a famous poem, that "The best lack all conviction, while the worst/Are full of passionate intensity"?

Youth Seeking Identity

It is a time of troubles for all, but perhaps it's easier for the old whose habit patterns firmed up in a healthier era than for the young who are searching for a value system and cannot find one. Depression, in the vocabulary of many young people, does not mean the economic malaise which this country staggered through during the nineteen thir-

Adapted from the November 1972 and December 1972 issues of *The Freeman*.

ties; it means the somber mood in which they hang question marks around life, wondering if it really is worth living. They are trying to find meaning for their lives in terms of the values their elders lived by—or on any other terms—and they are not having much luck. We sometimes find their behavior rather bizarre; the long hair, the weird clothing, the haphazard life styles. But perhaps these symbolize a message they are trying to get across to us. Some of the so-called hippies, by deliberately being ill-housed, ill-clothed, and ill-fed, may be practicing a charade whose message is that the More Abundant Life, as defined in New Deal terms, is not a proper goal for man. Perhaps they have a suspicion that reality is wider and deeper than the physical universe revealed to common sense—as religion has always maintained—and so they experiment with mind-expanding drugs. They grope after some form of religious expression, but still they drift.

Now, we know something about the rise and fall of civilizations. In our schoolbooks we read about "The glory that was Greece, and the grandeur that was Rome." Toynbee, Spengler, and Dawson have made us aware of dead civilizations on other continents. A civilization comes into existence cradled in dominant ideas, launched by deeds of heroism and self-sacrifice, and it maintains itself in a tonic condition only so long as it has solid grounds for believing in itself and its destiny. But civilizations wane; Rome fell; Spengler predicted the decline of the West. We need not buy a single one of Spengler's theories, but it is hard to argue against his phrase—the West is in decline. Great numbers of people in this favored land no longer believe in the things that made Western civilization unique.

An animal species which has flourished in a given area may be wiped out by a disease, or it may be decimated by a predator, or a climatic change may destroy its food supply. Every one of these afflictions has beset primitive peoples in times past, but a civilization does not founder for any of these reasons. A civilization goes under when its people, for one reason or another, lose contact with the big keynote ideas of their culture.

Ideas Make Us Human

Wherein lies the great difference between the human species and every other? We have much in common with other forms of life, especially with the warm-blooded vertebrates. In structure we bear some resemblance to the manlike apes, but the critical difference in the domain of ideas far outweighs any resemblances. If a chimpanzee has any thoughts at all about what it means to be an ape, they are rudimentary; he's a pretty good animal without even thinking about it. But no man is fully human unless he maintains a lively contact with a set of ideas as to what it means to be a person.

This is where our disease has set in, in the realm of ideas. The perilous days we are living through are not the result of a drying up of the food supply, which is more abundant than ever. There's been no marked change in the physique of modern man, and disease is not a menace. Nor are we beset by predators. The malaise from which we suffer has impaired the ideas which instruct us what it means to be men and women, and we function poorly in consequence. People of our race built the Parthenon, constructed the great systems of philosophy, painted the ceiling of the Sistine Chapel, wrote the plays of Shakespeare, and the music of Bach; and we can't figure out how to teach our kids tolerance and mutual respect without busing them all over town! Something is definitely wrong with us, and it won't be right with us until we come to terms with six big ideas. I'll mention them briefly now and deal with them at greater length later on. They are the right convictions about free will, reason, self-responsibility, beauty, goodness, and the sacred. We have "blown it" at every one of these points, and that's more than enough to account for the sorry spectacle modern man has made of himself. It also points the way to recovery. Let's, first of all, hear a portion of the indictment leveled at us by contemporaries.

Downgrading Man

The human race is getting a bad press these days, and we love it. Norman Cousins told us a while back that "Modern Man is Obsolete," and we conferred a couple of distinguished editorships on him in a frenzy of approval. Robert Ardrey writes a book to demolish what he calls The Romantic Fallacy and argues that our forebears were killer apes, whose blood lust still surges in our veins. And so great is the demand for preachments of this sort that the book has gone through 17 printings! The creature we used to refer to as the glory of creation is, when you scratch the surface little more than a *Naked Ape,* Desmond

Morris tells us. This. book has gone through six printings and there are two paperback editions. Knowing a good thing when he sees it, Morris writes a second book, *The Human Zoo*. The Nobel Laureate in biology, Albert Szent-Gyorgyi, goes Morris one better with a book entitled *The Crazy Ape*. And it is common knowledge that this odious race fouls its own nest, pollutes the environment of its neighbors, wars ceaselessly on its own kind, destroys wildlife, watches Lawrence Welk, and votes Republican. The creature once regarded as little lower than the angels is now ranked several degrees below the beasts!

The books whose titles I have listed above purport to be in the realm of science. In the realm of the admittedly fictitious there is a new school of novelists who aim, in their stories, to reveal man as the pitiable slob he really is. A critic comments that "From Cervantes to Hemingway, storytellers have assumed that man has hopes and aspirations, and that they could be expressed meaningfully. Bosh, says the new school. Man is a blob, creeping and leaping about in a world he cannot control, his words meaningless or hypocritical or both."[1]

Immortality of the Soul

How different the outlook of a great writer like William Faulkner, in these words from his speech accepting the Nobel Prize in 1950: "I believe that man will not merely endure; he will prevail. He is immortal, not because he alone among creatures has an inexhaustible voice, but because he has a soul, a spirit capable of compassion and sacrifice and endurance."

Brave words such as these are in danger today of being drowned out by the sheer bulk of the other message, which, through the numerous outlets it has contrived, produces the enervating atmosphere of misanthropy in which we struggle for survival. Take the movies. We are given films which degrade our species by focusing on the sordid, the silly, the ugly, the cowardly, the disgusting; as if all elements of the dramatic were lacking in characters who exhibit nobility, heroism, kindness, or even common decency. Another tack is taken in such a film as "The Hellstrom Chronicle." The mere ability to film those astonishing pictures of the insect world represents the culmination of the work of many geniuses, but this heartening thought is squelched by the narrator who tells us toward the end of the film that they really

144 / Edmund A. Opitz

do organize things better in the insect world, and human beings should learn from wasps and ants to submerge their individual talents for the greater glory of the hive and termitary!

The examples I have cited from works of popular science and the realm of entertainment might be multiplied many times, and they represent no more than the fraction of the iceberg that pokes itself above the surface of the water. The huge mass below the water line represents the mood, outlook, trend, or drift that sways the multitude.

In many previous ages lonely thinkers and poets sounded the note of pessimism, voiced their despair, and vented their hatred of life. But they were read and heard by only a handful of their contemporaries; they did not reach the multitudes. The masses of men in previous ages were comfortably insulated against ideas of any sort; most of them couldn't read and the range of the human voice limited the size of the audience. The traditional religious belief gave men's lives meaning and even dignity, and most human energy was used up in producing enough to live on.

Catering to the Masses

Things are different now. Antihuman sentiments, dislike of humanity, hatred of life, are epidemic among present-day intellectuals, and the idea that life may not be worth living has percolated down to the masses of people. This is a new situation in history. The masses of men are relatively inarticulate but only a mass audience can make a book a best seller, or award a golden record to some singer, or enable a film to gross ten million dollars. The people, books, songs, ideas which ride the crest of fashion today are held there by popular support; whereas, formerly, the artist and composer wrote for wealthy patrons. Joseph Haydn composed magnificent music for the Esterhazys; but Leonard Bernstein writes his *Mass* for the masses. We are dealing with a perverse attitude toward life which has infected major sectors of Western culture at every level. In the year 1929, Joseph Wood Krutch wrote a stunning little book entitled *The Modern Temper,* using the word "temper" in the sense of frame of mind, or outlook. His major point was that educated people had come to assume that science had exposed as delusions the values and standards upon which Western Civilization had been founded, and that the decline of the West was due to Western man's loss of faith in himself. The prevalent belief, he argued, is that men are animals and animals are machines.

What men believe about themselves is an important factor in the success or failure of their efforts. A golfer who firmly believes he can sink a putt is more likely to do so than one who believes he'll miss the cup. A swimmer like Don Schollander tells how he gets himself "psyched up" before a race and tries to make his opponents feel like losers in a war of nerves. It is a notorious fact in baseball that certain pitchers have the "Indian sign" on a particular batter; he's a dangerous hitter except against this one pitcher. The right beliefs, in short, inspire right action.

I don't know what an elephant believes about himself; I suspect that he doesn't believe anything about himself, one way or the other. I think it would not matter; he'd go on being the same old elephant he always was. Sometimes we say of a pet Saint Bernard who tries to crawl up into our lap that "Bodo thinks he's a kitten." But we know we're joking; and even if this was said seriously, we know that Bodo remains a dog no matter what he thinks he is.

With the human species it is different: Human beings do not attain their full stature as persons unless they are reinforced by the proper ideas and beliefs about the meaning of being a person. We share our physical being with other mammals; biologically speaking, we are anthropoids. By virtue of our genetic equipment we are clever, adaptable hominids; but no one of us realizes his full potential as a man or woman unless he knows what it means to be human. If we so misread human nature as to regard our species as nothing more than the fortuitous product of natural and social forces, then we have impaired our chances of achieving the most uniquely human qualities within our capacity.

Environmentalism

If it is generally believed that man is merely the product of his environment—the individual a passive outcome of the time and place into which he was born, the human race a consequence of accidental chemical and physical events of a few million years ago—when such beliefs pervade a culture, the result is pessimism and resignation. The sense of individual responsibility is dead in a man who regards himself as a passive creature of his circumstances. The only people who prove superior to their circumstances, who surmount environmental handicaps, are those whose beliefs about the human species endow men and women with the creative energy to overcome life's difficulties.

It may sound as though I am endorsing a "think and grow rich" formula, or the like. Actually, I am talking about the big picture; the dominant world view entertained by a culture, the prevailing ideology, the real religion. The dominant world view today is some form of materialism; explicit where Marxianism has taken hold, implicit elsewhere. Let me document this assertion from a statement entitled "What I Believe" by C. P. Snow; novelist, scientist, member of the peerage, writing in the current issue of the *Britannica Roundtable* (Vol. 1, No. 3). A publication such as this is no vehicle for publishing radical departures from orthodoxy; Baron Snow's statement is printed because his point of view is commonplace among people who regard themselves as being in step with up-to-date ideas. Snow writes as follows: "I believe life—human life, all life—is a ... fluke which depended on all manner of improbable conditions happening at the same time." But if all life is a chance occurrence, so is Baron Snow's life. And if Snow's life is a fluke how can his thinking be anything but a series of flukes? His thoughts then are random events, without rational foundation. "All that happened," he continues, "is within the domain of the laws of physics and chemistry. ... it was a completely material process. ... A few million years ago, subject to the laws of statistical chance, the creatures that were our direct ancestors came into existence. ... Speech and what we call conscious intelligence accrued. ... We are still an animal species, but much cleverer than all others." Snow goes on to add, rather wistfully it seems, "It has been a very unlikely process, with many kinds of improbability along the way."

Nature's Passion for Order

Now, old Mother Nature has a passion for order. She has an aversion to disorder, and the Laws of Probability simply record Mother Nature's gyroscopic tug to keep things on course. The Laws of Probability record that the number of male and female children born is roughly equal. Flip a penny fifty times and it will come up heads on the average of about every other throw—twenty-five times out of fifty.

Make a thousand random throws of a pair of dice and the Laws of Probability can tell you approximately how many times they'll come up snake eyes, and how many times you'll get box cars. Numbers between two and twelve are within the system, and each of the eleven possible numbers will appear a certain number of times according to the laws of statistical chance.

But let's pose this question: In a thousand random throws of the dice how many times will we get seventeen? How many times will the dice turn into a rabbit? The answer is that this would never happen; spooky questions like this imply belief in magic. Now suppose we ask the same question, but say that the dice have been thrown once a second for a billion years. Now how many seventeens and how many rabbits? The answer of any sensible person is "None!" to both questions. The number seventeen and rabbits are outside the system of the little spotted cubes called dice.

When a man like C. P. Snow declares that nonlife becomes life due to the operation of the Laws of Probability over immense time, he attributes magical properties to mere duration. He assumes that dice do turn into rabbits if the time span be measured in billions of years. And when he invokes another huge block of time to account for the transformation of the nonmental into the mental and the nonrational into the rational he is endowing the mere sequence of days, centuries, and millennia with miracle-working efficacy.

Monkeys vs. Shakespeare

We've all heard the assertion—intended to illustrate what mere chance and time can accomplish—that if a thousand monkeys were seated at a thousand typewriters and banged away for a thousand years they would reproduce every one of Shakespeare's sonnets. The premise upon which this wild illustration is based is that a Shakespearian sonnet is nothing but a mechanical arrangement of black letters on white paper. There are indeed letters on paper, but there is one other special ingredient in these sonnets: Shakespeare's genius. There is no place for genius in the world view of the materialist who professes to believe the mind is an offshoot of matter. A poet simply marks the location where a poem occurs, according to B. F. Skinner: "The poet is also a locus, a place in which certain genetic and environmental causes come together to have a common effect."[2] And besides, the genius is a salient individual who stands out above the crowd when really he should be content to seek "social gains!"

What men believe about themselves has a great deal to do with determining the success or failure of their efforts in the several departments of life, and when influential segments of the literate population embrace notions about the universe which demean man by depriving him of his most distinctive characteristics the culture is thrown off base.

Let me now probe a little deeper along this line. I shall argue that six major ideas, together with body, brain, and nervous system, transform what Snow calls "an animal species, but much cleverer than all the others" into a full-fledged member of the human species. A creature with anthropoid features who completely lacks these ideas is not of our species even though he walks, talks, and dresses like a man. Fortunately, in consequence of the animal health and grace in even the worst of men, it is almost impossible for any person to eliminate from his make-up all traces of these ideas; some influence remains to keep us reachable.

Now then, six big, potent, interrelated ideas, without which man is not man.

1. *Free Will.* Man's gift of free will makes him a responsible being.

2. *Rationality.* Man is a reasoning being who, by taking thought, gains valid truths about himself and the universe.

3. *Self-responsibility.* Each person is the custodian of his own energy and talents, charged with the lifetime task of bringing himself to completion.

4. *Beauty.* Man confronts beauty in the very nature of things, and reproduces this vision in art.

5. *Goodness.* Man has a moral sense, enabling and requiring him to choose between good and evil.

6. *The Sacred.* Man participates in an order which transcends nature and society.

Each of these big ideas is in trouble today. The attack on them has been gathering momentum for a couple of centuries and the case against has just about carried the day in influential circles.

It is no secret that a great many philosophers and scientists deny free will and affirm determinism; it is also a fact that no one can really bring himself around to believing that he is an automaton. A philosopher who announces himself as a determinist presumes to offer us a conclusion he has arrived at after observation, after marshaling the relevant evidence, after reflection, and as the end result of a chain of reasoning. Each of these steps reflects the action of a free being, and these free actions can never be pieced together so as to contrive an unfree result. Man's will is free; it is so free that it can deny this freedom!

Take the case of Baruch Spinoza. If any man ever lived free it was Spinoza; he was the "inner-directed" man par excellence. But Spinoza's own experience clashed with the new world view of Mechanism—the notion that the universe is constructed along the lines of an intricate piece of clockwork. Ideology overcame experience and Spinoza denied that his will was free. I quote from Proposition XLVIII of his *Ethics*:

> There is no mind absolute or free will, but the mind is determined for willing this or that by a cause which is determined in its turn by another cause, and this one again by another, and so on to infinity.
>
> The mind is a fixed and determined mode of thinking, and therefore cannot be the free cause of its actions, or it cannot have the absolute faculty of willing and unwilling; but for willing this or that it must be determined by a cause which is determined by another, and this again by another, etc. Q.E.D.[3]

Free Will

If the individual does not have free will, then he is not at liberty to reject determinism! But where will a man find a position from which he might judge whether his will is indeed free, or not. The answer is: Only as he looks within himself, at the workings of his inner life; by introspection, in other words. Now introspection is rather frowned upon today as a means of getting at the truth, as not being in accord with scientific technique. Early science viewed nature from the standpoint of the external observer, as a theater-goer views a play. The man occupying the seat in the first row of the balcony is observing the drama unfold upon the stage; he is detached from the action, is not involved in the play, his standpoint is objective. The world view that grew out of science is assumed to be the way the universe looks to an outsider who is not part of the action, merely looking in upon it.

Once this approach is adopted, what follows? Let me answer by quoting from Jacques Barzun's great book, *Science: The Glorious Entertainment:* "Pure science was engaged in sketching, bit by bit, the plan of a machine—a gigantic machine identical with the universe. According to the vision thus unfolded, every existing thing was matter, and every piece of matter was a working part of the cosmic technology."[4] Thus emerged the ideology bearing the label Mechanistic Materialism, and human beings schooled in this ideology come to think of themselves as mere cogs in the world machine. And just as every gear and cog in the machine is moved by another, so is every human action the mere effect of a previous cause, and so on. Observe a man's actions from the outside and you see only his body and limbs in motion; nothing that you can see from the outside gives you any assured knowledge of what is going on inside him. You cannot observe his will from the outside, nor his mind. You might guess what's going on, but that's the best you can do.

A Hidden Inner Life

There is one region of the universe which will always be beyond the ken of the external observer, and that is the region of the inner life. Each man's inner life is concealed from all the world; he alone has access to it. Millions of people can view the same eclipse of the sun, but only one person can know your inner life, and that is you. Truth about the will in action can be known by introspection only; it will never be disclosed to those who adopt the standpoint of the external observer and refuse to shift their perspective. If there is indeed freedom of the will, this is a truth which, in the nature of the case can be known only as each person knows it first hand in himself. Let a man look within himself and he knows with solid assurance that he is capable of exercising freedom of choice in situations where real alternatives are open to him. Which of us has not wrestled with dilemmas of the type: "I want to do this; but I ought to do that"? We know, in this context, that the will is free.

There's an old story about Galileo, who assured one of his contemporaries that the ring around Jupiter was composed of satellites; "I've seen them through my telescope; take a look and see for yourself." The friend had figured out that the ring was solid and refused to put his eye to the glass, the only posture from which he could test his theory. The free will, if it operates at all, operates only within, and those who are so wedded to the standpoint of the external observer that they refuse to look within, effectively bar themselves from ever obtaining any knowledge of the matter.

The consequence of this state of affairs is unfortunate. It is "unscientific," the average man is led to assume, to believe he has free will, and that decisive action on his part can make a real difference in life. He is taught that he is determined by heredity, or environment, or race, or childhood traumas, or poverty, or by some other factor that limits his capacity for free choice; and his ability to choose is impaired because he thinks he doesn't have it! The initiative is given over to environment and man only reacts; he doesn't act. Adjustments to the environment, comfort, and ease then come to be the goals of life. If we accept the dictum of a great economist that "the end, goal or aim of any action is always the relief of a felt uneasiness," then we have given up on life, for we'll never rest easy until we're dead! To live is to strive for greater intensity of life, and this means that we may choose adventure, heroism, suffering, and maybe even death.

The issue of free will constitutes a battleline of first importance. A people among whom the flame of life has burned so low that their philosophers preach determinism will be severely handicapped in the game of life. They will find it difficult to put their trust in reason and, as we might expect, reason itself is now under attack from several quarters.

Rationality

The second of the big ideas which make man man is this: Man is a reasoning being who, by taking thought, gains valid truths about himself and the universe. The attack on the rational mind comes from several quarters. Philosophical materialism and mechanism assumes that the ultimate reality is nonmental; only bits of matter or electrical charges or whatever are, in the final analysis, real. If so, then thought is but a reflex of neural events. "Our mental conditions," wrote T. H. Huxley, "are simply the symbols in consciousness of the changes which take place automatically in the organism."

Evolutionism, popularly understood, is materialistic and mechanical. So viewed it conveys the idea that living things began as a stirring in the primeval ooze and became what they are now by random interaction with the physiochemical environment, moved by no purpose, aiming at no goal. Darwinism offers an account of organic change which has no need of intelligence to guide it.

From popular psychology comes the notion that reason is but rationalization, that conscious mental processes are but a gloss for primitive and irrational impulses erupting from the unconscious mind. Psychoanalysis discredits mind by subordinating intellect to the id.

From Marxianism comes the notion that class interest dictates a man's thinking. There is one logic for the proletariat and another for the bourgeoisie; and the mode of production governs the philosophical systems men erect, and their life goals as well. The unfortunately placed middle class forever gropes in darkness, unable to share the light revealed to Marx and his votaries.

Convictions about the reality of reason and free will develop in the context of our vision of the ultimate nature of things. And here I bring up again the ideology of Mechanistic Materialism. There are several kinds of Materialism, the most prominent today being Dialectic Materialism, the official religion of Marxianism. However, the several brands of Materialism differ only in nonessentials; they agree that all forms of consciousness arise, develop, and disappear with changes in the material world. Every variety of Materialism downgrades mind; it makes mind an offshoot of matter, a derivative of material particles, an epiphenomenon.

"Man is but the outcome of accidental collocations of atoms"

Let Bertrand Russell tell us in his own words: "Man is the product of causes which had no prevision of the end they were achieving; his origin, his growth, his hopes and fears, his loves and his beliefs, are but the outcome of accidental collocations of atoms. . . . Brief and powerless is Man's life; on him and all his race the slow, sure doom falls pitiless and dark. Blind to good and evil, reckless of destruction, omnipotent matter rolls on its relentless way."[5] Of course, if matter is the ultimate reality, mind is discredited. But if this discredited instrument is all we have to rely on, how can we put any confidence in its findings? If untrustworthy reason tells us that we cannot trust reason, then we have no logical ground for accepting the conclusion that reason is untrustworthy! Well, I don't trust the reasoning of people who champion the irrational, and I do know that our reasoning powers may be—like anything else—misused. But when human thought is guided by the rules of logic, undertaken in good faith, and tested by experience and tradition, it is an instrument capable of expanding the domain of truth. Reason is not infallible, but it is infinitely more to be trusted than nonreason!

Self-Responsibility

The third great truth is that each man is the custodian of his own energy and talents, charged with bringing himself to completion and having a lifetime to do the job. Gifted with reason and free will, the human being must take himself in hand in order to complete his development: most animals, on the other hand, simply mature, brought to full term by innate drives. Human beings are not thus programmed, and occasionally we have to act against inclination and instinct and inertia if we would achieve our goals. This is simply illustrated in sports, where the successful performer forces himself to train even on those days when he'd rather be doing something else. The bike club I ride with held a century run over a six-mile course. A couple of youngsters turned up in full regalia and rode off, one pacing the other, looking very professional. Quite a few miles later I noticed that one of the young men had dropped out, so I asked the other what happened. "I train every day whether I want to or not," he replied, "he just goes out when he feels like it."

There you have it on a small scale, but the same principle applies to life. "That wonderful structure, Man," wrote Edmund Burke, "whose prerogative it is to be in a great degree a creature of his own working, and who, when made as he ought to be made, is destined to hold no trivial place in the creation."

The persistent downgrading of life, during recent centuries has reduced man to a cosmic accident inhabiting a fourth-rate planet, lost in the immensities of space and time, in a materialistic universe devoid of values. This dubious vision has not been vouchsafed to the birds and the beasts, but only to human beings. Only man among all the creatures of the planet has been able to take all time and all space within his purview and draw conclusions of any sort. And it is a perverse kind of silliness for a creature gifted with the ability to understand and explain to bemoan his littleness in the face of the unimaginable vastness of the cosmos. Whose mind is it that comprehends all this? What creature controls an enlarging domain? Man confronting the universe as astronomer, physicist, geologist, engineer, is entitled to stand tall; would that he might do as well in other departments!

Beauty

In the area of aesthetics, for example, to illustrate the fourth vital idea. Here man confronts beauty in the very nature of things, and reproduces his vision in art. In a materialistic age it comes to be believed that particles of matter in motion are the only realities, which means that beauty is unreal. "Beauty," we are told in the familiar phrase, "is in the eye of the beholder." How did it get there? we want to know, unless loveliness—as every great artist has taught us—is real, and out there waiting to be experienced.

What shall a painter resort to when the ideology of the age convinces him and his potential public that matter is the ultimate reality and beauty a mere illusion? Let Picasso answer:

> When I was young I was possessed by the religion of great art. But, as the years passed, I realized that art as one conceived it up to the end of the 1880's was, from then on, dying, condemned, and finished and that the pretended artistic activity of today, despite all its superabundance, was nothing but a manifestation of its agony.
>
> As for me, from cubism on I have satisfied these gentlemen (rich people who are looking for something extravagant) and the critics also with all the many bizarre notions which have come into my head and the less they understood the more they admired them. . . . Today, as you know, I am famous and rich. But when I am alone with my soul, I haven't the courage to consider myself as an artist.[6]

One more quotation, this time from Joseph Wood Krutch, generalizing about modern artists:

> They no longer represent anything in the external world, because they no longer believe that the world which exists

outside of man in any way shares or supports human aspirations and values or has any meaning for him.[7]

Art once celebrated the greatness of the human spirit and man's aspiration for the divine; great art reconciled man to his fate. "We are saved by beauty," wrote Dostoyevsky. Art now is the reaching out for bizarre forms of self-expression by more or less interesting personalities; or it becomes outright buffoonery and charlatanism.

Goodness

The fifth big idea has to do with ethics; it is the conviction that moral values are really embedded in the nature of things, and that men have the capacity and are under the necessity of choosing the good and eschewing evil. Given a revival of belief in reason and free will I am confident that ethical questions will be brought within the human capacity to resolve. But if we succumb to the attacks on reason and free will, and if we accept the ideology of Materialism we will seek in vain for some substitute for ethics. We reduce morality to legality; we confuse what is right with what works; or what advantages us, or what pleases us. These things, including utilitarianism and relativism, boil down to ethical nihilism, for if nothing is really right, then nothing is really wrong either.

The Sacred

The sixth big idea pertains to the human experience of the sacred—a dimension which transcends the workaday world. This encounter evokes awe, reverence, a sense of the sublime; and it produces—in the intellectual sphere—the philosophy known as Theism. Theism is the belief that the universe is not merely brute fact, but that a mental/spiritual principle is at the heart of things; the finite mind in each of us is somehow grounded in an infinite Mind. In one perspective, Theism encompasses all the other ideas; and in another perspective, if our thinking is right on the previous five ideas, Theism is an immediate inference.

We resist the word "God" because for most people the notions of their childhood still cling to it, and these notions they have outgrown while they have not permitted their ideas of God to grow with them.

But if one rejects the idea of God, he has no logical stopping place short of the idea of Materialism; and if he goes this far, he has embraced an ideology which shortchanges his own mental processes. Mind, reason, logic, and God are all bound up together. Santayana was once referred to as an atheist, and he replied, "My atheism, like that of Spinoza, is true piety towards the universe, and rejects only gods fashioned by men in their own image, to be servants of human interests." Genuine Theism demands that we be "a-the-istic" toward the false gods.

Theism contends, as a minimum, that a Conscious Intelligence sustains all things, working out its purposes through man, nature, and society. This is to say that the universe is rationally structured, and this is why correct reasoning pans a few precious nuggets of truth .

Acceptance of the Creator reminds men of their own finitude; no man can believe in his own omnipotence who has any sense of God's power. And finite men, aware of their limited vision, have a strong inducement to enrich their own outlook by cross fertilization from other points of view.

When theistic belief is absent or lacking in a society, men are beguiled by the prospect of establishing a heaven on earth. They vainly dream that some combination of political and scientific expertise will usher in utopia, and they use this future possibility as all excuse for present tyranny. Under Theism, they modestly seek to improve themselves and their grasp of truth—thus making the human situation more tolerable, more just, more enjoyable—confident that the final issue is in God's hands.

But won't men perversely use Theism as an excuse for intolerance and even persecution, as indeed has happened in history? Of course they will, for there is no good thing that cannot be misused. But reflect on the deadliness of the alternative as exhibited by regimes which make atheism official. Communism, during its first fifty years in several countries, has taken a toll of at least eighty-four million lives!

What is Man? the creature from Mars might ask. And our answer would be that man is a being with an anthropoid body and six ideas. What if he loses contact with one or more of these ideas? our questioner continues. In that case, we answer, his humanity is thereby that much diminished.

Diminished man has come to the fore at an accelerating rate during the past century. In statecraft, he was unable to resolve minor differences between Western nations and thereby prevent them from tearing each other to pieces in the cycle of wars which began in 1914. In religion, we have a split between the "death of god" trend, on the one hand; and, on the other, an emphasis on push-button salvationism. In education, there is agreement on one point only, that there is a crisis in the schools; but there's no consensus as to cause and cure. Philosophers have abandoned the great tradition in philosophy to embrace one fad after another; positivism, linguistic analysis, existentialism. Then there is the "treason of the intellectuals," many of whom have found communism and socialism irresistible; who resolved that there should be no more war in the Thirties but decided a few years later that war was a wonderful thing. And in personal life, at a time when the male is giving his worst performance, unable to reconcile women to their roles in life, the female wants liberation so she can imitate the male!

It goes without saying that as I list a portion of the indictment against modern man, I have in mind statesmen, artists, philosophers, theologians, intellectuals, as well as ordinary men and women, who have kept the faith, who have not lost their heads. I am not certain that the madness from which we suffer has run its course, and that we've turned the corner, but I am enough of an optimist to have confidence that the corner is within sight, and that there is sufficient health in us to make it.

---

1. *Time,* October 13, 1958.

2. *Saturday Review,* July 15, 1972.

3. Spinoza, pp. 74–5 of the Everyman's Library edition of *Ethics* (New York: E. P. Dutton & Co., 1925).

4. (New York: Harper & Row 1964), p. 21.

5. From the essay "Free Man's Worship." Reprinted in *Selected Papers of Bertrand Russell* (New York: Modern Library, 1927), pp. 3, 14

6. Quoted by Joseph Wood Krutch in *And Even If You Do* (New York: Wm. Morrow & Co., 1967), p. 186.

7. *Ibid.,* p. 185.

III. ECONOMIC FREEDOM

Thinking About Economics

Man is not simply a spiritual being; he is a spiritual being who feels hunger, needs protection from the cold, and seeks shelter from the elements. In order to feed, house, and clothe himself, a person must work. Augmenting his labor with tools and machinery, he converts the raw materials of his natural environment into consumable goods. He learns to cooperate with nature and use her forces to serve his ends. He also learns to cooperate with his fellows, his natural sociability reinforced by the discovery that the division of labor benefits all. "Trade is the great civilizer." There's an unbroken thread that runs from these primitive beginnings to the complex economic order of our own time: it is the human need to cope with scarcity, to satisfy creaturely needs, to provide for material well-being.

The visible signs of this endeavor are all about us; factories, stores, offices, farms, mines, power plants. These are the locations where work is performed, services rendered, goods exchanged, wages paid, money spent, and so on. This is the economy, and in the free society the economy is not under government control and regulation.

In the free society the law protects life, liberty and property of all men alike, ensuring peaceful conditions within the community. This lays down a framework and a set of rules, enabling people to compete and cooperate as they go about the job of providing for their material well-being. When government performs as an impartial umpire who interprets and enforces the agreed upon rules, then the uncoerced economic activities of people display regularity and harmony—as if guided by Adam Smith's invisible hand!

The Capitalistic Economy

In a society where people are free, the economy is referred to as capitalistic. Some prefer the term free enterprise; others like the private enterprise system, or the private property system, or the market economy. Now, of course, no society has ever been one hundred per cent free, which means that we've never had a completely free market econ-

---

From the May 1979 issue of *The Freeman*.

omy. Some people have always seized and misused political power to rig the market in their favor. Obviously, it is not the market's fault if some people choose to break the rules.

The appalling thing is that many intellectuals mistake these deviations from free enterprise for free enterprise itself! And so they condemn "capitalism." But the "capitalism" they condemn is actually the failure of certain people to live up to the rules of capitalism—the system of voluntary exchange among uncoerced people. We're aware of human frailties and shortcomings; we know that it's easier to preach than to practice, easier to announce a set of ideals than to live up to them. Economic theory provides us with a description of the way an economy would work among a people who exercise individual liberty and practice voluntary association. It is this theory we seek to understand and explain, and it is the deviations from this ideal that we seek to correct.

Every person of good will wants to see other people better off; better fed, better housed, better clothed and well provided with the amenities. So everyone wants the economic order to function efficiently. But how important is it that the economic order be free from bureaucratic direction and political controls? Does it do any harm if we allow the economic order to be quarterbacked by government? Let's examine a concrete example to indicate the serious secondary consequences of government control.

In the economic sector of our society there is a multi-billion dollar industry engaged in the production of newspapers, magazines, and journals of opinion. There is also the book trade. Those who publish and distribute the printed word constitute The Press, and one of the important freedoms cherished in our intellectual heritage is Freedom of the Press. The concept is now extended to cover the media—radio and television—where the same principle applies.

Freedom of the Press means simply that the government does not tell editors what to print and what not to print—nor does it dictate to purveyors of television commentary. Some editors print stuff they think will sell. Some editors are men of strong conviction trying to promote a cause they believe in; others are party hacks thumping the tub for some ideological idiocy like Communism, or anarchism, or the New Left, or whatever. But not a single editor in the country is out crusading for government censorship of the press; except indirectly!

Editorial Inconsistency

A large number of editors, writers, and commentators who demand freedom for themselves in one breath, demand government regulation of business and industry with the next! If, at the urging of The Press, government continues to extend its controls over one business after another, how can anyone believe that government will respect the editorial room as a privileged sanctuary, and keep its hands off that section of business known as The Press? Socialize the economy and The Press becomes a branch of the government bureaucracy, free no longer.

The fact that The Press actively cooperates in its own entrapment makes the end result even more bitter. It is one thing to go down fighting; it is something else to cooperate in your own demise. Political control and regulation of the written and spoken word means excessive influence over the minds and thoughts of people. It means eventually a ministry of Propaganda and Information, and an Office of Censorship.

If you get the impression that I don't think highly of some of the people involved with The Press, you'd be correct; they are—with notable exceptions—a sorry lot. They, along with their counterparts in the University and in the Church—with notable exceptions—are guilty of that "treason of the intellectuals" denounced by the French writer Julien Benda in his 1927 book of that title. The intellectuals' treason in the modern world, wrote Benda, is to abandon the pursuit of truth and to seek political preferment instead.

Lest you think I am being unduly harsh on some of those who refer to themselves as Intellectuals, I shall quote a few words of C. S. Lewis:

> It is an outrage that they should be commonly spoken of as Intellectuals. This gives them the chance to say that he who attacks them attacks Intelligence. It is not so. They are not distinguished from other men by an unusual skill in finding truth nor any virginal ardour to pursue her. . . . It is not excess of thought but defect of fertile and generous emotion that marks them out. Their heads are no bigger than the ordinary; it is the atrophy of the chest beneath that makes them seem so.[1]

A Vital Connection

I use The Press to point up the vital relationship between intellectual freedom and economic freedom. Freedom of thought, bound only by the rules of thought itself; freedom of belief, in terms of the mind's own energy; freedom of utterance, guided by logic and within reason—these spiritual freedoms are of the very essence of our being. When they are threatened directly all of us rush to their defense. My point is that they are threatened indirectly whenever—and to whatever degree—their material and economic support is straitjacketed by government regulations and controls.

The same analysis would apply to the Academy and to the Church. If the government owns the campus and pays the professor's salary, the teacher becomes a political flunky, no longer free to research, write, and teach according to his best insights and conscience. And when private property is no longer regarded as the *sine qua non* of a free people, when private property suffers increasing encroachments by government, then church properties, too, become politicized. And, as taxes increase and disposable individual income diminishes, private voluntary funding of churches correspondingly declines and religious programs suffer. Accept economic controls, and what then becomes of Academic Freedom and Freedom of Worship? In short, freedom is all of a piece; philosophy is not the same as digging a ditch, but socialize the ditch digger and the philosopher begins to lose some of his freedom. Freedom of the marketplace and liberties of the mind hang together as one depends on the other.

The great philosopher George Santayana reflected sadly that, in this life of ours, the things that matter most are at the mercy of the things which matter least. A bullet, a tiny fragment of common lead, can snuff out the life of a great man; a few grains of thyroxin one way or the other can upset the endocrine balance and alter the personality, and so on. But the more we think about this situation and the more instances of this sort we cite, the more obvious it becomes that the things Santayana declared matter least, actually matter a great deal. They are so tied in with the things which matter most that the things which matter most depend on them!

Economic Liberty Paramount

In precisely the same way, economic liberty matters a great deal because every liberty of the mind is joined to freedom of the market, economic freedom. There's an old proverb to the effect that whoever controls a man's subsistence has acquired a leverage over the man himself, which impairs his freedom of thought, speech, and worship. The man who cannot claim ownership over the things he produces has no control over the things on which his life depends; he is a slave, by definition. A man who is not allowed to own becomes the property of whoever controls his means of survival, for "a power over a man's support is a power over his will," wrote Hamilton in *The Federalist*. Economic planning implies the power to regulate the noneconomic sectors of life.

F. A. Hayek puts it this way in his influential book, *The Road to Serfdom:* "Economic control is not merely control of a sector of human life which can be separated from the rest; it is the control of the means for all our ends."[2]

In a totalitarian country like Russia or China the government acts as a planning board to assign people to jobs and direct the production and distribution of goods. The whole country is, in effect, a gigantic factory. In practice, there is bound to be a lot of leakage—as witness the inevitable black market. But to whatever extent the State does control the economic life of the Russian and Chinese people it directs every other aspect of their lives as well.

The Masses Content to Drift

The masses of people everywhere and at all times are content to drift along with the trend; they pose no problem for the planner. But what happens to the rebels in a planned economy? Suppose you wanted to publish an opposition newspaper in a place like Russia or China. You could not go out and simply buy presses, paper, and a building; you'd have to acquire these from the State. For what purpose? Why, to attack the State! You would have to find workmen willing to risk their necks to work for you; ditto, people to distribute;

ditto people willing to be caught buying or reading your paper. A *Daily Worker* may be published in a capitalist country, but a *Daily Capitalist* in a Communist country is inconceivable!

Or take the orator who wants to protest. Where could he find a platform in a country in which the State owns every stump, street corner, and soap box—not to mention every building?

Suppose you didn't like your job, where could you go and what could you do? Your job is pretty bad, but it is one notch better than Siberia or starvation, and these are the alternatives. Strike? This is treason against the State, and you'll be shot. Listen to George Bernard Shaw, defending Socialism, writing in *Labor Monthly,* October 1921: "Compulsory labor, with death as the final penalty, is the keystone of Socialism." Shaw was a vegetarian because he loved animals; perhaps he was a Socialist because he hated people!

Point One: *Economic freedom is important in itself, and it is doubly important because every other freedom is related to it.*

To have economic freedom does not, of course, mean that you will be assured the income you think you deserve, nor the job to which you think you may be entitled. Economic freedom does not dispense with the necessity for work. Its only promise is that you may have your pick from among many employment opportunities, or go into business for yourself, and as a bonus the free economy puts a multiplier onto your efforts to enrich you far beyond what the same effort returns you under any alternative system.

Under primitive conditions a family grows its own potatoes, builds its own shelter, shoots its own game, and so on. But we live in a division of labor society where individuals specialize in production and then exchange their surpluses for the surpluses of other people until each person gets what he wants. Most of us work for wages; we produce our specialty, and in return we acquire a pocketful of dollar bills. The dollars are neutral, and thus we can use them to achieve a variety of purposes. We use some of them to satisfy our needs for food, clothing, and shelter; we give some to charity; we take a trip; we pay taxes; we go to the theater, and so on. The money we earn is a means we use to satisfy our various ends.

These interlocking events—production, exchange, and consumption—are market phenomena, and the science of economics emerged, as Mises put it, with "the discovery of regularity and sequence in the concatenation of market events."

Economics Concerns the Means to Achieve Human Goals

Economics has often been called a science of means. The economist, speaking as an economist, does not try to instruct people as to the nature and destiny of man, nor does he try to guide them toward the proper human goals. The ends or goals people strive for are, for the economist, part of his given data, and his business is merely to set forth the means by which people may attain their preferences most efficiently and economically. Economics, as Mises says, "is a science of the means to be applied for the attainment of ends chosen." And a "science never tells a man how he should act; it merely shows how a man must act if he wants to attain definite ends."[3]

When people are free to spend their money as they please, they will often spend it foolishly—I mean other people, of course! As consumers they will demand—and producers will obediently supply—goods that glitter but are shoddy; styles that are tasteless; entertainment that bores; and music that drives us nuts. Nobody ever went broke, H. L. Mencken used to say, by underestimating the taste of the American public. But this, of course, is only half the story. The quality product is available in every line for those who seek it out, and many do. The choices men make in the economic sector will be based upon their scales of values; the market is simply a faithful mirror of ourselves and our choices.

Now, man does not live by bread alone, and no matter how much we might increase the quantity of available material goods, nearly everyone will acknowledge that there is more to life than this. Individual human life has a meaning and purpose which transcends the social order; man is a creature of destiny.

As soon as we begin talking in these terms, of human nature and destiny, we move into the field of religion—the realm of ends. A science of means, like economics, needs to be hitched up with a science of ends, for a means all by itself is meaningless; a means cannot be defined except in terms of the ends or goals to which it is related. The more abundant life is not to be had in terms of more automobiles, more bathtubs, more telephones, and the like. The truly human life operates in a dimension other than the realm of things and means; this other dimension is the domain of religion—using the term in its generic sense. Or, call it your philosophy of life, if you prefer.

If we as a people are squared away in this sector of life—if our value system is in good shape so that we can properly order our priorities—then we'll be able to take economic and political problems in our stride. On the other hand, if there is widespread confusion about what it means to be a human being, so that people are confused as to the proper end and goal of human life—some seeking power, others wealth, fame, publicity, pleasure or chemically induced euphoria—then our economic and political problems overwhelm us.

If economics is a science of means, that is, a tool, we need some discipline to help us decide how to use that tool. The ancient promise of "seek ye first the Kingdom" means that if we put first things first, then second and third things will drop naturally into their proper places. Our actions will then conform to the laws of our being and we'll get the other things we want as a sort of bonus.

Point Two: *Once we understand that economics is a science of means, we realize that economics cannot stand alone—it needs to be hooked up with a discipline which is concerned with ends, which means religion or philosophy.*

There is no easy answer to questions about the ends for which life should be lived, or the goals proper for creatures of our species, but neither is the human race altogether lacking in accumulated wisdom in the matter. Let me offer you a suggestion from Albert Jay Nock. Nock used to speak of "man's five fundamental social instincts," and he listed them as an instinct of expansion and accumulation, of intellect and knowledge, of religion and morals, of beauty and poetry, of social life and manners. He then makes the charge that our civilization, especially during the past two centuries, has given free reign only to the instinct of expansion and accumulation, that is, the urge to make money and exert influence; while the other four instincts have been disallowed and perverted. Our culture is lopsided as a result, and some basic drives of human nature are being thwarted.

Let's move to the next stage of our inquiry and ask: What is the distinguishing feature of a science, and in what sense is economics a science? Adam Smith entitled his great work *The Wealth of Nations* (1776); one of Mises' books is entitled *The Free and Prosperous Commonwealth* (1927). It is clearly evident that these works deal with national prosperity, with the overall well-being of a society, with upgrading the general welfare. These are works of economic science, insofar as they lay down the general rules which a society must follow if it would be prosperous.

General Principles

The distinguishing feature of a science, any science, is that it deals with the general laws governing the behavior of particular things. Science is not concerned with particular things, except insofar as some particular thing exemplifies a general principle. When we concentrate on a particular flower, like Tennyson's "flower in the crannied wall," we move into the realm of art and poetry. Should we want the laws of growth for this species of flower, we consult the science of botany. These books by Smith and Mises lay down the rules a society must conform to if it wants to prosper, they do not tell you as an individual how to make a million in real estate, or a killing in the stock market. This is another subject.

The question before the house in economic inquiry is: "How shall we organize the productive activities of man so that society shall attain maximum prosperity?" And the answer given by economic science is: "Remove every impediment that hampers the market and all the obstructions which prevent it from functioning freely. Turn the market loose and the *nation's* wealth will be maximized." The economist, in short, establishes the rules which must be followed if we want a *society* to be prosperous; but no conceivable elaboration of these rules tells John Doe that he ought to follow them.

Economic science can prescribe for the general prosperity, but it cannot tell John Doe that he ought to obey that prescription. That job can be performed, if at all, by the moralist. The problem here is to bridge the gap between the economist's prescription for national prosperity and John Doe's adoption of that prescription as a guide for his personal conduct.

A Science of Means

Economics is a science of means. It abstains from judgments of value and does not tell John Doe what goals he should choose. If you want to persuade John Doe to follow the rules of economics for maximizing the general prosperity you must argue that he has a moral obligation to conform his actions to certain norms already established in his society by the traditional ethical code.

This code extols justice, forbids murder, theft, and covetousness, and culminates in love for God and neighbor. This is old stuff, you say; true, but it's good stuff! It's the very stuff we need when constructing a proper framework for economic activity.

The market economy is not something which comes out of nothing. But the market economy emerges naturally whenever certain noneconomic conditions are right. There is a realm of life outside the realm of economic calculation, on which the market economy depends. Let me cite Ludwig Mises again, quoting this time from his great work, *Socialism*. Mises speaks of beauty, health, and honor, calling them moral goods. Then he writes: "For all such moral goods are goods of the first order. We can value them directly; and therefore have no difficulty in taking them into account, even though they lie outside the sphere of monetary computation."[4] In other words, the market economy is generated and sustained within a larger framework consisting of, among other things, the proper ethical ingredients.

Point Three: *The free market will not function in a society where the sense of moral obligation is weak or absent.*

Nearly everything on this planet is scarce. There are built-in shortages of almost everything people want. For this reason we need a science of scarcity, and this is economics—a science of scarcity. Goods which are needed but not scarce, such as air, are not economic goods. Air is a free good. Economics deals with things which are in short supply, relative to human demand for them, and this includes most everything we need and use. Our basic situation on this planet is an unbalanced equation with man and his expanding wants on one side, and the world of scanty resources on the other.

Human Wants Insatiable

The human being is a creature of insatiable wants, needs, and desires; but he is placed in an environment where there are but limited means for satisfying those wants, needs, and desires. Unlimited wants on one side of this unbalanced equation; limited means for satisfying them on the other. Now, of course, it is true that no man, nor the human race itself, has an unlimited capacity for food, clothing, shelter, or any other item singly or in combination. But human nature is such that if one want is satisfied the ground is prepared for two others to come forward with their demands. A condition of wantlessness is virtually inconceivable, short of death itself.

What does all this mean? The upshot of all this is that the economic equation will never come out right. It's insoluble. There's no way of taking a creature with unlimited wants and satisfying him by any organization or reorganization of limited resources. Something's got to give, and economic calculation is the human effort to achieve the maximum fulfillment of our needs while avoiding waste.

Let me, at this point, offer you a little parable. This story has to do with a bright boy of five whose mother took him to a toy store and asked the proprietor for a challenging toy for the young man. The owner of the shop brought out an elaborate gadget, loaded with levers, buttons, coils of wire, and many movable parts. The mother examined the complicated piece of apparatus and shook her head. "Jack is a bright boy," she said, "but I fear that he is not old enough for a toy like this."

"Madam," said the proprietor, "this toy has been designed by a panel of psychologists to help the growing child of today adjust to the frustrations of the contemporary world. No matter how he puts it together, it won't come out right."

Relative Scarcity

Economics is indeed the science of scarcity, but it's important to realize that the scarcity we are talking about in this context is relative. In the economic sense, there is scarcity at every level of prosperity. Whenever we drive in city traffic, or look vainly for a place to park, we are hardly in a mood to accept the economic truism that automobiles are scarce. But of course they are, relative to our wishes. Who would not want to replace his present car with a Rolls Royce if it were available merely for the asking?

These simple facts make hash of the oft repeated remark that "we have solved the problem of production, and now we must organize politically to redistribute our abundance." Economic production involves engineering and technology, in that men, money, and machines are linked to turn out airplanes, or automobiles, or tractors, or typewriters, or what not. But resources are limited, and the men, money, and machines we employ to turn out airplanes are not available for the production of automobiles, or tractors, or anything else. The dollar you spend for a package of cigars is no longer available to you for a hamburger.

The economic equation can never be solved; to the end of time there will be scarce goods and unfulfilled wants. There will never be a moment when everyone will have all he wants. "Economics," in the words of Wilhelm Roepke, "should be an anti-ideological, anti-uto-pian, disillusioning science,"[5] and indeed it is. The candid economist is a man who comes before his fellows with the bad news that the human race will never have enough. Organize and reorganize society from now till doomsday and we'll still be trying to cope with scarcity. This truth does not set well with those who have the perfect solution in hand—and the woods are full of such. No wonder economists are unpopular!

Point Four: *Things are scarce, and therefore we need a science of scarcity in order to make the best of an awkward situation.*

The modern mind takes the dogma of inevitable progress for granted. Most of our contemporaries assume that day by day, in every way, we are getting better and better, until some day the human race will achieve perfection. The modern mind is passionately utopian, confident that some piece of social machinery, some ideological gadgetry, is about to solve the human equation. Minds fixed in such a cast of thought, minds with this outlook on life, are immune to the truths of economics. The conclusions of economics, in their full significance, are incompatible with the facile notions of automatic human progress which are part of the mental baggage of modern man—including many economists!

I'm not denying that there is genuine progress in certain limited areas of our experience. This year's color television set certainly gives a better picture than the first set you bought in, say, 1950. The jet planes of today deliver you more rapidly and in better shape than did the old prop jobs—although there's some truth in the remark of some comedian: "Breakfast in Paris, luncheon in New York, dinner in San Francisco—baggage in Rio de Janeiro!" Automobiles are more luxurious, we have more conveniences around the house, we are better equipped against illness. There is real progress in certain branches of science, technology, and mechanics.

But are the television programs improving year by year? Are the novels of this year so much better than the novels of last year, or last century? Are the playwrights whose offerings we have seen on Broadway this season *that* much better than Shakespeare? Has the contemporary outpouring of poetry rendered Homer, Dante, Keats, and

Browning obsolete? Is the latest book on the "new morality" superior to Aristotle's *Ethics?*

Are the prevailing economic doctrines of 1979, reflecting the Samuelson text, sounder than those of a generation ago, nourished on Fairchild, Furness, and Buck? Are today's prevailing political doctrines more enlightened than those which elected a Grover Cleveland? Henry Adams in his *Education* observed that the succession of presidents from Washington, Adams, and Jefferson down to Ulysses Grant was enough to disprove the theory of progressive evolution! What would he say if he were able to observe the recent past?

The dogma of inevitable progress does not hold water. Perfect anthills may be within the realm of possibility; but a perfect human society, never! Utopia is a delusion. Man is the kind of a creature for whom complete fulfillment is not possible within history; unlike other organisms, he has a destiny in eternity which takes him beyond biological and social life. This is the world outlook of all serious religion and philosophy. The conclusion of economics—that life holds no perfect solutions—is just what a person who embraces this world view would expect. Economic truths are as acceptable to the religious world view as they are unacceptable to the world view premised on automatic progress into an earthly paradise.

Another Dimension Transcends the Natural Order

If there is another dimension of being which transcends the natural order—the natural order being comprised of the things we can see and touch, weigh and measure—and if man is really a creature of both orders and at home in both, then he has an excellent chance of establishing his earthly priorities in the right sequence. He will not put impossible demands on the economic order, nor will he strive for perfection in the political order. Earth is enough, so he'll leave heaven where it belongs, beyond the grave! The effort to build a newfangled heaven on earth in countries like Russia and China has resulted in conditions that resemble an old-fashioned hell. Let us strive for a more moderate goal, let us work for a tolerable society—not a perfect one— and we may make it!

Point Five: *Economics tells us that the Kingdom of God is beyond history.*

Economics is a discipline in its own right, but it has some larger meanings and implications. Its very nature demands a framework in which there are religious and ethical ingredients. Establish these necessary conditions—together with their legal and political corollaries—and within this framework the economic activities of men are self-starting, self-operating, and self-regulating. Given the proper framework, the economy does not have to be *made* to work; it works by itself, and it pays rich dividends in the form of a free and prosperous commonwealth.

1. *The Abolition of Man,* pp. 34–36.
2. *The Road to Serfdom,* p. 92.
3. *Human Action,* p. 10.
4. *Socialism,* p. 116.
5. *A Humane Economy,* p. 150.

Religion and the Free Economy

Imagine yourself in conversation with a new acquaintance. The exchange of ideas goes well for a time, and then the talk drifts around to economics. This brings forth a series of denunciations from your companion, who declares that economics belongs in the same category as voodoo and witchcraft. You rise hotly to the defense of your favorite subject, and the battle is joined. Within five minutes it becomes evident to the innocent bystander that the economics you are defending is not the economics your adversary is attacking. The thing he knows as "economics" is the set of conjectures and prescriptions drawn from the Marx, Keynes, Galbraith well; whereas for you, "economics" connotes the body of thought associated with men like Adam Smith, Mises, and Hayek. It's possible that your acquaintance has never heard of the Austrian School, but his general "feel" for things has already made him *simpatico*. He has rejected unsound ideas, and this opens up the possibility that he might accept sound ones. But even if he repudiates the Austrian School along with the Keynesian, you and he now have the same referent and are no longer talking past each other; you're that much ahead.

And so it is with the great themes of religion and God; the same words stand for different things to different people. Take religion: Men and women in every age and clime have sought to relate to an unseen order; call it the spiritual realm, if you prefer, to distinguish it from the social order and the order of nature. We live in some society, we are in touch with nature—and we also participate in a dimension which transcends them and us. People seek to come to terms with this unseen order by means of an enormous variety of attitudes, beliefs, and practices. These numerous, diverse, and sometimes contradictory activities are then pulled, hauled, and pounded into a single category bearing the label "religion." This taxonomic barbarism—this crude labeling—will not satisfy the philosophically-minded, who know that much if not most of what is labeled religion is more properly called magic, superstition, or ideology. Just as most of what is popularly

From the May 1975 issue of *The Freeman*.

understood as economics is anti-economic, and a lot of what passes for science is really scientism.

Strange Views of God

The well-nigh universal misuse of the term God is another stumbling block. God—in popular mythology—is the tribal deity, the Man Upstairs, Big Brother in the Sky, a transmogrified U.N. Secretary, a cosmic bellhop up there to run our celestial errands for us, and so on. We have to be a-theist-ic with reference to these ideas of God before we can confront a more adequate idea. Santayana put it well. Chided for his "atheism," the great philosopher gently stated his position: "My atheism, like that of Spinoza, is true piety towards the universe, and rejects only gods fashioned by men in their own image, to be servants of human interests." We resist the word God because for most people the notions of their childhood still cling to it, and these notions they have outgrown while they have not permitted their ideas of God to grow with them. Once this growth is allowed to occur, we become aware that genuine Theism demands that we be a-theist-ic towards the false gods.

Every living thing needs food and shelter and symbiotic relation to its kind, and so do we, but only a human being asks such questions as Who am I? What am I here for? Is there meaning in the totality? What is my destiny ? These are religious questions, and a creature who has never asked himself these questions is a defective hominoid. Philosophical religion is the uniquely *human* concern, and if our assessment of human nature fails to take religion into account—together with its corruptions into magic and superstition—we achieve only a warped and partial understanding of man and his checkered career upon this planet.

The subject presently under discussion is not theology as such, it is the relation between religion and the free economy; or, the bearing of Theism on the free market/free economy way of life. So, let us shift gears.

An important distinction is to be drawn between the market and the market economy; the former is universal, the latter is rare. The market comes into play wherever there is a society, for no people is so primitive as not to engage in trade and barter. There's a lively market in Russia and China. The market yesterday, today, and forever; but not the market economy: This human institution is very rare. Only occasionally has the market been able to institutionalize itself as the market economy. This is a most desirable transmutation; if it is to occur certain conditions must be met. In this paper I shall discuss five of these conditions, in an effort to deal with the question: On what does the market economy depend?

• *First,* there must be firm convictions widely held about the reality of Mind and the capacity of Reason to ascertain truth.

• *Second,* there must be belief in Free Will.

• *Third,* there must be a firm commitment to the idea of inherent rights; for it is obvious that unless we believe in an interior, private domain natural to the human person we will not structure government so as to protect it.

• *Fourth,* there must be firm convictions about the reality of a moral order whose mandates are binding upon all men alike.

• *Fifth,* there must be a sound philosophy of man and his destiny, and a hierarchy of the life goals appropriate to human nature.

Now we know what we are looking for; we are searching for a world view which meets these five conditions. I shall begin with the self-evident truth that some portion of your being is mental and attempt to draw out the full implications of this fact. There is the physical you, but in addition to your body, which is matter, you have a mind or intellect which is nonmaterial. The two interact; your state of mind affects the health of your body, and vice versa. A change in body chemistry or damage to brain cells may impair memory and darken the intelligence. Now, just as our eyes are given us to see with, we have a mind to think with. Possessing minds, we can remember the past, we can anticipate the future, and we can reason about the present. By using our intellect we can begin to understand and explain things. In virtue of our minds we are conscious beings; and not only that, we are self-conscious, aware that there is no way of understanding our mental processes except by other mental processes. We have the capacity to think about thinking, which means that the mind, in reflecting upon itself, is both measure and thing measured.

The Origin of Mind

What account shall we give of this remarkable instrument, the human intellect? What is its origin, its nature, its place in the totality of things? The consensus today is that mind is merely an off-shoot of matter; "there is only one world, the material world, and thought is a product of matter." This Marxist dogma is echoed by Behaviorists, such as B. F. Skinner, for whom thinking is a physical process. In other words—and to put it graphically—your brain cells ooze mind just as your scalp extrudes hair! Now, if we accept some such assumption as this—that your body originates your mind—the inescapable inference is that each person's mind is as private and unique as his fingerprints. And if this be the case, then each person's mind is locked within his skull.

Now, if the mind of each one of us is a strictly individual reflex of physical processes, it is difficult to imagine how mind so conceived could possibly be a means of communication between persons. And if the communications gap were somehow bridged, what information could be transmitted? Only information as to the inner state of the organism which produced the mind.

Ordinarily, we demand more of the mind than this; we expect our intelligence and our powers of reason to expand the boundaries of knowledge in the realm outside our skulls. This leads to the question: What must the universe be like if these expectations are to be fulfilled? Briefly, if by taking thought and using our powers of reason we are to acquire truths about the universe, the universe must be rationally structured; there must be some resonance between the thinking which goes on inside us and the rationality present in the nature of things. The mind in us can be trusted to reach reliable conclusions about the world outside only if the material world—nature—embodies a non-material element akin to our minds, that is to say, a pattern, a structure, a meaning. This position may be called Theism.

Mind is Ultimate

Theism is the belief that a mental/spiritual dimension is at the very heart of things; it is the conviction that mind is ultimate, and not matter; that mind is at least as ancient in time and as fundamental in significance as protons, electrons, and neutrons. Mind is a primary thing; not something secondary and derived. Push analysis as deep as possible and there is this elemental, primordial, original thing, mind; there is nothing nonmental beyond mind from which mind derives. The nonmental part of us, our physical body, is in a sense continuous with the material universe; at some point in time nature will reclaim the atoms which now comprise "this muddy vesture." In a similar fashion, it is contended, the mental part of us is continuous with that part of reality which is non-material; minds are linked to Mind. Anything short of this constitutes a subordination of mind to matter, a position which is self-stultifying.

Let me restate the argument thus far: If we choose to think at all we have no choice but to trust our thought processes. There's simply no way that you can think your way to the conclusion that thought is untrustworthy; a reasoned case against reason is a contradiction in terms! You can no more disown your own mental processes than you can stand outside your own feet. This is not to say that every chain of reasoning of yours or mine invariably arrives at assuredly true conclusions. No, we are imperfect creatures and our reasoning is frequently flawed—as we discover when we go back over it to check for logical coherence. But the checking process itself is an appeal to reason, and there is no higher court beyond reason until we appear at the Great Assize!

In short, a direct frontal attack by reason can never succeed in toppling mind from its pre-eminent place in the total scheme of things. If the intellect is to be downgraded the critical faculties must first be dulled, then redirected onto externalities, things. The universe is full of things so exciting that many Moderns come to regard them as more real than the mental activities that make us aware of them! Mind is awareness, which means that the intellect itself rarely gets into our sights when we are using it in the process of knowing something. We don't attend to it when we use it to attend to something else, just as we don't see our eyes when we are seeing something with them.

No Physical Measure

Awareness can't be quantified, and to the degree that we are obsessed with size, quantity, velocity, measurement, and the like—preoccupations of the laboratory—to this extent will we conclude that the universe must ultimately be defined in these terms: the quantitative alone being fully real, the mind, therefore, is given a second-class status. Our minds work so well that we forget we have them, and so we are intellectually disarmed when some learned fool comes along and tells us that the mind is a fiction and thinking only reflex activity.

Accept the premise that mind is not an ultimate and original ingredient of this universe and you assure the rise of a world view wherein reason is assumed to be untrustworthy.

Conversely, if we do acknowledge that mind is an ultimate and original ingredient of the universe—existing in its own right, independent, not derived from something non-mental—an interesting result follows. What are the characteristic earmarks of intellect or mind? The mental is characterized by awareness, conscious intelligence, rationality, creativity, will, purpose. Possessing intellects we have a principle of explanation, an ordering power. Having reasoned to this point we discover that we have arrived at the God of the philosophers, a concept of Deity which is the cornerstone of religion. Discard this concept— that something akin to the mental in ourselves is intrinsic to the universe—and the human intellect is imperiled. Accept the opposite outlook, which we may call nontheism, and the cults of unreason revive.

The Diminished Mind

Nontheism diminishes mind. It regards mind as a mere off-shoot of matter, an epiphenomenon, a secondary thing derived from that which is primary and fundamental—elementary particles. The mythology of nontheism tells us that the universe was mindless for billions of years, and that only after the appearance of the higher primates did this later comer, mind, stumble by accident onto the planetary scene. A few hundred thousand years ago the nonmental chanced to give rise to the mental the nonrational happened to turn into rationality, and lo, *homo sapiens*. This incredible pedigree downgrades mind by giving it an unreasonable origin, and then it compounds this error by asking us to believe that this discredited instrument can somehow be relied upon to reach trustworthy conclusions! Anti-theism makes matter the master of mind; it reduces our mental processes to the level of secretions from a gland; it degrades the search for truth into a movement of material particles—and thus refutes itself.

Nontheism of some variety—not spelled out this way, as a rule—is the prevailing ideology, and it is hostile to the idea that mind exists in its own right. It declares that matter is primary, mind only secondary, and so it is only natural that nontheism reduces truth to a matter of feeling and opinion. Reason, logic, intelligence—along with mind— are reduced to a second-class status, and without these props and stays the free society hasn't got a chance. The only philosophy which gives Mind and Reason their due is what I refer to as Theism.

Now, it is of course true that not everyone who entertains the Theistic position automatically draws the conclusions which I think are implicit in the premises. Human nature being what it is, this fact should cause no surprise. The point is that Theism leans in the right direction; whereas, there's no way to extract the ingredients necessary for a free economy from the polar opposite view, Materialism.

Another cornerstone of the free society is the concept of free will. Nontheism, carried out to its logical end, is some form of materialism, and materialism logically connotes the idea of a cosmic machine and the inexorable, inevitable workings of cause and effect sequences. This is the philosophy sometimes labeled Mechanism. There's no room for the human creative act within this closed system, and if man is not a freely choosing person, it's pretty silly to try to defend the free society, as one where people enjoy maximum liberty to choose and pursue their life goals.

Laws of the Market

Of course, the world view I espouse, Theism, acknowledges the realm of natural or scientific law—nature—the domain in which "there prevails an inexorable interconnectedness in physical and biological phenomena." Theism recognizes, in addition, the social order where the laws of the market (laws of praxeology) operate. For the nontheist, this is all there is, nature and society; man is totally contained within these two orders; he's a product of his natural and social environment; there's nothing more. For the Theist, there's more; man's body is compounded of the elements to be found in the earth's crust, but he also possesses a mind *sui generis,* in virtue of which he participates in the unseen order which transcends nature and society. "Mind," Plato wrote in the *Philebus,* "belongs to the family of what we called the cause of all things." Man is able to break the chain of causation because he has a leverage from beyond nature and beyond society; his will is indeed free. Most people, if they had the choice, would choose more freedom rather than less, and they'd rather be prosperous than not. But mere wishing gets us nowhere when the conditions for freedom and prosperity are absent; and these conditions are lacking when the climate of opinion is hostile to mind, truth, and freedom of the will.

The intellectual outlook which excludes the unseen order also diminishes man himself, to the point where the idea of inherent rights is extinguished.

Only a handful of the world's people have ever believed in the idea of the inherent rights of persons, and not many philosophers; nor will mere assertion on our part convince anyone but ourselves of the validity of this idea. Individual rights are not self-evident, except to those who embrace a world view from which the idea of equal rights is an immediate inference. It will not do merely to declare that human nature is the source of man's rights, because the alert critic will call upon you to explain the origin of human nature. Is human nature the chance product of the natural and social environment? In which case there is logically no room for rights. Or, is human nature rooted in the ultimate nature of things, thus embodying a purpose of cosmic dimensions, a purpose needing human freedom for its fulfillment? Theism answers in the affirmative!

Rights Are Intangible

Now, John Doe's rights do not exist in time and space, as does his brain, for example, or his heart. These organs have mass and extension, and upon analysis they break down into various chemical elements. Not so a person's rights; these intangibles are part of the unseen order— if they are real at all—and those who deny the reality of an unseen order should be sufficiently logical to abandon the idea of inherent rights. Because the prevailing orthodoxy for a century or more has been positivism, scientism, materialism—the labels are many but the substance is the denial of an unseen order—the idea of inherent personal rights has a feeble hold on the modern mind. Reality consists of two orders only, it is affirmed, nature and society, and man is a creature of nature produced by the blind action of chemical and physical forces, shaped finally by his interaction with other people in society: there is nothing in John Doe's present makeup which was not first in nature and society, whose joint product he is. Can we locate rights in those places? No! We can no more attribute rights to nature than color to a musical note; and what is "society" that it could be endowed with rights?

What sort of a world view do we need, then, if we would validate the idea of equal rights for all persons? We need a metaphysic which includes an unseen order transcending the orders of nature and society.

If man participates in a transcendent order then the idea of inherent rights readily follows; but if man is merely a creature of nature and society . . . no way!

The human person is either an accidental end product of forces in the natural and social environment—the popular opinion today; or, man is what the theologian would call a created being. To affirm that man is a created being is to say that his life has an ultimate meaning and the individual counts; it is not to say that God materialized him in a flash, like Houdini pulling a rabbit out of a hat. The doctrine of creation is another way of affirming that the whole show makes sense, and is purposeful; and man, therefore, has a reason for living. The late Archbishop of Canterbury put the doctrine of creation in theological terms: "the world exists because God chose to call it into being and chooses to sustain it in being." This is Theism, and it is the only world view hospitable to the idea of inherent or "natural" rights.

What Social Arrangements?

Let's assume now that our doctrine of man includes an affirmation of his inherent rights, natural or God-given. What kind of social arrangements most fully acknowledge each person's inner and private domain?

The Declaration of Independence says that legitimate governments are those limited to securing men in their rights, and this position has many adherents even today, myself included. But there are those among our contemporaries who maintain that government per se violates rights by its very existence.

To illustrate their zero-government position, these people ask us to suppose that John Doe decides to put down his stakes in Podunk and buys the house and lot at 10 Main Street. Along comes the tax collector and forces John to cough up his prorated share of the cost of Podunk's government. This tax, it is alleged, constitutes an invasion of John Doe's right to live and every taxpayer in the country is similarly violated. Will this allegation hold water? Nary a drop! Consider: Each of these millions of taxpayers lives at some definite location, his home address; and each of the alleged violations takes place at that same spot. The assertion that the assessment collected from John Doe at 10 Main Street is a violation, implies that John has some prior, inherent right to locate at 10 Main Street.

Logically, there cannot be a violation of a right unless there was a right in the first place! Presumably, Doe bought the property at No. 10 and acquired a legal "right" to live there; but if it be argued that he has a natural, inherent right to live at a given place—like 10 Main Street—why was he required to buy his way in? The same twisted theory that views the tax as a violation would have to view the purchase as a violation also. But the argument is wrong on both counts. Your right to live, properly understood, means that you have the same rights within a society as anyone else; equal rights for all. If you have chosen to live in Podunk because of its plus features, your choice logically embraces its minus features as well. It's a profit and loss world.

Moral Convictions

The idea of equal rights has close affinities with firmly based moral convictions, and it is Theism again—with its belief that the nature of things has an ethical bias—which supplies grounds for drawing a radical distinction between right and wrong, good and evil. No people, in the absence of an adequate moral code, can move from the mere urge to be free into the free society, nor can they maintain levels of freedom once reached by their forebears. What is right? and What is good? are perennial questions, and most emphatically they are not the same questions as What is useful? What is pleasurable? profitable? legal? What benefits the community? and the like. These are interesting questions, but they are not ethical questions; calling them such does not make them so.

Ethical relativism and ethical nihilism are part of the prevailing orthodoxy; they are the dead ends where axiological inquiry arrives if the opening premise denies the reality of anything beyond the natural and social orders. If there is no unseen order which transcends nature and society, then our moral code must anchor its authority in either the social order or the natural order. Now, nature does have its mercies, but it is also "red in tooth and claw"; it's the scene of a constant struggle for survival. Surely, the law of the jungle does not provide a model which human beings should seek to emulate. And if someone declares that society or a segment thereof is the source of moral authority, we must ask, Which society? or Which faction within society? Only the totalitarian nation can give a clear-cut answer here, and it is not a pretty one.

This position, moreover, presents a logical difficulty. It begins with the assumption that there is no reality beyond nature and society, and concludes that we ought to conform our action to nature's or society's mandates. Whence this imperative? It is not from within nature that we receive a mandate to obey nature; only if the code transcends both nature and the individual can the message be derived that the individual should live according to nature. And it is precisely such a code that is denied by all varieties of nontheism. Ditto in the case of society's mandates.

The next expedient of the nontheist confronting his moral dilemma is to assert that every individual is an end in himself; therefore he should pursue his own advantage and further his own interests; he should "do his own thing." The Theist believes that man didn't just happen; he is a created being. Those who deny this affirm that man is the accidental end product of the physical and social environment. And it would take a pretty hard sell to convince anyone that a mere end product really is an end in himself, thereby possessing inherent rights and immunities which everyone else should respect. Only if we acknowledge the mystery and sacredness of personhood—because each person participates in an order that transcends nature and society—do we have the ingredients for a moral code; only then do we have a set of rules, in terms of which each person has maximum opportunity to pursue his private goals and a reason for not aggressing against his fellows—even when an act of aggression appears to give him an advantage or serve his immediate interests. Throw out the rule book, and the admonition "do your own thing" puts the weak doing their thing at the mercy of the strong doing theirs.

What Is the Purpose?

Now for our final point. I have argued that Theism is the only philosophy which validates mind, supports free will, provides for inherent rights, and supplies a moral dimension. What does Theism have to say about the purpose of life and the goals appropriate for creatures cast in our mold? We do know that people who are not pursuing the goals proper to man come to feel that life is meaningless; and if life is meaningless—Albert Camus' point—then power has no limits. "What shall I do with my life?" is a question that dogs each of us in the course of our three-score-years-and-ten.

Shall we seek pleasure, power, truth, wealth, or what? Unquestionably, life is to be enjoyed and laughter is good for us; but it is notorious that those who work at having fun don't have much; the serious pursuit of pleasure is a contradiction in terms. What about power? It is a heady thing to wield power, but the corruptions wrought by power afflict both the powerful and their victims.

Truth and beauty? The search for truth and beauty is on a higher level than most pursuits, but there are disquieting trends in modern philosophy which downgrade truth by limiting it to the experimentally verifiable, and reduce beauty to a pleasing emotion. Logical positivists discredit mind by denying that thought is an independent source of knowledge. As the Oxford philosopher A. J. Ayer puts it, "... there are no 'truths of reason' which refer to matters of fact." Deny the reality of an unseen order which transcends nature and society, and truth is a casualty; men lose contact with the pursuits which make life worthwhile.

Let the Market Decide?

Sometimes another tack is taken; some people tell us that the market and the pursuit of maximum profitability provides both a goal for individual life and a guide to conduct. What shall the individual do with his talents, his time, his energies—his life? Why, let the market decide; let each person find out what other people most urgently want from him by noting what they are willing to pay, and then conduct himself so as to maximize his profits! Reflect on the fact that "the market"—in the eyes of any given person—is simply "other people"; so what this position boils down to is equivalent to advising each person to let other people determine how he should live and what he should live for! Society, then, is an enormous altruistic stew, in which "every one is the servant of all and all the masters of each." Any person who finds himself sunk in this predicament cannot rescue himself unless he has a purchase on a value system which transcends society. Only Theism offers such a value system, one which helps us choose the goals proper for human living.

The free society/free economy does not just happen in human affairs; only occasionally has it emerged in history. The free economy is a contingent thing, dependent upon the cultivation and application of the right ideas, the right philosophy. Freedom needs a world view which makes mind central and gives truth its proper place; freedom needs to be buttressed by firm moral convictions, by the idea of inherent natural rights, and by belief in free will. And only a happy citizenry pursuing the goals proper to man will struggle to become free, or fight to retain such freedom as they already enjoy. The free society, in short, needs Theism. Of course we need sound economic and political theory as well, but it must be emphasized once again that a people which has embraced an untenable world view—one which denies the spiritual and the transcendent—will be seduced repeatedly by crazy schemes of reform and revolution.

Humane Values and the Free Economy

The average American is in favor of freedom and he'll tell you so in no uncertain terms. He wants Church and State separate, he would object if government were to censor the press, he doesn't want some bureaucrat dictating to professors what they should teach. But at the same time he wants government to control and regulate business; he thinks industry and trade need to be policed in order to protect the consumer from the wolves. Warming up to his subject he proceeds to catalogue the wickedness of people engaged in commercial activity, and especially the sins of "big business."

Strange to say, these turn out to be the same old sins one finds in every walk of life. Some men in the business world are wicked, no doubt; but so are some ministers, some professors, some publishers, some entertainers, and even some television commentators. There's no reason for singling out businessmen—except to provide a specious rationale for saddling economic life with ever more bureaucratic regulations and controls. This has adverse economic effects, of course, adding to the costs of doing business and making all of us poorer, but that's not the worst of it. When economic enterprise is not free every other freedom is in jeopardy.

Human liberty is a precious and a fragile thing. Human liberty cannot be won, or even sustained, on the economic level alone; but it can be lost on that level, and it is being lost there. Control the economic life of a people and you control every other aspect of their lives as well. "Power over a man's subsistence amounts to a power over his will." The truth of this ancient maxim has been pounded home in our time by the conditions of life behind the Iron Curtain.

Now, it is true that business is not the only sector of our society under fire. Our whole civilization—Western civilization—has been under siege for several generations and because our culture so largely embodies bourgeois values, the attack against business is reinforced by the revolutionary Communist thrust to unseat the bourgeoisie.

The bourgeoisie are the middle class—townspeople engaged in industry and trade—and their emergence in the modern period was

From the June 1978 issue of *The Freeman.*

188

opposed by the aristocracy, whose values were quite different. Few of us live next door to counts, dukes, or lords: the nobility is distant in time and space, glowingly enshrined in romance and myth. "The nobleman has courage, spends without counting, despises petty detail. There is a great air of freedom and unselfishness about the nobleman. He will throw his life away for a cause, not calculate the returns. That is the noble idea. In reality, he lives by the serfdom of others, and he broadens his acres by killing, and taking other people's land—'the good old rule, the simple plan. That they should take who have the power, and they should keep who can.'" These are Jacques Barzun's words.

Dr. Barzun continues, "The bourgeoisie opposed such noble free-handedness and supported a king who would replace 'the good old rule' by one less damaging to trade and manufacture—and to the peasants' crops. But the regrettable truth is that there is no glamour about trade. Trade requires regularity, security, efficiency, an exact *quid pro quo,* and an exasperating attention to detail. . . . There is nothing spontaneous, generous, or large-minded about it. Man's native love of drama rebels against a scheme of life so plodding and resents the rewards of qualities so niggling."

"What a convenient word is bourgeois!" Barzun observes. "How expressive and well-shaped for the mouth to utter scorn. And how flexible in its application—it is another wonderful French invention!"

The Working Class

The free enterprise system—or what is popularly called "capitalism"—has a special affinity for the type of man we'd call bourgeois or middle class. Industry and trade have never been the preoccupation of any aristocracy, which dislikes to sully its hands with ordinary work. Most of the world's work today is done by those who have risen from the ranks, largely by their own efforts, in societies which have no rigid caste barriers to prevent upward mobility.

The emergence of the businessman during recent centuries was not a solitary adventure; the freeing of the business sector of Western society went hand in hand with the expansion of other liberties we cherish. The story is a familiar one, and it begins with the religious revolution of the sixteenth century which led eventually to the separation of church and state, and freedom of worship. Free speech and freedom of the press were parts of this liberating movement, and eventually—as Mercantilism gave way before the current of ideas released by Adam Smith, Edmund Burke, and others—economic enterprise was freed from political regulations and controls, and came under consumer guidance.

Consumers—by our millions of daily decisions in the marketplace to buy this or not buy that—project a pattern; and these buying habits of ours give entrepreneurs the clues they need to direct production into this channel or that, in an effort to please customers. In the free economy the consumer is sovereign. You may regard your product as the best gismo available anywhere at any price, but if the consumers don't like it they buy elsewhere and you go out of business. You, as an entrepreneur, have no power over customers except your ability to persuade and the quality of your product. This is the free market economy, and it is an integral part of the free society.

Everyone's Business

Freedom, we hear it said, is everyone's business, so each of us really does have a stake in freedom-in-general. To the extent that anyone's freedom is lost, everyone's freedom is in jeopardy. But there are particular freedoms, and when a particular freedom is attacked you'd expect those directly involved to rush to its defense. And this is what you do find in most instances. When religious liberty is threatened, churchmen unite to oppose the threat. When freedom of the press is imperiled newsmen band together. Any impairment of academic freedom is challenged by teachers, and intellectuals do battle on behalf of free speech. And when freedom of economic enterprise is being throttled by governmental controls, businessmen and business organizations mobilize to resist the attack. Right? Wrong!

Businessmen, all too often, are unwilling to speak out vigorously, even in self-defense—as the celebrated economist Joseph Schumpeter has scathingly pointed out: "Perhaps the most striking feature of the picture is the extent to which the bourgeoisie, besides educating its own enemies, allows itself in turn to be educated by them. It absorbs the slogans of current radicalism and seems quite willing to undergo a process of conversion to a creed hostile to its very existence. . . . This is verified by the very characteristic manner in which particular capitalist interests and the bourgeoisie as a whole behave when facing direct attack. They talk and plead—or hire people to do it for them; they snatch at every chance of compromise; they are ever ready to give in; they never put up a fight under the flag of their own ideals and interests—in this country there was no real resistance anywhere against the imposition of crushing financial burdens during the last decade or against labor legislation incompatible with the effective management of industry."

I can imagine an ideal society where each sector was alert to rebuff threats to any other sector; where clergymen would go to bat whenever freedom of the press was threatened, and publishers jealously guarded academic freedom, and professors fought for freedom of medical practice, and doctors resisted every bureaucratic invasion of the marketplace, and businessmen cherished freedom of religion. In real life, however, things do not happen this way.

It is partly the fault of business itself that the freedom most gravely threatened right now is the freedom of the economy, on which not only our prosperity depends, but much else besides. Those immersed in the grubby details of the marketplace often lose sight of the big picture; the head of a business worries about falling sales and how to meet the next payroll, but here, in this serene academic environment, we can sit back and theorize.

Better Understanding, the Best Defense

The best defense of the free economy is a better understanding of the free economy, shared by more people. So let's put capitalism to the test. Put aside, for the moment, any opinions you may entertain about the free enterprise system we now have, and let's draw up some plans for an ideal economic order. If we were starting from scratch what requirements would we lay down for an economic order that would meet with our approval? I'm going to suggest that there are four major demands we should make of any economic system, and after we have spelled these out a bit each of us can decide for himself whether our present system falls short and how it might be strengthened and defended.

A good economic system has four characteristics:

1. A good economy produces goods and services efficiently.
2. A good economy allocates rewards equitably, to all participants.

3. A good economy broadens the scope for individual free choice.

4. A good economy functions in harmony with religious and moral values.

There's no argument on the first point; our present economic system does deliver the goods, as even its enemies admit. The American economy has never been wholly free; it has operated under various political restraints from the very beginning. But compared to the politically planned economies of other nations our relatively free economy has been a paragon.

Producing and exchanging in a largely free country has bestowed a prosperity upon America that the world envies. Americans started poor. There was little per capita wealth two hundred years ago; but our forebears had an abundant faith in the nation's future under God, a strong belief in themselves, and they practiced the Puritan work ethic. This was the land of opportunity, and millions of the poor and oppressed of other nations migrated here to make their own way in this "land of the free." By and large they succeeded; never have so many advanced so far out of poverty in so short a time.

There have been evils in American life, and some are there still—along with errors, shortcomings, and blindspots. But what other nation is entitled to cast the first stone, or the second, or the third? If the American Dream has faded, if there is tarnish on our idealism, where lies the fault? The Church and the School are the institutions charged with the responsibility for things of the mind and spirit, and if we have lost that vision without which the people perish, if our value system is in disarray, we surely can't blame business and industry—which merely reflect the consensus.

The Goals of Life

The goals of human life, the ends appropriate for creatures such as we, are the primary concerns of religion and education. The increase of material well-being may be the *means* for achieving the good life; it is certainly not the *end* for which life should be lived. The economic order has the modest role of supplying our creaturely needs efficiently so that we may have the leisure to pursue our personal goals. In America the economy has performed its role commendably. It is not to be blamed for the failures of other institutions.

The relatively free economy we have enjoyed in America has brought unparalleled prosperity, but an affluent society is not necessarily a just society. And so we come to the second test we wish to put to the free enterprise system: Does it allocate the rewards fairly and equitably?

In a free society every one of us is rewarded by his peers according to the value willing buyers attach to the goods and services he offers in exchange. This is the market in action. This marketplace assessment is made by consumers, and we all know that consumers are ignorant, venal, biased, stupid; in short they are people very much like us! This does seem to be a clumsy way of deciding how much or how little of this world's goods shall be put at this or that man's disposal.

Isn't there an alternative? Yes, there's an alternative, and it occurred to people more than two millennia ago. We'll invite the wise and the good to come down from Olympus to sit as a council among men, and we'll appear before them one by one, to be judged on personal merit and rewarded accordingly. Then we'll be assured that those who make a million really deserve it, and those who are paupers belong at that level; and we'll all be contented and happy. What lunacy! The genuinely wise and good would not accept such a role, and I quote the words of the highest authority declining it: "Who made me a judge over you?"

The marketplace decision that this man shall earn twenty-five thousand, this one ten, and so on, is not, of course, marked by supernal wisdom; no one claims this. But it is a million miles ahead of the alternative, which is to recast consumers into voters, who will elect a body of politicians, who will appoint bureaucrats, who will divvy up the wealth—by governmental legerdemain. This mad scheme backs away from the imperfect and lurches into the impossible! There are no perfect arrangements in human affairs, but the fairest distribution of material rewards attainable by imperfect men is to let a man's customers decide how much he should earn; this method will distribute economic goods unequally, but equitably.

We do live in an affluent society, and the fact is that the prosperity generated by our relatively free institutions has been widely shared by the American people. There are the rich, there are the less well-to-do, and there are still some poor; but this allocation of rewards represents the choices of people themselves—as reflecting their buying habits. But the question still remains; do we have a lopsided society in which a handful of people have accumulated the bulk of the wealth produced in our economy? Dubious statistics are offered to demonstrate that 10 percent of the people own two-thirds of the wealth, or three-quarters, or 90 percent, or whatever. Is there any truth in such figures, or do they tell a lie?

There's a fairly simple way to check this out for yourself. Take home ownership. Is it a fact that a handful of people own the homes most of us live in? To the contrary; 45 million homes are owned by the families that occupy them. Assuming the family unit to consist in father, mother and one child this accounts for 135 million persons. Millions of other Americans can afford to own their homes, but choose instead to rent an apartment or a house. Take automobile ownership: 82 million people own their own cars and 33 million own two or more cars. There are 130 million licensed drivers in the country.

Eighty-three million housing units have electric refrigerators; there are 125 million television sets, 55 million of them color; 70 million homes have washing machines; and there is a radio for every man, woman, and child in the country. And as for food, we are the only nation in history whose number one medical problem is overeating! I do not know who concocted the first share-the-wealth scheme. It was ages ago, and it was a pipe dream from the beginning. It is a pipe dream still for most of the world's people. But in America that dream has come true—in large measure. Capitalism—the free economy—has produced material abundance, and the benefits of our prosperity are enjoyed by almost every man, woman, and child in the country—as well as by millions of people around the globe.

Let me pursue this point through one more stage. Most people, when they reflect on the matter, agree that there is no concentration of ownership in everyday things like houses, automobiles, and food. But when they get into the arcane world of the corporation, they are easily misled by those who have twisted "big business" into a four-letter word; they have been led to believe that the industry of this country is owned by a handful of stockholders.

Widespread Ownership

Pick any one of the giant corporations and examine its annual report. I picked Exxon, a fairly large outfit. The 1976 Annual Report reveals that Exxon is owned by approximately 700,000 shareholders;

that's roughly 5^1/$_2$ times as many owners as employees, and it's about as many people as live in the whole state of Delaware. That's a lot of people, but there's more to come.

Note the large number of stockholders who are not individuals but institutions. Every major church body owns shares of stock in industry, but in some statistics a denomination counts as but one stockholder. Several thousand colleges own stock, but each is counted as one stockholder. Your local Bank and Trust Company is a stockholder on behalf of its thousands of depositors; every insurance company owns stock on behalf of its millions of policy holders; every pension fund is invested in stocks. Pension funds, including labor union funds, now own about one-third of the total value of all the stocks listed on the New York exchange. The unions have come to own so large a share of American industry that Peter Drucker refers to this phenomenon as "pension fund socialism." In short, nearly every American owns a chunk of the corporate wealth of America!

Now, it is true, of course, that there are some enormously rich people in this country. What do they do with their money? Some of them spend their money foolishly, just as you and I would do if we were in their shoes. But any millionaire who wants to preserve his fortune and pass it along to his children and their children, has no choice but to invest it in industries which produce the incredible variety of goods which flood the marketplaces of America soliciting the patronage of the masses of consumers. No other society has ever allocated its rewards as generously, or so equitably.

Our present economic system, the system of free enterprise, has met our first two requirements; it has made us an affluent society producing over and above our own needs, an abundance that we have generously shared with the world; and every person who has participated in the production of goods and services shares equally in the fruits of his production.

The third test has to do with an aspiration deeply rooted in human nature; we want to be free; we want the freedom to choose. We want to be free to worship in the church of our choice, to choose our own schools, to read freely and speak our minds. We want to be free to be ourselves, even if this is to practice what others regard as our harmless eccentricities. We want to be free to choose our profession or place of employment. We want solitude when we choose to be alone, and we want the freedom to choose our associates—which includes the right to dissociate. These are some of the demands of human nature itself, this is how God made us. As Jefferson put it, "The God who gave us life gave us liberty at the same time." Therefore, the third demand we make of an economic order is that it manifest, in its operations, a creature who is a freely choosing being.

By Acts of Choice

Man's will is uniquely free. All other creatures—birds, beasts, fish, and so on—obey the laws of their nature willy-nilly. Only man has the capacity to disobey the deep mandates of his being. Ortega, the great Spanish philosopher, remarked that the tiger cannot be detigered but the human being is always in danger of being dehumanized. It is by acts of will, by acts of choice, that man is humanized; and this decision process, in the nature of the case, must be engineered by the individual concerned—by an act of inner resolve. Each person is self-controlling, he is in charge of his own life; and if a person refuses to assume responsibility for himself no one can exercise this role by proxy, from the outside.

The free society is our natural habitat; freedom accords with human nature, and the tactic of freedom as it applies in the economic sector is capitalism, the market economy. The economy is free when the productive activities of men respond sensitively to the needs of consumers, as these needs manifest themselves in people's buying habits. It is true, of course, that when people are free to spend their money as they please they will often spend it foolishly—other people, that is! They'll make mistakes. But isn't that one of the important ways we learn in life, by being free to make mistakes, picking ourselves up every time we fail and standing a bit taller every time we succeed?

The biggest mistake of all is to persuade ourselves that we can avoid the little mistakes people make in a free society by adopting a planned economy. A centrally planned nation is necessarily a command society. Individual persons are no longer free to make their own decisions, their private plans must be cancelled whenever they conflict with the overall political plan. This is a giant step along the road to serfdom.

No Guarantees

To have economic freedom does not, of course, mean that you will be assured the income you think you deserve, or the job to which you think you are entitled. Economic freedom does not dispense with the necessity for work. Its only promise is that you may have your pick from among many employment opportunities, or go into business for yourself. And as a bonus the free economy puts a multiplier onto your efforts, to enrich you far beyond what the same effort returns you under any alternative system.

The American economic system—free enterprise, capitalism, the market economy, call it what you will—has never been as free as the believer in the free society would wish. But it aspires toward freedom, as do most citizens of our country; and our economy has indeed been freer than the economies of other nations. But despite the restrictions and controls, our relatively free economy has (1) delivered goods and services efficiently; it has (2) allocated rewards equitably; and (3) it does expand opportunities for personal choice in society.

There is one final point. Americans are basically a religious people who try to bring moral values to bear on the issues of public life. Does a person have to put aside his religious and moral values while engaged in the sordid business of making a living—as some misguided voices declare? Or is there, as I believe, a vital relationship between market-place and altar? No man's judgment can rise above his understanding of the facts; and as I have pointed out, there is gross misunderstanding of the nature of business and the economy—especially, it seems, among those given to pronouncing moral judgments!

Biblical religion has at least three important and relevant criteria for judging social policy:

(a) the idea of justice voiced by the Old Testament prophets;

(b) the New Testament ideal of the sacredness of persons (i.e., Rights endowed by the Creator); and

(c) the Protestant emphasis on the importance of personal decision—you are closed to God's grace until you decide to open yourself up.

Put these ingredients together in the proper proportions—justice, the sacredness of persons, and the necessity of choice—and you have the free society. The political structures of a free society are designed to assure the inviolability of every person. They maximize his opportunity to pursue his personal goals, and they cultivate an economic order that is guided by consumer demand This was the social goal envisioned by the eighteenth-century Whigs, the men we refer to as the Founding Fathers. What they founded was prepared for by eighteen centuries of tutelage in biblical religion.

Questions Concerning the Morality of Capitalism

This may sound good, the critic tells us, but doesn't the psychology of capitalism take the wraps off greed, and doesn't capitalism elevate money-making to the chief end of man? And didn't Jesus condemn wealth?

The answer to all three question is No. As my first witness I call upon the eminent sociologist Max Weber, and quote from his celebrated book *The Protestant Ethic and the Spirit of Capitalism*. "The impulse to acquisition, pursuit of gain, of money, of the greatest possible amount of money, has in itself nothing to do with capitalism. This impulse exists and has existed among waiters, physicians, coachmen, artists, prostitutes, dishonest officials, soldiers, nobles, crusaders, gamblers, and beggars. It should be taught in the kindergarten of cultural history that this greed for gain is not in the least identical with capitalism, and is still less its spirit." Greed is a human frailty, to be condemned where found and overcome if possible. It is not the exclusive vice of any class or occupation. In any event, it has nothing to do with the efficient production of goods and services in the capitalist order and their equitable distribution.

My second witness is the eminent theologian Reinhold Niebuhr. Late in life, after being converted away from socialism, Niebuhr made a sage comment on the profit motive. Even the minister is economically motivated, he wrote, "when he moves to a new charge because the old one did not give him a big enough parsonage or a salary adequate for his growing family."

We can better understand Jesus' attitude toward material possessions if we contemplate a seeming paradox: Jesus had harsh things to say about the three R's; the three R's in this case being Religion, Righteousness, and Riches! We learn from the Gospels that something which resembles religion, but which is ritualistic and external, may immunize us against the real thing, which is inward and spiritual.

Which of us does not feel, at times, the exasperation which caused a member of Parliament to blow his top and say: "Thank God for the Church of England; it's all that stands between us and Christianity!"

And by the same token, perfunctory righteousness —Pharisaism—may harden the heart and beget an uncharitable spirit. Riches, too, may pose a peril; but this is a matter of degree only, for it is just as common to be infected with a false philosophy of material possessions by a thousand dollars as by a million. Avarice is a common trait in all cultures and at every economic level. There are misers everywhere, and a miser is one who puts his trust in riches, and in so doing he treats means as an end.

This is the point of Jesus' parable of the rich man whose crops were so good that he had to build bigger barns. This good fortune was the man's excuse for saying, "Soul, thou hast much goods laid up for many years! take thine ease, eat, drink, be merry." There is a two-fold point in the parable; the first is that nothing in life justifies a man in assuming this attitude; we must never stop growing. It has been well said that we don't *grow* old, we become old by not growing. The second point is that a material windfall may tempt a man into the error of quitting the struggle for the real goal of life. Jesus condemned the man who put his *trust* in riches, who "layeth up treasure for himself and is not rich toward God." Which is not the same as condemning material possessions *per se,* or wealth held under proper stewardship.

Life is probative; our three score years and ten are a test run. As St. Augustine put it, "We are here schooled for life eternal." And one of the important examination questions concerns the economic use of the planet's scarce resources and the proper management of our material possessions. These are the twin facets of Christian stewardship, and poor performance here will result in dire consequences. As Jesus put it, "If, therefore, you have not been faithful in the use of worldly wealth, who will entrust to you the true riches?"

Economics, the science of means, needs religion, the science of ends. To inflate a means into an end is idolatry. In sober truth, no economic system can be anything more than a means. The ends for which life should be lived take us into another dimension, into the domain of our moral and religious life. As created beings we are de-signed to achieve a transcendent end: "Thou hast made us for Thyself, and our hearts are restless until they find rest in Thee." But if we are to live as we should live during this life, we must be free; and one of the imperatives of the free life is freedom of economic enterprise.

Perspectives on Religion and Capitalism

The two major terms in my title are subject to extravagant misunderstanding and occasional abuse. Some of this is natural, due to limited knowledge; much of it is willful and ideological. It is appropriate, therefore, that I try to elucidate at the very beginning how the term "religion" is to be used in this paper. The meanings I attach to "capitalism" will be clarified as we proceed.

It is my understanding that religion, at bottom, is not one sector of human experience; it is more like a common core. A college or university, for academic purposes, may have a department of religion alongside departments of chemistry, history, mathematics, or whatever, and this fact may mislead. In actual living, and in its deepest sense, your religion is not one subject among other subjects; your religion is the fundamental way you approach, understand, and evaluate all subjects. It consists of your first principles, the truths you regard as self-evident, the basic axioms you take for granted, and through which you view everything else. Your religion colors your outlook upon the universe, affecting the way you look upon life, your relation to other people, your treatment of things.

Religion is many faceted; it has its history, its doctrines, its exercises, its rituals, its ecclesiastical structures, and so on. But the central core of every religion is its vision of the cosmos, its understanding of the nature of ultimate reality. For the purpose of this paper I shall put aside several important elements of religion and use the term as equivalent to worldview, or *Weltanschauung*. Everyone entertains some image of the entire scheme of things, a mental picture of what the totality—in the final analysis—is like. Some have pictured the universe as an immense and intricate piece of clockwork, a mechanism; others regard it as a gigantic organism, or as the great ocean of being, or as a featureless Absolute. Everyone operates in terms of some image of the nature-of-things, for to be human is to be a metaphysician. My own world-view is that of Christian theism.

From the December 1981 issue of *The Freeman*.

A Creative Intelligence

Those who entertain the religious—or theistic—worldview conduct their lives on the premise that a Creative Intelligence is working out its mighty purposes through nature, in history, and above all, by means of persons. The Divine Intelligence is creative, as witness the continuing emergence of novelty on the world scene; the Divine Creativity is intelligent, because wherever we look we find a deft and ingenious adaptation of means to ends. There is order, beauty, elegance, economy, and balance from one end of this universe to the other. Human beings may come to a sense of kinship with this Creative Intelligence by aligning themselves with the movement and configuration of its thrust.

At the same time we may become keenly aware that vast stretches of this universe appear to be indifferent to us. I refer to the natural order, the realm of nature subject to the laws of physics, chemistry, and the other sciences. Cause and effect operate inexorably in nature, independent of our fears and wishes. A stone falls to earth in response to the tug of gravity, and we have no choice but to adjust our actions to this and other physical laws. Natural forces affect our actions, and natural disasters cause human injury and sometimes death. The natural world piques our curiosity, and we seek to understand it so as to cope with it more successfully. Nature will never surrender unconditionally to man, but nature's stubborn otherness provides a necessary condition for the exercise of human freedom.

The nature we confront is a nonhuman Other, and this Other is neutral, so far as we as individuals are concerned; the rain falls on the just and the unjust alike. But if this were not so—if the Other were responsive to the conflicting and the constantly changing whims of billions of human beings, submissive to our rituals and incantations—if the Other were not largely neutral and/or indifferent it would be chaotic.

Actually, the Other is an order, a vast and comprehensible order consisting in discoverable patterns and recurrences. The neutral orderliness of nature provides a basis for understanding and explanation; it affords a significant measure of predictability, allowing us to plan our lives and achieve our goals. A neutral order provides the necessary condition for exercise of the freedoms and powers proper to human nature. And as we come into a working relationship with the Other a sense of kinship begins to develop.

Let me illustrate: A man confronts a portion of the Other in the form of a body of water: a pond or a stream. He complains because the water is cold, wet, and indifferent to him; furthermore, the water is an obstruction, impeding him as he wades through it. But this same water, to an expert swimmer, is the necessary vehicle for his freedom as a swimmer. The swimmer does not complain about the water's friction, even though it does impede his progress through it and slows his speed. For him the friction of the water is the same thing as its buoyancy, and without the buoyancy swimming would be impossible. The exhilaration our athlete derives from a vigorous swim begets his belief in the friendliness of at least this little segment of the cosmos— which now appears to have been constructed just for his delight. The relation is symbiotic. There is resonance between ourselves and the Other.

The realm of nature out there may sometimes appear arbitrary, indifferent to human values, or even antagonistic. But shift perspective even slightly and we realize that if nature were not neutral—that is, if nature could be bent to the human will we would not be free beings. If nature were not largely recalcitrant and unyielding, we free beings would have no incentive to cooperate intelligently with it, making use of its forces to advance our purposes—simultaneously strengthening our own powers and refining our skills as we do so.

Human Capacity for Choice

It is obvious that we human beings do not merely react mechanically to external stimuli—we are capable of a creative response to our environment. B. F. Skinner and his behaviorists declare that human beings are capable of little more than a Pavlovian reaction to a stimulus; they speak for themselves. They don't speak for us, for at the very core of our being we bear the imprint of the Creative Intelligence which is back of all things. We are gifted with free will, and it is this capacity for choice which makes us partakers of the primordial creativity.

Let me offer you some words of the great Russian religious philosopher Nicholas Berdyaev: "God created man in his own image and likeness, i.e., made him a creator too, calling him to free spontaneous activity and not to formal obedience to His power. Free creativeness is the creature's answer to the great call of its creator. Man's creative work is the fulfillment of the Creator's secret will."

Human nature is threefold; we are implicated in nature, we are part of some society, and we are touched by the sacred. We human beings, with a portion of our being, are directly geared into nature. Drop us from a height and gravity operates on us just as it does on a sack of grain. The chemical processes going on inside our bodies differ little from the way those chemicals interact outside our bodies. We are largely within the same network of causal sequences which characterize nature.

We are natural beings, but that's not all we are. We are also social beings, involved in history. Occurrences in nature are explained in terms of causes; actions in history and society are explained in terms of choices. Society is our natural habitat. Society is a spontaneous order—as F. A. Hayek has taught us—emerging out of human choices but not resulting from conscious human design.

Social order—comprising both the written and the unwritten law, together with custom, convention, habit, and taste—social order may occasionally appear to stand athwart the individual to frustrate his immediate intentions. But everyone knows, on sober second thought, that our very survival as individuals depends on social cooperation under the division of labor; human beings are interdependent. Everyone, therefore, has a personal stake in the fashioning, the strengthening, and the refining of the structures of a free society. The free society provides the optimum environment for every productive, peaceful person.

Participants in a Divine Order

There are natural elements in our makeup, and everyone carries a portion of some society in his very being. And there is a third thing. Analyze human nature and you discover elements in it which are not reducible to either nature or society, important as those facets of human nature are. We participate in an order of reality which is beyond nature and beyond society. Call this the sacred order or the divine order, if you wish; or call it God—the unconditioned Creative Intelligence in which all contingent existence, including our own, is grounded.

The word "supernatural" has been battered beyond use, and in any event, it is completely "natural" for the person to bear the marks of sacredness in his own being. This fact has important political implications. In the eighteenth century, this central sacredness in the person—

as he is conceived within the theistic worldview—was politically translated. The sacred in persons found secular expression as the idea of inherent individual rights "endowed by the Creator," the rights referred to in our own Declaration of Independence.

Given the idea of individual rights, in virtue of what a person genuinely is in his true being, it is the task of political philosophy to fashion a legal structure designed to protect every person's private domain, secure the rights of all persons equally, and maximize everyone's opportunity to choose and pursue his personal goals. A uniquely religious political philosophy oriented toward these ends was called Whiggism in the eighteenth century, and Liberalism during much of the nineteenth. Whiggism and Liberalism endeavored to protect each person in his life, his liberty, and his property. The free economy, or capitalism, is the natural counterpart to Whiggism; you get capitalism in the second place when you have Whiggism in the first place. Whiggism lays the necessary political ground work for the set of economic arrangements called capitalism.

The Capitalistic Order

As nineteenth-century Classical Liberalism turned into the diametrically opposed thing called liberalism today, the economic order became less and less free market as governmental regulations and controls progressively expanded over the economy. Capitalism—ideally—means simply private property, individual liberty, and the voluntary exchange of goods and services between freely contracting parties.

Capitalism is what happens in the realm of industry and trade when force and fraud are eliminated from that realm. It involves peaceful competition for the privilege of serving consumers better, with a reward in the form of profit going to anyone the consumers believe has served them well. Capitalism is the only productive economic order, and the only equitable one; it submits everyone's offering of goods and services to the collective judgment of his peers and rewards him according to his contribution—as his peers assess it.

I firmly believe that a society of free people is impossible if economic actions are fettered and controlled by the government bureaucracy. The free market economy, or capitalism, is the only way free people can organize their bread and butter activities—business, industry, and trade. This mode of economic activity—capitalism—enjoys a symbiotic relationship with the legal system and political structures called Whiggism in the eighteenth century. Whiggism and capitalism are the two sides of the same coin; you can't have one without the other.

Whiggery goes back to the seventeenth century—although Lord Acton made a good point when he referred to St. Thomas Aquinas as the first Whig. The Puritan religious movement in seventeenth-century England spawned a political arm of Dissenters and Nonconformists in opposition to the court party, whose members were contemptuously called Whiggamores—a Scottish term for horse thieves. Whiggery bore its best fruit on these shores, in the Declaration of Independence, the Constitution, and *The Federalist Papers*.

Whiggery in America

Whiggery gave rise to political structures designed around the sovereign individual person, to secure his rights, protect his private domain, and afford him maximum scope to pursue his personal goals. These legal and political structures—which are the earmark of a free society—represent the secular projection of a religious vision of man and the universe unique to Western civilization.

The introduction of Christianity into the Classical World of two thousand years ago had important political consequences, for this religion taught that only a part of man is social; a portion of his being is God's. That which is God's is sharply marked off from that which is Caesar's. The realm which is Caesar's becomes a mere province in the all-encompassing Kingdom which is God's.

There are half-gods, false gods, and tribal deities—idols all. We worship the gods of power, wealth, fame, or pleasure—or whatever else evokes our highest priorities. Some god you must have. Whatever thing you value so much that you would sacrifice all other values to it; whatever elicits your ultimate devotion; that which you invest your most ardent emotions in—this is your god. The nation state in our time usurps a god-like role as the arbiter of men's destiny. It is a chief characteristic of the twentieth century that multitudes of men and women in the worldwide mass movements of our time—secular faiths like Communism, Fascism, and Naziism—have consecrated first-rate loyalty and devotion to fifth-rate dictators.

Every human being is capable of first-rate loyalty and dedication, and logically we need to match this up with a first-rate object, the Object of ultimate concern—the one true God. Only the Supreme Being, God, merits the utmost devotion and consecration of which human beings are capable.

Religious Premises

If there is to be a society—in the sense of a culture—there must be a measure of agreement as to the relation between God and man, and as to the nature of man and his proper end. There must be some agreement as to what constitutes justice, honor, and virtue. The source from which a society derives its understanding of these matters is its religion. In this sense, every society is cradled in some religion, Christian or otherwise. The culture of China is unthinkable without Confucianism; Indian society is the expression of Hinduism; and Islam is composed of followers of Mohammed. In like fashion, our Western culture stems from the Judeo-Christian tradition; we are a branch of Christendom.

Our own institutions and way of life are intimately related to the basic dogmas of the Christian religion. From this faith we derive our notions of the meaning of life, the moral order, the dignity of persons, and the rights and responsibilities of individuals. Ours is a religious society, but it has its counterpart in a secular state. The Constitution forbids an official church, an act which permits religion to exercise its unique authority directly, unhampered by ecclesiasticism.

Capitalism Under Fire

The word "capitalism" itself has always been controversial, having been brought into use by Marxist writers for polemical purposes. Werner Sombart, a Marxist, claims to have been the first to use the term "capitalism" systematically in his analyses published around the turn of the century. The term still has pejorative connotations, as many people use it, including those who prepare ecclesiastical pronouncements.

The World Council of Churches was launched at a meeting of churchmen in Amsterdam in 1948. This ecumenical group appointed a commission on The Church and the Disorder of Society, chaired by one of my former teachers, John C. Bennett. The report of this commission kicked up a considerable stir because it recommended that "The Christian Churches should reject the ideologies of both *laissez faire* capitalism and communism. . . . " When the press asked Dr. Bennett what he had in mind as the middle ground between Communism and capitalism, he said it was British Trades Union socialism.

Precisely what did Mr. Bennett and his commission think they were rejecting when they turned their backs on capitalism? Well, they told us, by listing the four earmarks of the thing they dismissed. I quote from their report. (1) "Capitalism tends to subordinate what should be the primary task of any economy—the meeting of human needs—to the economic advantages of those who have most power over its institutions; (2) it tends to produce serious inequalities; (3) it has developed a practical form of materialism among Western nations in spite of their Christian backgrounds, for it has placed the greatest emphasis upon success in making money; (4) it has also kept the people of capitalist countries subject to a kind of fate which has taken the form of such social catastrophes as mass unemployment."

Everyone who has had even a limited exposure to the economic thought of men like Mises, Hayek, Friedman, or Hazlitt recognizes the flavor of schoolboy Marxism in these allegations. If there is a form of social organization which gives economic advantages to the powerful at the expense of the rest of us, makes money grubbing the highest good, and periodically throws masses of people out of work—then every person of good sense and good will would oppose that system.

But if you really want to dismantle the thing Dr. Bennett and his cohorts ignorantly label "capitalism," there's only one way to do it, and that is to labor on behalf of the free society on all three of its levels; the free market economy, the Whig political structures which sustain it, and the theistic *Weltanschauung* on which all the rest depends.

The Rule of Law

Whiggery insists on the Rule of Law—one law for all persons alike, because all are one in their essential humanness. Equality before the bar of justice means maximum liberty for all persons. In *The Wealth of Nations,* Adam Smith speaks of his "liberal system of liberty, equality and justice." People are free to the extent that such ideals come to prevail in practice, and the only economic arrangement compatible with a free people is the market economy, or capitalism properly understood.

I should like to speak for a moment about the important distinction between principle and practice, or theory and history. Many good illustrations of this point are to be found in the history of the Church over the past nineteen centuries, where we find several instances of a wide discrepancy between Gospel Christianity and the practices of the Church in certain eras. The Church has occasionally sanctioned tyrannous political rule, it has lent its support to persecutions, inquisitions, and crusades. It has forgotten its primary mission while pursuing secular ends like wealth and power.

In the economic realm, too, principle is sometimes obscured by malpractice. The late Wilhelm Roepke put it this way: "We must make a sharp distinction between the principle of a market economy as such ... and the actual development which during the nineteenth and twentieth centuries had led to the *historical* form of market economy. One is a philosophical category, the other an historical individuality ... a nonrecurrent compound of economic, social, legal, political, moral and cultural elements. ..."

The theory of free market economics is one thing; the way some people used or misused such economic freedom as was available to them in 1870 or 1910 or 1960 is something else again. A listing of the misuse or abuse of any specific freedom cannot be made part of a case against that freedom, for a mere multiplication of instances does not constitute proof one way or another. The case for freedom of the press does not stand or fall, depending on any evidence you might muster that editors are idiots and reporters knaves.

It is absolutely certain that freedom will be misused, simply because we are human beings. The fact that people sometimes misuse their freedom is indeed bad, but to try to correct the misuse of freedom by the denial of freedom would be infinitely worse. If there were a Richter Scale to measure social dislocation, the misuse of freedom would be one or two; the denial of freedom would be seven or eight—disaster.

Take this matter of academic freedom—a principle nobly exemplified by many educational institutions. Academic freedom does not justify the expectation that you will have Einsteins in the physics department, Nobel prize winners in chemistry, or a Whitehead in philosophy. Academic freedom could be justified on its own terms even if it could be demonstrated that the majority of professors had mail order degrees, turned up tipsy in class, and never cracked a book. Given these conditions on a campus there would be good grounds for a faculty house-cleaning; but a catalogue of these bad conditions does not add up to the first step in the argument against the principle of academic freedom.

Academic freedom is a sound principle even if many teachers are incompetent and others betray their profession. We defend freedom of speech and freedom of the press even though we are dismayed by the inferior quality of much of the spoken and written word. Freedom of worship is a good thing and we stand for separation of Church and State even though some of the results are not to our liking. And by the same token we believe in freedom of economic enterprise—even though consumer demands and producer responses to them fall short of the Good, the True, and the Beautiful. As do the efforts of some contemporary philosophers, I dare say.

Economic Freedom

Economic freedom is to be cherished for itself, just as we cherish every one of our liberties. But economic freedom is doubly important because it sustains all the rest; economic freedom is the means to every one of our other ends. Economic freedom represents our livelihood, and whoever controls our livelihood has acquired critical leverage over every other aspect of our lives as well.

We stress private property as an absolutely essential ingredient of a society of free people, an ancient bit of wisdom which Alexander Hamilton referred to twice in *The Federalist*. In the 79th Paper Hamilton wrote: "In the general course of human nature, a power over a man's subsistence amounts to a power over his will." Control the economy and you control people. So it is not simply for the sake of economic freedom and the prosperity it creates that we argue that business, industry, and trade should come within the Rule of Law and be freed from governmental dictates, and bureaucratic regulations.

Incidentally, the free economy does not go unregulated—operating within the Rule of Law, the economy is regulated by the buying habits of consumers. We defend economic freedom—voluntary exchanges of goods and services between freely contracting parties—

because every one of our more important freedoms depends critically on private property and free exchange.

It is my contention that a society of free people has a free economic order as an essential element of it. John Maynard Keynes, in back-handed fashion, lends support to my contention by declaring that his theory of economic planning adapts nicely to a totalitarian political order. In a Foreword to the 1936 German translation of his *General Theory,* Keynes had this to say: "The theory of aggregate production, which is the point of the following book, nevertheless can be much easier adapted to the conditions of a totalitarian state than ... under conditions of free production and a large degree of laissez-faire."

Axioms of a Free Society

Capitalism—the free economy—appeared on the political foundation laid down during the eighteenth century by Whiggism in a period when the cultural climate of the West was at least vestigially Christian. The intellectual soil of Europe still bore the marks of centuries of tilling by the teachings of the Church. Theism had yielded to Deism in the eighteenth century but Deism was not secularism, and Deism did lay great stress on the three basic axioms of a free society: (1) each person is endowed with certain rights; (2) each person is gifted with free will; and (3) there is a moral law binding on all persons alike.

The eighteenth century's faith in reason really constitutes a fourth axiom; this was the belief that the universe is rationally structured, and so, by taking thought, unaided by revelation, we could convincingly prove that human beings possess inherent rights, free will, and a conscience which attaches them to the moral law. These four items constitute the heart of the religious *Weltanschauung.* If your image of the cosmos has these ingredients—reason, rights, free will, and the moral law—you have the proper religious foundation for the free society, of which the economic expression is capitalism.

The nineteenth century brought about a complete change in worldview, from Deism to Materialism. The latter finds its explicit and most familiar exposition in the Dialectical Materialism of Marx. The worldview of Marxism has no genuine place for reason, free will, the moral law, or the sacredness of persons. The same is true of every other variety of Materialism. Materialism sometimes goes by other labels, such as Naturalism, or Secularism, or Positivism, or Humanism.

Whatever the name, the thing here discussed is the theory which maintains that reality is reducible, ultimately, to mechanical arrangements of material particles. This is the nontheistic *Weltanschauung,* logically denying everything the theistic *Weltanschauung* affirms: inherent rights, reason, free will, and the moral law. Some Materialists may assert one or more of these religious axioms, but none of these axioms can logically be grounded in a universe consisting ultimately of nothing more than material particles, electrical charges, or whatever.

We hear much talk these days about "rights," but to call something a "right" does not make it a right. Privileges, granted or withheld at the discretion of the state, may be called "rights," but this notion is worlds apart from the idea of individual sovereignty in virtue of a sacredness in the very being of each person.

Free Will and Morality

Free will is incompatible with philosophical Materialism. If man is wholly natural, and if Nature is all-there-is, and if Nature is the realm where cause and effect operate inexorably, then men and women are as much caught up in causal sequences as water, stones, gases, and everything else. It follows that free will is a delusion, determinism a fact. "Man is unconditionally subject to the natural conditions of his environment," a leading thinker tells us. Man does not act; like everything else in nature he is acted upon; he merely reacts.

A mechanistic universe has no moral dimension; there is no right and wrong *per se*. But people can't avoid making moral decisions; human beings are habituated to thinking in moral terms, or perhaps the human mind is so constructed that it cannot function outside the moral categories. Those who assert that the universe lacks a moral dimension frequently argue that the social system determines what is right and what is wrong—which is to subordinate ethics to politics.

Again, one hears it said that each person decides for himself what is right and wrong for him. The inference is that the private will of each person is his only "authority"—there being no external norms or standards universally binding, to which the will and actions of every person should conform. Every man rolls his own and does his own thing. Whim, impulse, instinct, inclination, are the spurs of action. "If it feels good, do it," is the contemporary folk wisdom conveyed by bumper stickers.

If the cosmos provides no clues for human conduct; if justice is of merely human contrivance, representing the interest of the powerful, then no one has any moral obligation to do anything when he happens to feel like doing something else. By the same token, no one has any warrant for telling anyone else what he ought to do, or not do. This is what each person decides for himself, each getting his kicks in his own way, each doing whatever turns him on. The old covenant has been shattered, the rule book discarded.

Having reached this point, the argument is hoist with its own petard. The weak doing their thing are at the mercy of the strong doing theirs. The unscrupulous doing their thing is why good guys finish last. Some people get their kicks by preventing other people from getting theirs, and there is no rule to say them nay. Those who want to live and let live are put under the thumb of those who strive for ascendancy over others because for these latter the exercise of power "feels good." You cannot tell those who hanker after power that tyranny is "wrong," because they will tell you that wielding power is "their thing," which you have been at such pains to tell them to pursue!

The nontheistic world view has no real niche for the concepts of inherent rights and free will; it has discarded the norms without which no genuine ethical decision is possible; it makes reason the tool of class interest. Materialism is the appropriate ideology for a totalitarian society, but the Materialist who seeks to provide a rationale for the free society has saddled himself with an impossible task.

The Moral Foundations

Economic arguments for capitalism fall on deaf ears unless people, on other grounds, have first embraced a philosophy of man and society which incites them to seek their own good while working for the well-being of the whole community, that is to say, when they have given proper weight to the argument for the free society based on ethics, inherent rights, and free will.

The ethical argument for the free society limits governmental power by surrounding it with moral restraints. There is not one law for magistrates and another for citizens; rulers and ruled are alike under the moral law. Statutes must conform to a higher law, or divine law, superior to the enactments of legislators, discovered by reason and intuition.

The argument from inherent rights views society's political agency as having the negative function of securing each person's private domain, protecting his life, liberty, and property, in order that he might have maximum freedom to pursue his personal goals.

The argument from free will is that the free society-free economy—Whiggism-Capitalism—provides the only social arrangements consonant with the nature of a creature gifted with the capacity to choose. The fact that each person is in charge of his own life, responsible for making the countless decisions required to bring his life toward completion, requires social conditions of maximum opportunity for choice. Human nature and the free society are complementary, two sides of the same coin. A society humane and just needs economic arrangements to match, and this means capitalism.

The free economy does not beget itself; the free economy appears only after we have the free society. And the free society emerges only after generations of exposure to the idea that there is a sacredness in persons which, in the political and economic spheres, demands liberty and justice for all. It is a mandate of our better nature as well as a requirement of our religion, that we work toward a society which every person has the widest possible scope to exercise his capacity as a freely choosing person, guiding his life by reason, within the moral law.

Liberalism and Religion

Classical Liberalism created a revolutionary new view of the political State, its nature and proper functions. We may better understand this sea change in political thought if we contrast the secular state of liberalism with its polar opposite found in the ancient world. The great authority on the ancient city, Fustel de Coulanges, tells us that "the state was a religious community, the king a pontiff, the magistrate a priest, and the law a sacred formula." The Greek *polis* was Church and State in one, Julius Caesar was Pontifex Maximus; the citizen was bound to the State body and soul. When civic and religious obligations are combined and owed to the same institution we have that absolute power dreaded by Lord Acton.

It was the great achievement of Classical Liberalism, with its roots in the post-Reformation era and mood, to desacralize the political order, thus stripping the State of its religious and moral pretensions. Holy empires and sacred monarchies claiming transcendent sanction have prevailed throughout history, and the State was venerated as an order of salvation. From now on, however, the sanctions of the State were to be much more modest, its objectives limited to constabulary functions; "the night watchman State," as a critic dubbed it.

No longer would the State assume responsibilities beyond its competence for the moral and spiritual regeneration of men and women. "It is not for a disdain of spiritual goods that liberalism concerns itself exclusively with man's material well-being," writes Mises in *Liberalism,* "but from a conviction that what is highest and deepest in man cannot be touched by any outward regulation" (p. 4). The tutoring and renewal of the human mind and spirit would, from now on, be the task of Church and School—in the broadest sense—so these institutions were pried out from under the State's umbrella and assumed the autonomy they must have if they are to achieve their purposes.

"Separation of Church and State" is repeated endlessly and mindlessly among us, so that the idea of a secular State is now commonplace. But it was a novel idea in the seventeenth century, and it has not taken root anywhere in the world except in regions responsive to the

From the November 1985 issue of *The Freeman.*

influence of classical liberalism. What was the seed idea which eventually germinated as the concept of a secular State? And what was the milieu in which the seed took root? It was a milieu in which an aura of sanctity might be attached to virtually anything; trees, rivers, stones, animals, as well as to the social order itself. And of course there were priest-kings, divine monarchs, and holy emperors.

The Old Testament records a sharp break with this mentality, a new departure which removes the idea of the holy from nature and society and rests it exclusively with the transcendent deity: "I am your Lord, your Holy One, the Creator of Israel, your King." H. Frankfort, in his *Kingship and the Gods,* elaborates: "In the light of Egyptian, and even Mesopotamian, kingship, that of the Hebrews lacks sanctity. The relation between the Hebrew monarch and his people was as nearly secular as is possible in a society wherein religion is a living force." The distinction between civic and sacred is sharpened in the New Testament, especially in Jesus' rejoinder to a trap question: "Render unto Caesar that which is Caesar's, and unto God that which is God's." The realm of Caesar, the State, is now shorn of its lofty conceits. The State is a necessary and useful institution, but there's nothing divine or sacred about it. Only God is holy, and there is something of the divine in persons; but not in the social order—the State is secular.

There is a private domain in man, touched by the sacred, to which only the individual has rightful access. Invasion of this self by any other constitutes a violation, and the State's apparatus of compulsion is set up precisely to punish trespasses of this sort. Wanton killing is the most flagrant of violations and it is the law's business to punish murder. Stealing is a violation of the bonds of ownership and is the ground for laws against theft. And because no person can be held accountable for his actions, nor realize his potential, unless he is free, the law seeks to secure equal freedom for all persons. In short, each person has inherent rights, derived from a source beyond nature and society, to his life, his liberty and his property; and it is the function of the Law to secure these rights.

The State's ability to punish evil should not create any expectation that the State can enforce good. Goodness must be voluntary, and the most the State can do on behalf of goodness is to curb evildoers and thus create "a free field and no favor" where right thinking and well doing of every variety can take root.

The State began to get out of the religion business early in the modern era; the press got free, and speech was unfettered. Adam Smith demonstrated that the economy did not need political controls, but only the Rule of Law, which preserved social cooperation under the division of labor. The best things in life began to flourish in regions outside the domain of politics: family, friendship, fellowship, conversation, work, hobbies, art, music, worship. . . .

It was a noble vision, but it did not promise utopia and thus disappointed those who demanded a heaven on earth. A little more realism on this point and the vision may yet take hold again.

Socialism—Substance and Label

Americans appear to like most everything about socialism except the name. Let a politician lift a plank out of the old time Socialist Party platform, paint it red, white, and blue to disguise its origin, and the voters will go on a stampede until they find some office for him. Socialism, thus domesticated, is safe and sane enough for a Fourth of July oration. But if an opinion poll is taken by these same voters it reveals that they are as hostile to the socialist label as they are friendly to its substance. "For the great majority of Americans," laments a pair of certified thinkers who jointly edit a socialist monthly, "'socialism' is little more than a dirty word."

Thus is was necessary for Mr. W. Averell Harriman, when he directed the mutual security program, to explain away foreign "socialism" for the inquiring members of a Senate committee. "Now this word [sic!] 'Socialist Party' is much misunderstood here, because it is a general term. In many countries the Socialist Party is what we would call here the New Deal Party or a Fair Deal Party and not the theoretical socialist of the historic kind."

This confusion about socialism as between substance and label bespeaks the need of a definition. As a first step, turn to Webster's dictionary. There we read this: "Socialism: A political and economic theory of social organization based on collective or governmental ownership and democratic management of the essential means for the production and distribution of goods." This definition may be sharpened to read as follows: "A conviction or belief that organized police force—government—should dictate the creative activities of citizens within a society by the ownership and/or control of the means of production and exchange."

Such definitions as these are all right as far as they go, but they omit an important fact about socialism: that it is a substitute religion for many people, arousing all the emotional response and ethical fervor of genuine religion. It is a dream of the kingdom of God on earth— but, as von Huegel observed, "without a king and without a God."

From the February 1960 issue of *The Freeman*.

It was such a religion to H. G. Wells, for example. Wells stands about halfway between Karl Marx and the present. He was active among the early Fabians in Great Britain and wrote a book, *New Worlds for Old,* about fifty years ago. In it he said,

"Socialism is to me a very great thing indeed, the form and substance of my ideal life and all the religion I possess. I am, by a sort of predestination, a socialist. I perceive I cannot help talking and writing about socialism, and shaping and forwarding socialism. I am one of a succession—one of a growing multitude of witnesses, who will continue. It does not—in the larger sense—matter how many generations of us must toil and testify. It does not matter, except as our individual concern, how individually we succeed or fail, what blunders we make, what thwartings we encounter, what follies and inadequacies darken our private hopes and level our personal imaginations to the dust. We have the light. We know what we are for, and that the light that now glimmers so dimly through us must in the end prevail."

This apocalyptic mood was shared by Americans in the early decades of this century. One of these was the prominent socialist, George D. Herron. He wrote, "There is approaching—and it is not so far off as it seems—a world arranged by the wisdom hid in the human heart; a world that is the organization of a strong and universal kindness; a world redeemed from the fear of institutions and of poverty. Even now, derided and discouraged as it is, socially untrained and inexperienced as it is, if the instinctual and repressed kindness of mankind were suddenly let loose upon the earth, sooner than we think would we be members one of another, sitting around one family hearthstone, and singing the song of the new humanity."

In Aristotle's View

These harbingers of a terrestrial paradise by legislative fiat are not without antecedents. Aristotle encountered them. Proposals for legislative interference have "a specious air of benevolence," he says, causing an audience to accept them with delight, supposing, "especially when abuses under the existing system are denounced as due to private property, that under communism everyone will miraculously become everyone else's friend." But Aristotle comments, "the real cause of these evils is not private property but the wickedness of human nature."

The men for whom socialism is a kind of religion, see it as the fulfillment of mankind's age-old dream of justice and good will on earth. Lenin brought to fruition the seeds planted as far back as the Old Testament prophets! Harry Laidler, of the League for Industrial Democracy, opens his *History of Socialist Thought* (1927) with a chapter in praise of Amos, Hosea, Isaiah, Jesus, and St. Augustine. This tactic of marshaling the great figures of our religious tradition under the banner of socialism is designed to make the critic of modern socialism appear in opposition to the spiritual giants of our race.

The Methods Kill the Dream

But the dream of justice and good will among men is by no means the exclusive possession of socialists; it is a dream shared by all men of generous instincts. It is possible to demonstrate, moreover, that the good things, both material and spiritual, that we desire for all men are undermined by methods socialists use to attain them. The socialist dream is shattered by the operational imperatives of socialist performance. This is not only true of Russian practice; it is implicit in socialist theory.

Socialists propose to realize their dreams by putting the productive powers of men under the direction and control of the state. Socialists prefer to speak of the social ownership of property. But society— which means all of us—cannot act as a whole to own and control property; it must act through its enforcement agency, which is government. The men who comprise the governing agency in any society are a small minority within that society.

In practice, therefore, a socialist society is one in which the vast majority of men are controlled by the tiny minority which has power to direct their economic activities. We might put the matter differently by saying that the socialist dream is based on the delusion that men's other freedoms will be enhanced if they are deprived of economic liberty. By eliminating economic liberty and replacing it with a planned economy socialists hope to usher in a brave new world.

It hasn't worked out that way in practice because the theory is all wrong. "Economic control is not merely control of a sector of human life which can be separated from the rest," writes F. A. Hayek, "it is control of the means for all our ends." Eliminate economic liberty in a society and you begin to institute a master-slave relationship. The

guiding ideals which ushered in the modern period aimed at the liberation of the individual; from ecclesiastical corruption, from political
tyranny, and from economic bondage. These movements of liberation
converge and the individual is more firmly fettered than ever before.
What a strange denouement! How did it happen?

Chronic Discontent

Socialism, as mood, theory, and practice, is a result of the material
abundance made possible by the Industrial Revolution. Millions of
people had toiled close to the soil for millennia, only to be rewarded
by a bare subsistence, at best; at worst by plague and famine. Until the
modern era, poverty was hardly more attributed to human arrangements than to cosmic setting; one seemed about as fixed as the other.
Generations toiled, fed, bred, and died; and, because of the general
conviction that such was man's fate, entertained little hope of bettering
their circumstances. The expectation of unimaginable progress was
released by the revolutionary changes which mark the modern period,
a period characterized until recently by expanding political liberty,
invention and technology, capitalist production, and relative material
abundance. Men ceased to yearn for compensatory delights in the
world to come and began to dream of getting their New Jerusalem
now in "England's green and pleasant land."

Secular hopes grew wildly, and material progress seemed to justify
them. Conditions of existence were ameliorated. Life expectancy increased; many diseases were eliminated. Populations have increased at
an accelerated rate since 1800; but in spite of this, the additional
mouths were better fed and the additional bodies were better housed
and clothed. But this was not enough. For those whose expectations
can only be summed up by one word, "More!" no additional incre-
ment is ever enough.

Given this mood, discontent becomes chronic in the modern
world. Material progress must forever trail behind expectation because,
in the nature of things, economic goods are always in short supply.
This does not reflect a human failure; it is a built-in feature of the
universe. A thing is not an economic good unless it is scarce relative
to human demand for it. Human demands, being limitless, invariably
outrun supplies, which are naturally limited. This simple fact is widely
overlooked, with the result that a sense of grievance has become en-

demic among large numbers of people. It is simply a reflex of the contrast between a utopian vision and actual living conditions.

Being poor is endurable, and besides, poverty is a relative matter. But the feeling that one is being *kept* poor raises an issue of an altogether different sort; justice is involved. Embracing the practical possibility of a heaven on earth is the first false step; belief in a conspiracy which prevents it from arriving is the second. A mind which entertains the first foolishness is ripe to be infected with the second.

A sense of grievance is, of all human emotions, the easiest to exploit; and exploited it was, by grievance collectors and demagogues. Political power had been wrested from the kings and distributed according to the democratic formula. But after the flow of exaltation over popular sovereignty had worn off, it was noticed that the anticipated new dawn had not broken. The immediate inference was that someone must be holding it back. The bottleneck could not be political—the democratic revolution assured that; therefore, it must be economic. A conspiracy of capitalists prevented the arrival of utopia! Obviously, we needed an economic revolution.

"Das Kapital"

The word "capitalist" was a Marxian term, imported into the language for polemical purposes and as a term of abuse. The "capitalist" was the owner of the factories, machines, and tools. He employed people to run his equipment and then, in his depravity, stole everything they produced except for the pittance they needed to stay alive.

This "surplus value" theory would never have been broached—or, if broached, would never have caught on—except that the mentality of the period consisted of a utopian expectation, a sense of grievance, and a belief that the masses were victims of a conspiracy. Out of this soil sprang modern collectivist movements, Marxian and otherwise.

But collectivism has been fed by another tributary as well, a nontheoretical one. Classic Liberalism distrusted the state, *per se*. On principle it threw up safeguards to protect society from undue extensions of political power. But the democratic principle does not address itself to the problem of limiting political authority; it is concerned only to get the state operating under popular auspices, or majority rule. If a majority wants the state to undertake some function, there is nothing in the democratic principle to forbid it, however unjust it might be,

222 / *Edmund A. Opitz*

or however violative of the principles of liberalism, which make for limited government.

Perpetuation of Power

The nature of political action is constant, regardless of the auspices under which it operates. It is of the nature of power to want to perpetuate itself and, following this mandate, every government seeks to create the means of its own support. The Court at Versailles, under the old regime, was largely a group of wastrels depending on government handouts for their mode of life. Their consumption was nothing if not conspicuous. Political subventions, under a democracy are more subtle, but the feeling spreads that everyone is entitled to all he can get.

Government comes to be regarded as a benign omnipotence possessing the magical properties of an Aladdin's lamp. If properly approached—by means of a lobby or pressure group which knows which buttons to push, which levers to pull—it delivers the goods as obediently as a vending machine. Government is a tool capable of accomplishing anything a majority can be mustered to demand. "Majority" is a technical term among political pros, referring to a numerical figment used by a literal minority to justify a handout from the public treasury. Democracy and majority rule become a screen behind which insiders operate under the formula: *Votes and taxes for all, subsidies for us*.

Given popular acceptance of the Service State—a political authority presumed to be responsive to majority demand, and it is inevitable that democratic governments would get into the business of dispensing economic benefits—advantage for some at the expense of others.

Pyramiding Special Pleaders

There is only one way for mankind to live and improve its economic circumstances, and that is by applying its energies to nature and nature's products. Goods are produced in this way and in no other. But once produced, the goods of some men may be acquired by other men through political manipulation. Let government perform this service and the trek to Washington is on. Once on, it will grow in geometric progression as group after group organizes to apply political pressure to get something for nothing: organized labor, the farm bloc, veterans, regional groups, educationists, the aged, and others.

Business and industry, strictly speaking, have to do only with the deploying of economic factors and resources—somebody making something, transporting it, exchanging it. A businessman or industrialist, pursuing his aims as an entrepreneur, seeks to turn a profit. The appearance of a profit indicates that his talents are being employed in a manner approved by a significant number of people. Absence of a profit, on the other hand, ought to be his clue that people are instructing him to go into some other line. So long as a man produces and sells things people want at a price they are willing to pay, he operates according to the rules of economics. The vast majority of our millions of business enterprises are conducted in this fashion. All that is necessary to keep this operation going is for the law to inhibit and penalize cases of theft, fraud, and violence.

A "Fair Advantage"

The processes of production and exchange are self-starting and self-fueled and need nothing from government but protection from predation. It is in the interests of business-as-a-whole to maintain this climate of freedom. But the immediate interests of a particular businessman do not always coincide with the interests of business-as-a-whole. That is to say, businessman X might find it profitable for himself if his responsive, democratic government will intervene to give him a preferential position in the market by penalizing his competitors.

Such political intervention is contrary to the principles of Classic Liberalism and has the effect of giving some men an economic advantage at the expense of other men. Government intervention frustrates the workings of economic laws by forcing economic decisions contrary to the decisions of the unhampered market. The intervention annuls consumer choice, and the net result is economic advantage for political favorites.

Economic success under capitalism—the free market system—is measured by consumer satisfactions. If consumers are pleased with the goods and services provided by a producer, as demonstrated by their willingness to pay for them, the producer makes a profit. But in a political setup where the politicians stand by to confer economic advantage in return for lobbying and pressure group activity, material rewards may accrue to a man, even if consumers have returned a negative vote by not buying his goods or services.

When there is general acceptance of the idea that it is the function of the state to dispense economic privilege to its partisans, there will be competition among "businessmen" for political largesse. This is a departure from capitalism into the practice of an under-the-counter socialism. The practice has been all too prevalent during the past century, and is one of the main influences feeding into the socialist trend. No businessman wants overall socialism, but many a businessman wants a little piece of socialism where it is to his immediate advantage. Add up all these little pieces and the society is no longer liberal. It may be called liberal by some merely because the word has a favorable connotation, but it is not liberal in the limited government sense of the word.

The Costs of Freedom

Classic Liberalism meant freedom: Freedom to write and speak, to worship and teach, and, most neglected freedom of all, freedom of economic enterprise, i.e., consumer sovereignty in the marketplace. A believer in free speech accepts this principle even though he is fully aware that its exercise will result in campaign oratory, socialist tracts, uplift drivel, pornography, public relations prose, modern poetry, and the "literature" of a beat generation. The defender of free speech recognizes these things as corruptions of the divine gift of communication, but they are part of the price he is willing to pay for freedom. Freedom costs, and thus it cannot endure among a people who do not understand this or, if they do, are unwilling to incur these costs.

Accept the principle of religious liberty and things will happen which the civilized man will view with disgust. There will be holy roller revivals, store-front churches, unlettered Bible thumpers, bingo, and baked bean suppers. But the man possessed of a sensitive religious conscience is aware that it is not up to him to tell God the kind of instruments He can use to work His mysterious ways; and he wishes to make it plain that the opponent of religious liberty, if he is logical, must invoke a kind of inquisition to curb those expressions of religion he finds distasteful.

Acceptance of the principle of economic liberty means that the consumer has a right to demand, and the producer a right to supply, any item which does not injure another—as injury is defined in laws against theft and fraud. This means that poor taste and doubtful morals will find expression here just as they do in the kindred fields of speech and religion. A rock-and-roll performer will ride around in a pink Cadillac while a symphony orchestra has to beg for funds. A race track will be built where common sense would dictate a playground. People refuse to buy mere transportation; they want a chariot with lots of chrome and three hundred horses under the hood. Worse yet, when political subventions are available, some businessmen will seek to get "one up" on their competitors with government help.

Freedom costs, and the costs of freedom in the areas of speech, press, worship, and assemblage are generally acknowledged by a significant number of articulate people. These freedoms are not under assault—not in this country, at any rate. In the case of economic freedom the situation is different. Few people mistake the abuses of free speech for the principle itself; but the abuses of economic liberty loom so large in the modern eye that it cannot detect the market principle of which they are violations.

Properly Limited Government

Freedom, in sound theory, is all of a piece. It hinges on properly limiting government. A society may be called free when its government does not dictate matters of religion and private conscience, does not censor reading material, curb speech, nor bar lawful assemblage. But mere paper guarantees of these important freedoms are worthless if there is governmental control and bureaucratic planning of economic life. The guarantee of religious freedom is worth little if the devotees are denied the economic means to build their temples, print their literature, and pay their spiritual guides. How meaningful is freedom of the press if there are no private means to buy paper and presses? And there is no full right to assemble if buildings, street corners, and vacant lots are government owned. "Whoso controls our subsistence controls us."

If government is properly limited, men are free. In a free society a certain pattern of economic activity will be precipitated. This pattern will change constantly. It will respond as men have less or more political liberty. It will be modified as technology advances, taste is refined, and morals improve. Properly speaking, the economic pattern of a free society is capitalism, or the market economy. Under capitalism the people are economically free, exercising control over their own subsistence, and thus they become self-controlling in other freedoms as well.

Socialism and Beyond

Suppose you were asked to nominate the most influential figure in American politics during the first half of the twentieth century. Whose name would come to your mind? Would it be a President like FDR? A Senator like Henry Cabot Lodge? A Supreme Court Justice like Oliver Wendell Holmes? Or would it be a machine boss like Tom Pendergast?

Before we go on with this question, let's pause over the word "influential." Is political influence measured by the power of the office; by a man's standing in a popularity contest? Or is influence primarily an intellectual and moral force, measurable, therefore, only by assessing the extent to which a man's political and social ideals are actually translated into government policies and programs. The most influential figure must be an idea-man who insinuates his ideas into the ideological mainstream so that people thereafter play the political game with his deck. Viewing the matter in this light, my nominee for the most influential person in American public life since World War I is a man who never held public office. I refer, of course, to the late Norman Thomas. I fervently wish that this were not the case, for my own position is diametrically opposed to that of Mr. Thomas; but I think I know a winner when I see one.

Norman Thomas was the Socialist Party's candidate for the Presidency in 1928 and every four years thereafter for the next two decades, six national campaigns in all. He never got many votes. His greatest success was achieved in 1932 when all of 884,649 people put their X alongside his name.

These electoral contests were not very important for Norman Thomas; they did little or nothing to further socialism. A political party, in the American experience, is a private organization aimed at the capture of public office for its candidates. The American Socialist Party barely qualifies, for it has hardly ever engaged in serious politicking. Instead, it is organized and drilled for education and propaganda primarily; and this roundabout approach proved to be, in the end, immensely successful practical politics. The socialists in the course of

From the July 1969 issue of *The Freeman*.

227

a generation changed the American political climate so subtly yet so completely that by mid-century no matter which candidate won, socialism (small "s") could not lose! Socialism with a small "s" has become the new consensus, but capital S" Socialism has virtually expired giving birth to it! We will tell, briefly, the story of the rise and fall of Socialism, following this with an analysis of the auspices under which the drive toward collectivism proceeds today.

Principles, Yes; Party, No!

Norman Thomas and his friends, from the 1920s on, advanced the socialist cause by their devoted labor, day in and day out, year after year. They wrote books, pamphlets, and articles; they lectured before all kinds of audiences and made inroads among professors, clergymen, and millionaires. An incident recorded by Upton Sinclair is pertinent. Sinclair lived in Pasadena before World War I, and writes of a visiting European socialist who expressed unbelief when Sinclair told him that his circle of friends included socialists who were also millionaires. To prove his point, Sinclair said he would have a dinner party the next evening and invite some of his millionaire friends. The European was astounded to meet a dozen millionaire socialists, all rounded up on short notice from Pasadena and environs. Furthermore, because Socialism enormously strengthens the hand of government, it naturally appeals to politicians, Republicans as well as Democrats—and to the bureaucracy. These efforts by Thomas and associates paid off, and long before mid-century something like Socialism had become the American thing.

Thomas wrote a pamphlet in 1953 entitled "Democratic Socialism," in which he observed that "here in America more measures once praised or denounced as socialist have been adopted than once I should have thought possible short of socialist victory at the polls." But, as we have seen, the American voter decisively rejected socialism when it was offered to him under that label. A 1954 editorial in the *Socialist Call* noted that "an examination of the Socialist Party platform of 1928 and the Republican Party platform of 1952 shows how much of socialist ideas succeeded in permeating the mind of America, including business circles. In the 1930s," the editorial continued, "the United States accepted the basic principles of the welfare state. The final seal of acceptance appeared in the State of the Union message delivered by President Eisenhower to Congress in January of this year."

Norman Thomas was puzzled by the paradox of the comfortable acceptance of socialistic practices by the government while "socialism itself," he said, "is under much sharper attack, and the organized socialist movement is much weaker." In 1956, the Socialist Party candidate got 2,044 votes, and the party has not run candidates in '60, '64, or '68. It might seem the Socialist Party has been a Typhoid Mary, of sorts; it has been the carrier of an infectious set of ideas, inoculating others with the virus while remaining itself outside the pale. But this analogy does not walk on all fours; for while Norman Thomas has been transforming the Republican and Democratic Parties, the Socialist Party itself has been transformed. To take the measure of this transformation, let's look at the formation of this party at the turn of the century.

Born in Indianapolis, 1901

Perhaps the American Socialist Party has lived out its life span, for it was born nearly three-score-and-ten years ago. In the year 1901, on the 29th of July, 124 delegates representing various factions of socialism met in Indianapolis. The meeting is described by Morris Hillquit, the old-time socialist, in these words: "The convention has assembled as a gathering of several independent and somewhat antagonistic bodies; it adjourned as a solid and harmonious party. The name assumed by the party thus created was the SOCIALIST PARTY."

How many people were there in the United States in all the little socialist factions which sent delegates to Indianapolis? "No less than 10,000," says Hillquit. The active membership was undoubtedly much less than this, which is to say that the merest handful of earnest, dedicated people—who thought they knew what they wanted and worked to achieve it—succeeded in getting the most powerful nation in history to turn away from the methods of liberty and plunge into collectivism. The Socialist Party had succeeded so well by mid-century as to render itself unnecessary!

A party platform came out of this meeting in Indianapolis, full of rhetoric, as are all political documents, but containing also an unambiguous statement of socialist procedure: " . . . the organization of the working class and those in sympathy with it into a political party, with the object of conquering the powers of government and using them for the purpose of transforming the present system of private ownership of the means of production and distribution into collective ownership by the entire people."

Ends and Means

If we are to understand the nature and meaning of socialism, we must make a rigorous distinction between, on the one hand, the proclaimed socialist goal of a cooperative commonwealth which has no more war and no more poverty and no more injustice—and, on the other, the means which socialists would employ, or the techniques they would use, to achieve their goal. Ends versus means.

Up to a certain point, the ends and goals proclaimed by socialists of all denominations are the aims of all generous and fair-minded men. All men of good will seek to hasten the end of injustice and oppression; they want a more productive society in which each man enjoys the fruits of his own labor and where there is more material abundance for everyone. And because the economic order operates at peak efficiency only in a peaceful world open to trade and travel, economic considerations reinforce all the moral and religious imperatives favoring peace and opposing war. Immanuel Kant, writing at the dawn of the capitalist era, foresaw an era of peace in the nineteenth century and beyond as reliance on economic production and exchange to obtain goods supplanted the political struggle to get other people's goods by privilege and subsidy. "It is the spirit of commerce which cannot exist side by side with war," he maintained. This was a fundamental idea of Classical Liberalism whose spirit was expressed by Jefferson in his Second Inaugural, when he spoke of "peace, commerce, and honest friendship with all nations."

Armed with Power

The socialists appear to believe that they have a monopoly on the virtues, but in this—as in most everything else—they are quite mistaken. The unique thing about Socialism is not its professed aims; the unique thing about Socialism is the means it embraces for achieving its ends—means which include the authoritative direction and control of the lives of the masses of men by the few armed with political power. The original platform from which I have quoted announced the means Socialists would employ: They would form a political party and campaign until they were voted into power; and when they controlled the government, they would nationalize productive property.

True, the document does not speak of nationalization; it refers to "collective ownership by the entire people." Now, an entire people, all two hundred million of us comprising American society, cannot own anything collectively or in common; ownership is the right to the exclusive enjoyment and disposal of a good against all comers. If there is no one against whom such a claim might be pressed, the claim itself would not arise. Now, if everybody "owns" a thing, against whom will the entire people press their claim? "Collective ownership by the whole people" is a mere combination of words; it is not an intelligible idea. The absurdity of the notion of social ownership is humorously emphasized by the story of a sign in a public park in a midwestern city: "No baby carriages; no bicycles; no ball playing; this is your park." Obviously, the park does not belong to the one addressed but to the signwriter who lays down the rules for its use.

Nationalization of Property

Ownership can, however, be vested in society's enforcement agency—government. And the extension of government ownership is what mainly distinguishes Socialism from other schemes for the improvement of man's lot in society: Socialists would nationalize productive property. Into the hands of politicians and bureaucrats would come all titles to property; government would be the sole employer, and as the only employer, government would assign a task to each citizen and lay down the terms on which men would hold their jobs. If this sounds like the army, it is because Socialism is in fact a militaristic organization of society. Socialism involves a command type of operation and, because "whosoever controls a man's subsistence controls the man," a socialist society becomes a minutely regulated bureaucratic tyranny. When men lose the right to accept the best available job and to quit for whatever reason, they have lost a large and significant chunk of that free choice on which many other freedoms depend.

A New Kind of Tyranny

In 1884, Herbert Spencer foresaw the emergence of a new kind of tyranny in Western nations and wrote his prophetic essay, "The Coming Slavery." In 1912, Hilaire Belloc wrote *The Servile State,* predicting that when the Socialists got their way, the result would not be socialism, but a totalitarian order in which the masses would toil for those who possessed political power. Hayek wrote his stunning *Road to Serfdom* in 1944, by which time the appalling extent of slave labor in the Soviet Union was known to all men. But that evil thing, Communism, was not Hayek's culprit; he put the finger of blame on planning, even planning of a most benign intent. If a society has an overall plan, enforced by government, this will come into collision with the millions of private plans of individual citizens. Citizens, pursuing their personal goals as free men are in the habit of doing, resist bureaucratic stupidity, and the more stubborn citizens have to be made to see the error of their ways. The planned society needs enforcers, and in the nature of the case these are not gentle visionaries and scholars; they are the worst type of men, and it must be so, as Hayek demonstrates in a famous chapter entitled "Why the Worst Get on Top." Gentle American socialists used to lament that Stalin betrayed the Revolution; not so! Stalin was an authentic product of the Revolution.

The British accepted wartime planning under Churchill; and when a socialist government came to power after the war, the planned economy was extended to the edges of society. The catastrophic consequences for England were described by the Oxford economist John Jewkes in his book *Ordeal by Planning,* published in 1948. The American, Hoffman Nickerson, examined *The New Slavery* in his book of that title, published a year earlier; and finally even the American Socialist Party had to concede that it no longer believed in socialism—in the old sense.

The Socialist Party platform for 1956 contains the familiar windy rhetoric about eliminating war, hunger, and oppression; the socialist ends are about the same as they were half a century earlier. But the means are radically different. "Socialism," reads the platform, "is the social ownership and democratic control of the means of production. Social ownership, which includes cooperatives, is not usually government ownership." (It was simple government ownership, you will recall, to which the early socialists pinned their faith.) "Social ownership would be applied to large-scale business not to family farms or other individually owned and operated businesses of similar size. Democratic control is not administration by the central government but control by the people most directly affected. . . . "

The earlier socialist blueprint contained no private sector, but present-day socialists put the family farm in the private sector as well as businesses of comparable size. Now a family farm can cover four hundred acres and represent a capital investment of a quarter of a million dollars. The majority of commercial enterprises are much smaller, by comparison, than this, so this leaves several million businesses in the private sector. The present thrust of the American Socialist Party, therefore, is control of *"BIG* business," and this emphasis has so little sex appeal for Socialists that they've gone out of politics. The rationale for the planned society has been taken over by others. The trend toward collectivism still continues, but it is more deceptively camouflaged.

A Fanatic Faith

There's more to Socialism than its belief that productive property should be nationalized. Socialism is one of several ideologies which pin their faith to the notion that political reorganization will bring about a perfect human society: secularized versions of the Kingdom of God. Socialists do not modestly believe they have a remedy for *some* social ills; they think they have the cure for all! In this sense, Socialism is a modern, this-worldly religion. Listen to H. G. Wells, for example: "Socialism is to me a very great thing indeed, the form and substance of my ideal life and all the religion I possess." As a religion, Socialism promised a terrestrial paradise, a heaven on earth.

There is an unrealistic utopian streak running through the socialist mentality, generating a kind of fanaticism which makes it impossible to assess the realities and possibilities of human life on this planet. You've heard the brief prayer which runs: "Give me courage, O Lord, to change the things which need to be changed; the strength to endure those things which cannot be changed; and the wisdom to know the difference." The Socialists don't know the difference! They imagine an impossible state of perfection and then condemn the hard realities for not conforming to their dream. Everyone who has his feet on the ground recognizes the workings of sin, ignorance, and evil in human life. "History," said Edward Gibbon contemplating the decline and fall of Rome, is "a record of the crimes, follies, and misfortunes of mankind." But none of these things need be, cries the Socialist, and the revolution will eliminate them; in the classless society of the future every man will radiate kindness and intelligence and the world itself will be transformed into a new Garden of Eden.

I'm not exaggerating. Here is Karl Marx himself, in an early work entitled *The German Ideology*, writing on the theme which is so popular these days—the theme of alienation. In what Marx calls "a natural-grown society" (as contrasted with a society consciously planned), there arises the thing we call division of labor. Men are gifted in different ways and come naturally to specialize in various occupations. And there the trouble begins! "As labor comes to be divided," Marx says, "everyone has a definite, circumscribed, sphere of activity which is put upon him and from which he cannot escape. He is hunter, fisherman, or shepherd, or 'critical critic,' and must remain so if he does not want to lose the means of subsistence—whereas in the Communist society, where each one does not have a circumscribed sphere of activity but can train himself in any branch he chooses, society by regulating the common production makes it possible for me to do this today and that tomorrow, to hunt in the morning, to fish in the afternoon, to carry on cattlebreeding in the evening, also to criticize the food—just as I please—without becoming either hunter, fisherman, shepherd, or critic."

Utopian Strains

Now it is obvious to everyone that the material abundance we enjoy in modern America is due to specialized occupations and exchange. If every man were a jack of all trades, living only on what he himself produced, most of the earth's population would shortly starve and the lives of those who remained would be "nasty, brutish, and short." Marx never did accommodate himself to the idea of the division of labor, but Communist regimes, of course, have had to bow to reality. Nevertheless, the utopian streak is still there. Leon Trotsky ventured into never-never land when he wrote his *Literature and Revolution* in 1925. Consulting his crystal ball, Trotsky predicted a proletarian paradise in which "the average human type will rise to the heights of an Aristotle, a Goethe, or a Marx. And above this ridge, new peaks will arise."

Marx and Trotsky are bad enough, but theirs is a sober vision compared to that of Charles Fourier who inspired several utopian colonies in nineteenth-century America and converted Horace Greeley and other Americans to his views. Fourier would group society into phalanxes comprising 1,620 people each and when the world was thus organized man, beast, and nature would be wholly redeemed. "Men will live to the age of 144," wrote Fourier, "the sea will become lemonade; a new aurora borealis will heat the poles.... Wars will be replaced by great cake-eating contests between gastronomic armies." Whatever Fourier's mood when he wrote this, the man was obviously insane and thus comparatively harmless; but a kind of madness afflicts even the soberest Socialist. The proletarian paradise is out of this world; heaven cannot possibly be achieved on this earth. To *improve* the conditions of earthly life is every man's job; to *perfect* them is God's. Those who try to establish perfection on earth usurp God's role, and in the name of Man they subjugate men.

Some former Socialists acknowledge the validity of these criticisms, so they crusade for collectivism using a different tack. Thus the new consensus, shaped by the Socialist mold, but completely pragmatic rather than idealistic. Reinhold Niebuhr, the eminent theologian, was a Socialist most of his life. He left the Socialist Party some twenty years ago saying that its creed "contained even more miscalculations than the liberal creed which it challenged." Does this mean that Niebuhr came over into the conservative or libertarian camp? Not at all. Niebuhr now favors a mixture of freedom and planning, as he would put it, in order that no one of the three major foci of power shall come to predominate. It is the power of Big Business that is the primary object of Niebuhr's concern, and he thinks we need both big government and big unions to cope with Big Business. The position is that power in society assumes three forms—as business, government, and labor, and that each of these must be played off against the other. Let's submit this position to critical analysis, beginning with government.

Two Kinds of Power

Nearly every political theorist until the present day has identified government with the police power. The government of a given society was regarded as the power structure. The head of the government was the commander-in-chief of its armed forces, which were charged with the task of defending the society against foreign foes. The police protected citizens against criminals, and the legal system offered redress when collisions of interest occurred within society. The government has the power to tax, and various other responsibilities as set forth in the country's constitution. That which distinguishes a government from any other organization within society is that government alone is granted a legal monopoly of coercion.

Anyone not blinded by ideological prejudice knows that the power wielded by government is unlike every other species of power in society. Should you run afoul of the law you will quickly realize that the police, the courts, and the jails are not a branch of General Motors. The army fighting in Vietnam is not under the control of A.T.&.T.; and if some young man you know is drafted, he will be drafted by the government and not by Du Pont or Alcoa. You'll be paying your income tax when due, and you'll pay it to the government. If you fail to pay, you'll be visited by an agent of the I.R.S., not by a Fuller Brush man.

How, then, can a bright theologian like Niebuhr fail to sense the power with which government is endowed? Only because he is blind to the nature of business. Niebuhr has said that the "prestige and power [of] the giant corporation [with its] right to hire and fire . . . certainly makes big business a part of government." (*New Leader,* August 26, 1951) This is a beautiful example of logic turned inside out. The right to hire and fire is nothing more than an exercise of the right of an owner to say who shall be allowed to use his tools and under what circumstances. There's an automobile registered in your name; but if you are not permitted to use it yourself, nor to decide who shall be allowed to use it and when, then the car cannot rightly be called your property. (Either that, or you have teenage children!)

Attack on Business

Now, hiring and firing is not a unique function of government, even though government employs millions of civil servants. But if you cannot make your own decision as to who shall work for you in your own factory or store or restaurant or bank or whatever, then you are prevented from exercising the natural responsibility of ownership.

Niebuhr's curious observation boils down to the nonsensical assertion that big business, by behaving in a business-like fashion—by hiring and firing—thus demonstrates that it's part of government!

The attack is leveled against *BIG* business, and thus it slips under the guard of some people. The size of things is a factor in our judgment of them; we don't like things to depart too far from the norm. In fairy tales and folklore both giants and dwarfs carry overtones of the sinister. Bigness carries the suggestion of inordinate strength, and that is always a threat; so we like to have things the right size. But how do we decide what size is proper for a business? And *who* should decide? Should the government decide how big X industry should be? Or should the consumers of X industry's products decide? I have no hesitancy in saying that the size of a given business should be decided by the consumers. If consumers like a given product, they telegraph their fondness to the manufacturer who tools up to produce more of it, increasing his output until diminishing sales give him the clue to cut down.

The theory of the free market, or laissez faire, or Classical Liberalism, never contemplated an unregulated economy. Laissez faire opposed *government* regulation in order that the economy might be regulated by those most directly affected—the consumers. According to the theory of laissez faire, government was to act as an umpire to interpret and enforce the previously agreed upon rules of the game; government was intended to keep the game of competition going by punishing breaches of the rules. Within the rules, a given business or industry had complete latitude to expand or contract or fail.

"Bigness" Decried

So what *is* a big business? The world's biggest business engaged in the exclusive manufacture of French horns is the Sansone Company which employs about fifteen craftsmen in a loft just north of Times Square. This is technologically feasible. Now, an automobile might be handcrafted in a shop with only a few employees, and such a machine might win the "Indianapolis 500"; but the American consumer favors the kind of car that can be mass-produced by the millions, and so Ford, Chrysler, and G.M. employ hundreds of thousands of men. The appropriate size of an industry varies greatly according to the nature of the enterprise, but the final decision as to the right size of X industry properly rests with consumers. Unless, of course, the proprietor decides he wants to do custom work at his own pace and prefers to stay small.

If you recall your textbook in economics, you'll remember the equation: Land + Labor + Capital = Wealth. Human energy aided by tools and operating on natural resources produces wealth. Business and industry is somebody making, growing, or transporting things which consumers demand, or performing a service. Human laziness is a factor in economics, and it is a safe bet that men would not work as they do nor as hard as they do if they didn't have to. Men have to work, not because anyone forces them to work, but because the human race would perish if people gave up working. This is simply a fact of life; this is not coercion in the sense in which those unfortunate millions who have perished in Soviet slave labor camps have been coerced. Coercion is not part of the private sector. (Acts of coercion may occur in the private sector but only as criminality.) A unique and necessary feature of government, however, is that society has granted it a legal monopoly of coercion. Government is *the* power structure in a society. But a business cannot exercise power without breaking the law—or else it secures the connivance of government and operates a cartel.

Given a framework of law which preserves competition and peaceful trade, a business should be as big as consumers want it to be—as evidenced by their buying habits. And business, as such, has no power—not the coercive kind of power which is the type government must have. The position that we need big government and big labor to contain the threat of big business has the props knocked from under it if "big business" is seen to be a vague term, and when we realize that business as such is not a threat but rather an essential for maintaining the general prosperity.

Unions Are Special

What about "big labor"? The mythology surrounding this question is hard to penetrate, for it is a modern article of faith that to labor organizations is due the major credit for the fact that wages are higher today than they were fifty years ago, and hours of work less. But mere organization does not produce goods; only the application of human effort to raw materials, augmented by tools and machines (capital) produces goods. And our increasing efficiency in production is due to inventions, good management, and above all, to the machinery the average worker has at his disposal. On an average, there is a twenty-one-thousand-dollar investment of capital per worker in American industry. This is why Americans are more productive than workers in other parts of the world, such as Great Britain, where trade union organization has been much tighter than here and has been going on since the nineteenth century. Unions do not contribute to our prosperity; they detract from it; they institutionalize unemployment.

Furthermore, national legislation such as the Norris-LaGuardia Act and the Wagner Act have granted special privileges and immunities to unions to engage in acts of intimidation and violence which would jail nonunion perpetrators. This is a serious breach of the Rule of Law. And in bargaining with employers within the terms laid down by the N.L.R.B., the discussions proceed with one party's hands tied by partisan legislation.

Let me offer a striking analogy of this situation from the pen of the Harvard economist, Professor E. H. Chamberlin. He's writing about what is called "bargaining," and says: "Some perspective may be had on what is involved (in labor-management "bargaining") by imagining an application of the techniques ... in some other field. If A is bargaining with B over the sale of B's house, and if A were given the privileges of a modern labor union, he would be able (1) to conspire with all other owners of houses not to make any alternative offer to B, using violence or the threat of violence if necessary to prevent them, (2) to deprive B himself of any access to any alternative offers, (3) to surround the house of B and cut off all deliveries, including food, (4) to stop all movement from B's house, so that if he were for instance a doctor he could not sell his services and make a living, and (5) to institute a boycott of B's business. All of these privileges, if he were capable of carrying them out, would no doubt strengthen A's position. But they would not be regarded by anyone as a part of 'bargaining'—unless A were a labor union."

Intellectual Error

The intellectuals of our time are bemused by power. Irving Kristol is an intellectual and also a liberal of sorts, but he's nevertheless able to maintain his objectivity. "The liberal," he writes, "is pleased with the increasing concentration of power in the national government, because he sees in it an opportunity to translate his ideals into reality. . . . He is convinced—not always by evidence, often by self-righteousness—that he knows how to plan our economy, design our cities, defeat our enemies, assuage our allies, uplift our poor, and all in all, insure the greatest happiness of the greatest number. And for this knowledge to be effectual, he needs more power over the citizen than Americans have traditionally thought it desirable for a government to have." (*New Leader,* September 14, 1964)

The liberal is saying, in effect: "We're a lot smarter than the rest of you folks, and possess a keener sense of moral responsibility as well. Why, therefore, should we sit idly by while mankind mindlessly repeats the same damn fool mistakes over and over again?" Well, the worst mistake mankind continues to make is to turn its destinies over to some demagogue who in turn whips people up into mass movements. "People go mad in herds; they recover their sanity one by one." The mob intoxication wears off and then each person can locate for himself those loopholes in logic through which a tiny bit of his liberty trickles away, and he can plug the leaks with sound ideas.

Some conservatives and libertarians spend a lot of time attacking big government. The mythology surrounding big business and big labor can be stripped away; and when we've finished that job, big government remains, towering over us and watching us like Big Brother in Orwell's novel. But the excessive size of government is a secondary effect. A government must be large enough to accomplish its task, and during wartime or to cope with a crime wave it will naturally expand. Our criticism should be directed at government doing the wrong things and not at mere size, because whenever government starts doing the wrong things, it will overflow its boundaries and become too big. Government should be large and virile enough to keep the peace, to preserve individual rights, and punish anyone who injures his fellows—as injury is defined at law. But when a government attempts to run the economy and dictate the actions of peaceful people, it usurps improper authority, and thus grows to inordinate size.

Back to Fundamentals

Liberty in human affairs will never be wholly lost, nor ever wholly won. We've been on the losing end for some time now, but it is our great good fortune that whatever runs contrary to the natural grain of things will eventually bring about its own demise. Socialism as a consistent intellectual system has committed suicide, although its practical consequences are still with us. Now we are confronted with the shallow notion that big business is a power structure, as is big government and big labor; and we must somehow prevent the ascendancy of any one of these three powers. Upon analysis, this position is seen to be error piled upon error. A business is as big as consumers want it to be; and if they want it to fail, it fails. The power displayed by modern unions is a chunk of raw political power bestowed by national legislation on some people over other people. The bestowal of this kind of power is a violation of the principles of the free society and a breach of the Rule of Law. Finally, government has certain indispensable functions to perform and it should perform these tasks with vigor and integrity—and no others.

Once we have the ideas sorted out and rearranged in order, then what shall we do? How shall we act? Well, that's up to you, for in the nature of the case each man must answer for himself when it comes to deciding where he shall exert his influence. Bonaro Overstreet has set the idea to verse:

> You say the little efforts that I make
> Will do no good.
> They will never prevail,
> To tip the hovering scale
> Where justice hangs in the balance.
> I don't think
> I ever thought they would.
> But I am prejudiced beyond debate
> In favor of my right to choose which side
> Shall feel the stubborn ounces of my weight.

---

1. Morris Hillquit, *History of Socialism in the United States* (New York: Funk & Wagnalls, 1903, third edition), p. 229.
2. *Ibid.*, p. 338.
3. *Ibid.*, p. 343.

What You Don't Know Might Help You!

The practice of liberty in human affairs is an acquired skill and, like every other skill, the practice of liberty must be learned. Imagine a ballet performed upon a stage and involving a dozen dancers. Each dancer must perfect various motions and then learn a routine of steps so that the ensemble creates a moving work of art before our eyes. The dance must exhibit a pattern, else the performers—however skilled individually—would simply get in each other's way. The practice of liberty includes the knack of keeping out of each other's way, thus giving free play to the natural forces of social cohesion.

There is an aspiration toward liberty inherent in our very being; it's a corollary of the fact of our individuality. But this potentiality is not realized unless we learn techniques for expressing it. Liberty has to be learned—as well as earned—and like every other skill we acquire, it may be lost. The circus juggler who has learned to keep six plates in the air must work constantly to refine and improve his skill or he begins to lose it. And it is the same with liberty; liberty may be un-learned, and the unlearning of liberty goes on at a constantly accelerat-ing rate in our time. Perhaps we'd know why, if we knew more about the learning process itself.

Every one of you who plays golf, or bats a tennis ball, or bangs away on a piano has moments of frustration. It's not the occasional bad shot or wrong note that causes the irritation; it's the fact that our progress is so uneven. There's such a thing as beginner's luck, and it may be that after our first golf or tennis lesson we surprise everyone by making a number of good shots. And so we approach the second lesson with expectations keyed high—only to fall flat on our face. Everything goes wrong. We may experience similar frustrations in the course of the next several lessons, and then something seems to click. We hit the ball and it feels right. Enthusiasm flares, but the improve-ment doesn't last. Or, if it does, we seem to bog down again on this level. Sometimes there's a slump; but if we persist there is eventually another breakthrough, and then the struggle to consolidate our gains goes on once more.

From the December 1970 issue of *The Freeman*.

242

All learning takes place in somewhat this fashion. The psychologist speaks of "plateaus of learning," and if you draw a graph it will resemble a profile of a staircase with deep treads and low risers. The line does not show a steady rise; instead, it shows the learner slogging away on one level, and then a breakthrough to a higher level; more slogging, another breakthrough, until we reach our potential.

Unlearning is as much a part of life as learning. Sometimes we want to unlearn, but there is also the all-too-common involuntary unlearning of a skill we'd like to retain. The great pianist, Paderewski, once remarked that if he went a day without getting in his customary hours and hours of practice, he knew it. If he went two days without practice, the critics knew it. If he went three days, his friends knew it. Athletes have the same problem; once they've reached a peak and then lost it, the comeback trail is rough. Similar difficulties beset all human affairs.

Liberty in Our Time

Our subject is human liberty, and the fate of liberty in our world. When this country was young, the accepted belief was that men were by nature free, and that governments were instituted among men to secure that freedom by defending the rights of all men alike. "The God who gave us life gave us liberty at the same time," wrote Jefferson. Liberty now, in the twentieth century, is viewed as a permissive thing, to be exercised by the citizen at the discretion of his political masters within the lines laid down by the government. Liberty, once regarded as a birthright, now partakes of the nature of a political favor. The ways of liberty once learned by some of our ancestors, and in some measure applied by them in actual practice, were unlearned by other forebears of ours. And a good deal of learning and unlearning has been going on in this generation, perhaps even by us.

If we examine the learning process more carefully we realize that there's more to it than conscious effort, important as this is. A great deal of learning takes place behind the scenes, below the level of consciousness. We are learning between one practice session and the next. It is not by a mighty effort of will that you move from one plateau to another; if you practice correctly, the breakthrough will be accomplished for you. Here's an illustration of the way it works, taken from the writings of the great French mathematician of a generation ago, Henri Poincaré.

Poincaré on Insight

Poincaré was stumped by a certain problem, and for fifteen days spent an hour or two a day trying to work out a proof, with no results. Then, "one evening, contrary to my custom, I drank black coffee and could not sleep. Ideas rose in crowds; I felt them collide until pairs interlocked, so to speak, making a stable combination. [I dozed off, and] by the next morning I had established the existence of a class of Fuchsian functions . . . I had only to write out the results. . . . The idea came to me, without anything in my former thoughts seeming to have paved the way for it."

Poincaré is credited by other mathematicians with several important breakthroughs, which occurred in the manner described, in the form of sudden illuminations. These insights, he says, are "a manifest sign of long, unconscious prior work. The role of this unconscious work in mathematical invention appears to me incontestable." There's a condition—persistent prior work. Breakthroughs "never happen except after some days of voluntary effort which has appeared absolutely fruitless and whence nothing good seems to have come, where the way seems totally astray. But these efforts have not been as sterile as one thinks; they have set agoing the unconscious machine and without them it would not have moved and would have produced nothing."

Genius, as someone remarked, is 90 percent perspiration and only 10 percent inspiration. Sir Francis Galton, who did the pioneering studies of genius about a century ago, observed that his subjects were bigger, stronger, and more energetic than average men and women—otherwise they couldn't have performed the required prodigies of work.

The achiever, then, knows how to apply the pressure, and how long. He also knows that there is a time to let up, to relax the conscious effort and let a deeper wisdom take over. If we may use the word Application for the first stage, we might call this second stage Incubation; ideas apparently must ripen before they can hatch. In order to successfully negotiate this stage of learning—the period when nature takes its own course—we must practice the difficult art of letting things alone—which is quite different from doing nothing. Albert Jay Nock, who edited the old *Freeman*, from 1920 to 1924, had a stable of bright young writers under his editorial command. One day a friend said to Nock, "Albert, it's wonderful what you have done for these young people." "Nonsense," Nock replied, "all I've done is let them alone." "That may be so," was the response, "but things would have been different if someone else had been letting them alone."

The Notebook of Coleridge

The mind has a front end or top layer, and we consciously feed data into this part of our mind through our eyes and ears, by observation and experiment. Then the raw data of experience is mulled over and reflected upon. We talk it over with colleagues, argue it out with opponents, write it up, act it out. And all the while, learning is taking place. At the proper moment we shift gears and put the subconscious mind to work on the material the conscious mind has prepared for it. And if the conscious preparation is adequate, the rest of the job is taken care of with a finesse and expertise that is simply astounding.

Let me cite the case of Samuel Taylor Coleridge, one of the supremely gifted poets of our language. Apart from his published works, Coleridge left a notebook in manuscript, in a kind of shorthand, recording his reading and his observations. This notebook forms the basis for a classic study of Coleridge, really a study of the workings of the imaginative energy itself: *The Road to Xanadu,* by John Livingston Lowes. Incidents and phrases got into Coleridge's notebook and thence into his subconscious mind, to be transformed there by his genius, taking final shape in his poetry. "Every expression of an artist," writes Lowes, "is merely a focal point of the surging chaos of the unexpressed. And it is that surging and potent chaos which a document like the Note Book recreates." The word "chaos" here is not used with connotations of confusion or randomness; chaos is a term for the teeming, primordial raw material which challenges the artist to shape it into forms of beauty by the power of his imagination. "Unless a man has a little chaos in his soul," wrote Nietzsche, "he'll never give birth to a dancing star."

The Subconscious

Below the level of conscious mental activity there are deeper levels of the mind, and an enormous amount of hogwash has been written about the subconscious mind, some of it by amateurs but a lot of it by medical men engaged in the practice of psychiatry or psychoanalysis. I have been suggesting, by the two examples I have cited—Poincaré and Coleridge—that the mental processes which occur behind the scenes are mighty allies, able to accomplish beneficial results we could achieve in no other way. The subconscious mind is the silent partner of our rational faculties, wise and trustworthy. Turn to the popular literature of psychoanalysis, however, and the picture is quite different. There, one gets the impression that only the conscious mind is *us;* that each of us is shackled to an idiot; that the subconscious mind is a mere collection of drives, impulses, and emotions; that this unconscious part of us tyrannizes over our rational faculties and must be squelched.

Why these conflicting views? The main reason is that psychiatrists deal with sick people, and the subconscious mind of psychopaths may very well be as psychiatrists describe it. Geniuses and normal people do not ordinarily wind up in psychiatric clinics, and clinical findings, therefore, do not pertain to great poets and mathematicians—or to normal people.

We are not talking about achievement without tears, or learning while you sleep, or awakening your hidden powers. There are no short cuts. But we do have the assurance that if our conscious thinking is sound, persistent, and hard, our subconscious mental processes will cooperate to mobilize the constructive forces that bring about the final result.

The capacities of the human mind are almost limitless, and those of the human body are only slightly less so. The incredible feats of endurance, strength, speed, and skill that we witness on track, field, arena, and stage are beyond most of us. Only a handful of people will ever run a four-minute mile, no matter how hard they train, or win the heavyweight championship, or break 65 at golf, or perform on a trapeze, but almost anyone who wills to do so can play a good game of golf, or develop unusual strength, or multiply his endurance. The recipe is the same as that for acquiring mental skills—an alternation of hard workouts with rest, or Application followed by Incubation. Endurance, strength, and skill improve even when you do nothing—provided you preface the quiet time by intense effort. This physical partner of ours has enormous potential in many directions, but few people ever realize their potential. When reasonably fit, this physical partner of ours displays a remarkable wisdom in its workings. Through its organs of sight, hearing, and touch we are properly oriented toward our physical environment. There are two other sense organs: The sense of smell is not as important to us as to other creatures, but we know how important his taste buds are to an infant. I think it was Gerald Heard who suggested that a baby's motto might be: Seeing is believing, but tasting is knowing.

The Amazing Human Body

This body of ours performs sophisticated chemical operations with the raw material we take in as food, distributes nourishment to the tissues that need it, carting off the waste products. Chemical balances are maintained, temperature is regulated, foreign bodies are neutralized, wounds are healed—and all this is done quietly without fuss or stress, unless we interfere. We are "fearfully and wonderfully made," and the body performs miracles daily. There's a genius down inside us. The most awe-inspiring performance of that genius is the masterwork he accomplishes before we are born. The eminent biologist, Hudson Hoagland, delivered a paper at M.I.T., in 1967, in which occurs this passage: "Frank Crick has estimated that the amount of information contained in the chromosomes of a single fertilized human egg is equivalent to about a thousand printed volumes of books, each as large as a volume of the Encyclopedia Britannica. This amount of coded instruction packed into the size of a millionth of a pinhead is the remarkable material which transmits information from parent to offspring to tell the next generation how to make a person." Each one of us passed that test, else we wouldn't be here.

A skilled adult scientist in an expensive laboratory gets a do-it-yourself kit with various amino acids, colloids, and protein molecules. He combines these in a certain way and exposes the compound to electrical currents for a week or so. And then, for a short time his concoction appears to exhibit some characteristics of life. The scientist gets headlines. But each of us, when no more than a tiny speck, was brilliant enough to manufacture a person! Stupidity, of course, sets in shortly after birth and full recovery is rare.

Work and Wait

Learning something, whether it be the mastering of a new subject matter or the acquiring of a new skill, is more than conscious effort. Conscious effort is an indispensable part of the total learning process, however, for it is the spark that gets the machinery going. Learning is a dual process. It reminds us of an iceberg with much of its bulk below the surface. Go about the topside matters correctly, and events of great importance take place below the water line without any human agency directing, controlling, or managing them. This is a fact of great significance, to be taken into account in deciding the nature of this universe in which we find ourselves: *Things work for our benefit if we know how to cooperate with them and otherwise let them alone.*

The art of letting things alone applies to the complex interactions we have with nature. Each spring we are impressed anew with the exuberance of the earth, by its fruitfulness, its hospitality to the endless variety of living forms. Men poke seeds into the ground but plants grow by interacting with nonhuman forces; "God giveth the increase," as a pious old poet said. Make preparations of the right sort, work hard, and the good earth cooperates by focusing nature's powers of growth to put a multiplier onto your efforts. We have to overcome natural obstacles, but we enlist the help of natural forces to do so. "A mighty help in our contest with nature," writes Böhm-Bawerk, "is nature himself."

The Invisible Hand

Move now into our final example, which has to do with society and the economic order. Remember Adam Smith's famous metaphor of "the invisible hand"? What was the problem he sought to explain? He observed countless millions of people in the different nations of the world, engaged in thousands of different occupations and trades, each busy with his own affairs, pursuing his own aims. But what is the result of this seemingly chaotic situation? The result is an orderly transfer of goods and services; people are fed, clothed, and housed; the wealth of the world is brought within reach of all who enter into these multiple transactions. There is a marvelous harmony in this situation, just as if some invisible hand were guiding each person to produce the kinds and quantities of goods the market is calling for. It is the result of human action but not the execution of human design. The right kind of human effort in the marketplace enlists the help of an other-than-human intelligence. Anyone who has looked into the economic order must marvel at the intelligence displayed in the way the market works—intelligence manifesting itself in the precise adaptation of means to ends throughout the system. Yet no human agency is putting people through their paces; there is a spontaneous order which arises when men obey a few moral rules and otherwise act in freedom. Why do things happen this way? Because it's that kind of a universe!

Three-quarters of a century after Adam Smith, Frederic Bastiat mused over the miracle of the provisioning of Paris. Here are a million human beings who do not grow their own food, nor do they make most of the things they use. Yet food and other necessities appear as if by magic! No Napoleon commands these movements. "What, then, is the ingenious and secret power which governs the astonishing regularity of movements so complicated?" Bastiat asks. And he answers his own question, "That power is an absolute principle, the principle of freedom in transactions."

I have been stressing the point that there is wisdom and intelligence directing the events which happen below the surface, or below the level of conscious action. This is not to diminish the importance of willed effort; it is to suggest that we have to know when to let up and let go, trusting the forces of growth and cohesion we find at work in our bodies and minds, as well as in nature and the market. This willingness to take the plunge is a matter of mood—a mood of faith or confidence or trust or belief that the universe is on our side. But just as Adam Smith was writing his masterpiece a new and hostile mood was emerging in Western nations.

The Age of Enlightenment

The eighteenth century is referred to as the Age of the Enlightenment. It was a period of great *over*reaction to the ages of religion, a time when Man with a capital M was exalted into a god, able to fashion men in his own image. It was an age of optimistic rationalism, with all mysteries resolved. It was the age of the Rights of Man, confident of its power to wipe out an old society and manufacture a new one at will. A take-charge mood came to dominate many minds, a managerial mentality. The idea was that the world would fall apart if *we* stopped holding it together; things wouldn't work unless *we* made them work; everything was defective and had to be patched up, rigged out, put into functioning order.

This was the mood of the men who engineered the French Revolution, the rootless intellectuals of the day; but the mood was infectious and it has spread all over the globe, seeping into and out of every sector of life. It seeped into the theory and practice of medicine about a century ago. Certain medical theorists examined the human organism and found it a crude contrivance of pipes, tubes, levers, and dead weight. This botched mechanism could be kept going only if someone constantly patched and repaired it. Writing of this antiquated medical theory, an historian says: "This held that the body was a faulty machine and Nature a blind worker. The student made an inventory of the body's contents and found, as he expected, some out of place, some wearing out, some clumsy makeshifts . . . and some mischievous survivals left over." Medical practice, based on this theory, was to interfere with the body's working by probing, operating, removing, and altering. The practice often proved disastrous to the patient! Today's medical theory is quite different.

The Managerial Mentality

The managerial mentality gets into philosophy, and is especially marked among the Existentialists. One of them writes: "Being a man is deciding what man will be. . . . Man remains the author of his own destiny, the creator of his own values." Philosophy used to be the pursuit of truth for its own sake. No longer. The contemporary philosopher aims at knowledge for the sake of control. The primary target of the controllers is, of course, the economic order. The free market must go.

When this managerial mentality, this take-charge mood, pervades a society, it will kill the free economy where it finds it, or prevent it from emerging in countries which don't have it. When the mood is to manage, you'll have a managed economy, because everyone lacks confidence that the economic machinery will operate—unless it is directed, controlled, and planned. The belief is that some human agency must be in command or nothing will function. Social engineering is the order of the day; society is to be masterminded by men waving blueprints and armed with powers of enforcement. Nobody is to be left to his own devices; everybody is to be assigned a task so that society can be operated with mechanical precision.

But men are not robots or puppets; they have the gift of free will, and most people choose *not* to be the tools of other men—when they understand the issues. When they find themselves trapped in situations which demean their humanity they rebel, and their rebellion takes various forms. The rebellion sometimes moves in the direction of freedom, but more often the rebellion is just as mindless and bizarre as the things revolted against.

Ideas Come First

I have suggested that a false ideology has been percolating into Western societies for two centuries or more. How is it, then, that things appeared to go so well for a while—that is, during much of the nineteenth century—and only in our time has the situation gone to pieces? Well, the impact of ideas is never felt immediately. Imagine, if you will, that history is like a huge pipeline; like the Big Inch, say, which brings oil from Texas to the eastern seaboard. If a batch of oil is pumped into the western end of this line, and if it travels at twelve miles per hour, it won't reach New York until about a week later. Ideas work the same way; put them into the pipeline of history and it may be a generation or a century or longer before they surface.

Go back two millennia to the dawn of our era. The Roman Empire was authoritarian, and the new ideas about God and man and life promulgated in the Gospels largely disappeared into the pipeline—so far as their impact on the history of the first several centuries was concerned. The Roman Empire went from bad to worse and finally fell, and Europe was in a bad way for hundreds of years. The Middle Ages was a turbulent period whose major religious thrust was a blend of Caeserism and Christianity. A new style of personalistic Christianity emerged in the sixteenth and seventeenth centuries, the period which also saw the beginnings of Puritanism in England. The political arm of the Puritans was the Whig Party, whose later spokesman was Edmund Burke, and which became the Liberal Party in the early nineteenth century. Ideas were coming out of the pipeline, especially in nineteenth century America, where we enjoyed more religious, political, and economic liberty than any people hitherto. We are reaping the harvest of sound ideas put into the pipeline over the course of many centuries—including some brilliant ones added since *The Wealth of Nations.* We might mention *The Federalist Papers,* the writings of Burke, Mill, Bastiat, and Spencer, plus the important contributions of the Austrian School from Böhm-Bawerk to Mises which have refined and extended the science of economics with meticulous care, establishing its main points beyond dispute. In short, there are some good ideas in the pipeline in 1970, and if we keep on stuffing more of them into the near end they are bound to emerge in due course.

A Preponderance of Socialist Literature in the Past Century

But such good ideas as went into the pipeline during this period were overcome and nullified by the virulence and sheer bulk of the bad ideas. From the time of Marx to the present day the socialists and Communists have written a hundred books for every book written by a libertarian or conservative, plus a thousand pamphlets; and whereas the socialists and Communists offered a contagious vision of a new life for humanity, their opponents countered with the promise of two cars in every garage! It is bad that we have been losing in such a lopsided contest, but it would have been worse if we had won.

There are some good ideas coming out of our side of the pipeline, and they are getting better. But they are not good enough for the task at hand. They have taken on some of the protective coloration of the collectivists with respect to the ends and aims of human life, objecting merely to collectivist means.

The Jacobins promise to manufacture a new society from scratch and, with democratic controls on scientific power, bring about a heaven on earth—meaning the City of Man in which everyone is well-housed, well-clothed, and well-fed. All too frequently, defenders of the free market have responded: The City of Man is our goal, too, but we can show you how to have better housing, superior clothing, and tastier food! The fact is that the struggle goes deeper than economics; two ways of life are in conflict. You don't win a battle for the minds of men by promising to fatten their pocketbooks. You might say that if a man's heart is empty because life has lost its meaning, the full belly argument turns his stomach!

Two ways of life are locked in combat, so let's engage in some self-examination and self-criticism in order to raise our sights and change the terms in which the contest is viewed. Shifting gears, we begin with a solemn observation by the eighteenth-century philosopher, George Berkeley, after whom a certain university city on the coast was named: "He who hath not much meditated upon God, the human mind, and the supreme good, may possibly make a thriving earthworm, but will most indubitably make a sorry patriot and a sorry statesman."

Raising Our Sights

What do these three ideas—God, mind, and the supreme good—have to do with the free economy? I think I can demonstrate that they have a lot to do with it, and that unless they are taken into account, economic liberty is a vain hope.

The idea of God has to do with the ends or goals for which human life should be lived. The old catechism said that the chief end of man is to know God and enjoy him forever. But most economists have told us that economics is a value-free science, that it is neutral as to ends. Let men dedicate their lives to any end that catches their fancy; to the economist it's a matter of indifference. This is a typical line taken by economists, and it contains potential disaster for the free economy. Suppose the chosen end is power. Many men dedicate their lives to the concentration of political power in society, and then scheme to get that power into the hands of themselves and their party. Every minor success by the power-hungry nullifies the free economy at some point. It is suicidal for the economist to declare that his disciple is indifferent as to what ends in life men pursue.

Or take wealth. Suppose a significant number of men agree that the pursuit of wealth is the chief end of man. Making money in the free economy is laudable enough, being a token that you are providing people with things they want. But if money-making is accepted as a man's chief end then any means are justified if they further this end. The free economy is more productive than any other—on the whole; but you cannot promise any given individual that he'll better his own circumstances in the free market. Many people can do better for themselves if they operate a racket. Congresswoman Edith Green of Oregon has made a calculation which shows that a welfare mother with four children could in one year net $11,698 of relief funds; double the number of children and the ante is upped to $21,093. But this is peanuts compared to the subsidies some slick operators can get by political finagling. Proponents of the free economy will continue to lose unless human life is geared to the goals proper for man, and this makes the God concept a live issue.

Goals Proper to Man

Well, it may be asked, what are the goals proper for man? It is obvious that there is no pat, copybook answer to a question of this magnitude; what is important is that this question continues to be asked and that it can be wrestled with unceasingly. Albert Jay Nock addresses himself to the problem when he speaks of "man's five fundamental social instincts." He charges that only the instinct of expansion and accumulation, that is, for power and wealth, has had free play during the past century and more, while "the instincts of intellect and knowledge, of religion and morals, of beauty and poetry, of social life and manners, were disallowed and perverted."

There are many facets to human nature and we cannot afford to neglect any. The English philosopher C. E. M. Joad writes as follows:

> For a guide to the demands of our nature we should refer to the pursuits of our fathers. For what mankind has done uninterruptedly for thousands of years we may be assured that there is a natural itch in the blood. In all ancestral and customary pursuits, then, we should indulge, but in none of them overmuch. We should pray a little, fight a little, play a little, dig a little in the ground, and go on the sea in ships; we should make love, speak to our fellows in public, and expand in the company of our friends in private. Above all we should recognize that we have an instinctive desire for occasional solitude, and a need for country sights and sounds.

The Nature of the Mind

Berkeley's second point has to do with the nature of the human mind. Is the mind a mere offshoot of the brain or a tool of survival or an instrument of adaptation to society? In which case we are born, marry, work, die, and that's the end of us. Or is the manifestation of mind in each of us more than a mere adjunct to the brain and nervous system; is it something that endures when its physical partner perishes; is it an immortal essence? This is an issue which philosophers have debated for centuries, but I raise it here only because of its bearing on the free economy.

Shakespeare wrote of "this blessed plot, this realm, this England." That was nearly four centuries ago; a dozen generations have lived and died since those lines were penned, but hundreds of years ago men were proudly conscious of living in a nation with a long history. And today they boast that "there'll always be an England." The nation endures; individuals perish. The nation existed before any of us were born, and it will continue in existence after everyone here is dead. You hop aboard this ongoing reality, last out your three-score-years and ten, and that's the end of you. Suppose this version of the way things are is widely accepted, and suppose you find yourself out of step with the nation's consensus—as many of us would be at odds with today's establishment. If you—a fleeting fragment of an ancient and enduring nation—challenge the nation's consensus you would not only be pitting your puny self against your contemporaries but tackling past centuries and future generations as well. The encounter would be somewhat lopsided!

But there is another interpretation of the way things are, and according to this wiser reading of the human situation, kingdoms rise and fall, nations come and go, civilizations finally crumble, but the person is forever. When there are firm convictions along these lines the individual has an enormous leverage against any majority, any society, any nation. The nature of the human mind is a vital political question.

Human Motivation

Berkeley's third idea has to do with human motivation. What is man's supreme good? The traditional answer was: To please God. Since the eighteenth century the answer has been: The supreme good is to please yourself. The thing gets pretty fatuous in the ideology of some would-be defenders of capitalism who try to tell us that the aim of life is to please customers! What were our ancestors driving at when they spoke about pleasing God? Let me try to frame an answer in contemporary terms.

I have pointed out that each of us, in his prenatal stage, knew how to manufacture a baby. Quite a stunt! But the full stature of humanity is an achievement, not an endowment; all that being born confers upon us by way of natural endowment is the plastic and sensitive raw material needed for evolving a human being. Finishing the job is up to us, and it will take us a lifetime to do it—if we do it at all! Before birth we had the advantage of working by instinct: the formula was inside us. But after birth we have to look for a recipe outside, that is to say, we must look for a set of rules which are written into the nature of things. These rules for completing our growth are what our forebears spoke of as God's laws or Commandments. By discovering and obeying these commands, each of us furthers his own purposes and completes his own nature.

The Road to Chaos

When men cease to believe in an objective set of rules, then each person tries to make up his own rules as he goes along; he tries to please himself by "doing his own thing." But this is like trying to play baseball when each player decides for himself how many strikes are out, or whether to run bases clockwise, or whatever. "Doing your own thing" doesn't work out, for, if no external standards are acknowledged, the weak doing their thing are at the mercy of the strong doing theirs; the honest entrepreneurs doing their thing are at the mercy of political finaglers doing theirs; those who want to be let alone are harassed by those whose thing is meddling. Throw away the rulebook and chaos ensues. Putting the rules for living in the order of their priority is a live issue for the freedom philosophy. We have neglected this philosophical framework; and collectivist ideology, taking advantage of our neglect, has crowded into the vacancy.

Nature on Side of Freedom

It is encouraging to know that the nature of things is ultimately on our side. The aberrations we face are against the grain of things and will fall of their own weight—if we don't misguidedly prop them up. Does the opposition seem strong? Well, said Disraeli, "the dominant philosophy in any age is always the one which is on the way out." Collectivism in our time has changed into nihilism, and nihilism is as far as you can go into a dead end. From there, the way back is the way ahead.

The collectivism which has come to full flower in the totalitarian nations, which is growing in all countries, including our own, is a plague that reminds one of the witchcraft mania of the sixteenth and seventeenth centuries. How was that disagreeable episode transcended? Not by anti-witchcraft crusades nor by social pressures on behalf of civil rights for witches; witchcraft crawled back into the woodwork when it was confronted by a quite different tactic. Aldous Huxley, discussing the period, says "the theologians and inquisitors . . . by treating witchcraft as the most heinous of crimes, actually spread the beliefs and fostered the practices which they were trying so hard to repress. By the beginning of the eighteenth-century witchcraft had ceased to be a serious social problem. It died out, among other reasons, because almost nobody now bothered to repress it. For the less it was persecuted the less it was propagandized." A new understanding of the nature of the cosmos, a new world view, began to gain acceptance in the eighteenth century, and witchcraft, finding no foothold in it, withered on the vine.

Great Changes Come Slowly

History has a number of great turning points. We may not be able to agree on matters of historical causation, but all students are unanimous on one point: These great changes were in the works a long time before their effects were manifested on the surface.

In Victor Hugo's great novel *Les Misérables* there is a dramatic account of the Battle of Waterloo, after which Hugo reflects on the cosmic dimensions of that battle. "Why Napoleon's Waterloo?" he asks, "Was it possible that Napoleon should gain this battle? We answer No. Why? Because of Wellington? Because of Blucher? No, because of God! Bonaparte victor at Waterloo—that was no longer according to the laws of the nineteenth century. Another series of events was preparing wherein Napoleon had no further place ... Napoleon had been denounced in the infinite and his downfall was resolved. He bothered God. Waterloo is not a battle; it is the universe changing front."

A novelist may be allowed his liberties, but Hugo's main point is clear; every event on the surface of history has been manufactured at a deeper level by human initiative and intelligence cooperating with cosmic energies.

Whenever people of our general persuasion get together to assess the world scene the discussion sounds like an inquest; things are not going our way; the freedom philosophy is in disrepute, and things have fallen apart faster in recent years than any of us would have dared predict. Judge the events of our time from the newspaper or journalistic level and the mood is despair. But we know on second thought that many good and important things are happening at deeper levels. Probe below the surface and there are signs of hope. There are good things in the pipeline, and also good people.

258 / Edmund A. Opitz

It is difficult to assess the significance of contemporary events, although wisdom after the event is easy. Hindsight tells us that the voyage of *The Mayflower* three and a half centuries ago was one of the most important voyages in history, but few people of the time were even aware of it. It was just another trip for the seamen involved, writes William Baker, the naval architect who designed the present *Mayflower* after much research. Even the name, *Mayflower,* was a common one for merchant vessels in the seventeenth century, and the boats hired by the Pilgrims "were merely common traders." Baker researched the Port of London records and traced the voyages of *"The Mayflower,* Christopher Jones, Master," from August, 1609, to October, 1621. There are no entries for the year 1620. The Port of London official deemed this voyage to the New World not even worth recording! Nor is the name of their ship recorded by the men of the Plymouth Colony until 1623. The celebrated Bradford manuscript, written by the man who governed Plymouth Plantation during most of its first thirty-six years, was missing for generations and not published in full until 1856. Several centuries went by before the Pilgrims assumed their rightful place in American history.

A Vast New Outpouring of the Literature of Freedom

The events that disturb us today have been long in preparation; and the events that will correct these disturbances are in the making right now. They are, for example, in the books now being written and read. There are now well over one hundred titles listed in the FEE book catalogue. Apart from the handful of classics, every book in this list has been written since the end of World War II. Almost as many more books by brilliant libertarian and conservative thinkers have appeared during this same quarter century which are not included in the catalogue, and the writers of our side continue to provide a steady stream of material presenting the case for the free society.

People on our side didn't write these kinds of books during the 1850–1950 period; their creativity went into other channels. They were doing the work of the world while the socialists were writing the books. Our people were exemplifying the accomplishments of a society which at least gave lip service to the ideals of freedom, while the socialists were writing millions of words to extol the planned life and forming all kinds of organizations to bring about a collectivist order. Our forebears probably believed that the free way of life is its own rationale, but it is not so. Good deeds are not enough, we must supply a reason why. And that is just what is happening today, as libertarian and conservative literature pours off the presses.

The Inherent Stability of the Masses

There's something else below the surface of today's events, ready to be engaged in our cause, and that is the solid core of decency and common sense in the mass of men, covered over now and again, confused, but waiting to be enlisted. One often hears the despairing question, How can we win the masses back from liberalism? That's not our problem; the masses have never been converted *to* liberalism! To become a real liberal you have to go to graduate school! The average man, the man in the street, is not our problem. He may be mean, shiftless, ignorant, and a wife-beater when drunk, but he is not a collectivist and he is here by the millions, waiting to pin his emotions alongside the flag and cheer for the home team. Cardinal Newman was right: "There is always in the multitude an acknowledgment of truths which they themselves do not practice." When our side gets good enough, the multitudes will swarm in our direction.

We have a real mess on our hands, but no one can say it is not richly deserved. For the past couple of centuries we have bullheadedly made a wrong choice at every opportunity. We have discarded the tried and true and let ourselves be seduced by the myths of an immanent utopia. We have embraced phony values and followed phony leaders. And in consequence of our folly things are in a bad way, but not as bad as they might be. Things aren't as bad as they would be if Reality were neutral. It is our great good fortune that the nature of things is on our side, on the side of freedom, that is; and it's the collectivists' tough luck that their program goes against the grain. These are forces in us and in the universe which make for growth and cohesion; unobstructed they make for liberty. Let's join 'em!

Index

PRICE LIST
Religion: Foundation of the Free Society

Quantity	Price Each
1 copy	$14.95
2-4 copies	12.00
5-49 copies	9.00
50-499 copies	7.50
500 copies	6.00

Please add $3.00 per order for shipping and handling. Send your order, with accompanying check or money order, to The Foundation for Economic Education, 30 South Broadway, Irvington-on-Hudson, New York 10533. Visa and MasterCard telephone and fax orders are welcome; call (914) 591-7230 weekdays or fax (914) 591-8910 anytime.

About the Publisher

The Foundation for Economic Education, Inc., was established in 1946 by Leonard E. Read to study and advance the moral and intellectual rationale for a free society.

The Foundation publishes *The Freeman*, an award-winning monthly journal of ideas in the fields of economics, history, and moral philosophy. FEE also publishes books, conducts seminars, and sponsors a network of discussion clubs to improve understanding of the principles of a free and prosperous society.

FEE is a non-political, non-profit 501 (c)(3) tax-exempt organization, supported solely by private contributions and the sales of its literature.

For further information, please contact:

The Foundation for Economic Education
30 South Broadway
Irvington-on-Hudson, New York 10533
telephone: (914) 591-7230
fax: (914) 591-8910
e-mail: freeman@westnet.com